One thousand copies
of

William Trent
and
the West

have been printed
for
The Great Pennsylvania
Frontier Series
by
Wennawoods Publishing
This book is number

372

William Trent and the West

BY

SEWELL ELIAS SLICK

WENNAWOODS PUBLISHING
Lewisburg, Pennsylvania
2001

To

Max Harrell

Shirley Lou and Beverly Jean

TABLE OF CONTENTS

PAGE

Foreword _____ vii

CHAPTER

I. Ancestry and Early Activities _____ 1

II. In the Service of Virginia _____ 14

III. Virginia Service Resumed _____ 28

IV. Accepts a Virginia Military Commission _____ 42

V. Financial Troubles, Pennsylvania and Royal Service _____ 60

VI. Assistant Deputy Indian Agent of the Crown at Fort Pitt, 1759 _____ 72

VII. Assistant Deputy Indian Agent and Trader at Fort Pitt, 1760-1761 _____ 86

VIII. Life Around Fort Pitt, 1762-1763 _____ 102

IX. The Siege of Fort Pitt, 1763 _____ 111

X. Trader's Losses and Land Speculation _____ 127

XI. Land Company Promotion in London _____ 139

XII. Finale and Failure _____ 155

Bibliographical Note _____ 177

INDEX _____ 185

FOREWORD

This volume is the result of the author's deep and abiding interest in the early period of American history which dates from his childhood in western Pennsylvania. Under the able teaching and guidance of Professor Alfred P. James of the University of Pittsburgh that interest was greatly intensified.

Much of the material included in this study was submitted in a different form to the Graduate School of the University of Pittsburgh in partial fulfillment of the requirements for the doctor of philosophy degree.

It was with a great deal of reluctance that the decision was made to omit the documentation from the text in the interest of the general reader. To satisfy the curiosity of the scholar as to the sources used, an extensive bibliographical note has been added.

Space does not permit the listing of the names of all those persons who helped in some way in making this work possible. The librarians and the staffs of the libraries listed in the bibliography were most co-operative. A deep debt of gratitude is owed to all of them.

Especial mention should be made of Elisabeth Mellon Sellers, who graciously assisted in the task of editing. And last, but not least, the author is indebted to his wife for her assistance in typing the original manuscript and for help in reading the proof.

S. E. S.

Clarion, Pennsylvania

CHAPTER I

ANCESTRY AND EARLY ACTIVITIES

William Trent's father also bore the name of William. The elder Trent was born in Inverness, Scotland, and came to Pennsylvania in 1682. Soon after his arrival in America he became a prominent merchant in Philadelphia, where he engaged in business both as a private adventurer and as a partner with William Penn and his deputy, James Logan. As a shipowner and merchant, he carried on extensive trading operations. In the year 1703 alone, he handled nearly "300,000 hundredweight of tobacco and over 2,500 'skins' besides a large 'peltry account.' " The latter included almost seven thousand pelts of such animals as deer, elk, bear, wolf, otter, beaver, raccoon, marten, and mink. Trent also dealt in numerous other commodities, among which were wheat, flour, and corn. His largest shipment of wheat was said to have been fifty-five hundred bushels on one vessel and six hundred on another. Human chattels were dealt in too. It is related that he "often handled on commission cargoes of [white] 'servants,' as well as negroes." In his old leather-bound journal, covering the years 1703 to 1708, may still be clearly read the story of Trent, the merchant. His extensive business transactions included various adventures in cargoes sent to such places as Barbados, Jamaica, Boston, Milford, and St. Thomas, with investments ranging from less than £100 to over £2,200. In a letter to William Penn, Logan commended Trent highly for his skill and insight in trading enterprises and wrote of him as a successful merchant.

This prominent citizen of early Pennsylvania did not confine his activities to material pursuits. He was a devoted member of the Church of England, and in America he soon became actively associated with Old Christ Church in Philadelphia. In that church he served as a vestryman, and he was listed as one of the benefactors who contributed to the various needs of the parish. Possibly the best proof of the man's character and integrity is the fact that he, although a Church of England man, was fully accepted as a partner in various business ventures by Penn, as well as other Quakers, and, despite his lack of legal training, was elevated to the highest political offices in a colony completely dominated by the Society of Friends. The first high office to be filled by the elder Trent was that of provincial councilor; an original copy of his oath, bearing the date 1701-1702, is in existence today. He served as a member of the council for almost two decades. In April, 1706, the governor, at a council meeting, announced that he had received from the proprietor in England instructions to appoint a tribunal for the province of Pennsylvania and the Lower Counties (Delaware). Among the names of the five judges appointed was that of William Trent, Sr. Trent was also called to represent Philadelphia County in the assembly, and filled the legislative assignment from 1710 to 1720. During a part of that time he served as speaker of the assembly. When a law was passed in 1715 authorizing the creation of county courts for Chester and Bucks counties and a Supreme Court for the province of Philadelphia, Trent was one of the five jurists chosen to occupy the Supreme Bench. He acted as one of the presiding judges in that court for a number of years.

The real estate deals of the elder Trent were not numerous. They involved tracts of land ranging in size from two hundred to several thousand acres; but his operations were in no sense large, considered in the light of other land speculations of the eighteenth century. A number of old deeds, as well as other records, indicate their extent. Most of the holdings were located in and around Philadelphia, but there was one notable exception: in 1714 he purchased from Mahlon Stacy, the son of one of William Penn's associates and a proprietor of West Jersey, the old eight-hundred-acre Stacy plantation, bordering on both sides of the Assunpink Creek, upon which Trenton and South Trenton now stand. Some years after Trent had acquired the Stacy holdings he had a town laid out on the estate, which at first was called Trent's Town; as early as 1719, however, the name was written simply as "Trenton." To his adopted home in New Jersey, William Trent, Sr., is supposed to have removed with his family in the autumn of 1721. There he built a family mansion called Bloomsbury Court. This structure is still standing and bears the distinction of being the oldest house in the city of Trenton today. With the aid of Federal funds, it has been completely and carefully reconstructed according to its original specifications.

No sooner had Trent taken up his residence in New Jersey than the citizens proceeded to elect him to the New Jersey Assembly, and Governor William Burnet commissioned him colonel of a militia regiment. He had been in the assembly only about two years when he was chosen speaker. In that position he led a group that was seeking to have the province of New Jersey divorced from the province of New York, at least in judicial affairs. The assembly's request resulted in the appointment of Trent as the first chief justice of the province of New Jersey. In a letter to the Lords of Trade announcing the appointment, Governor Burnet said: "The present Chief Justice Mr. William Trent is universally beloved as your Lordships may observe by his being chosen their Speaker and I doubt not will answer my expectations in executing the office." But the governor was to be disappointed. Scarcely a year later Chief Justice Trent was taken ill; he died on Christmas Day of the year 1724, from what was diagnosed as a fit of apoplexy.

William Trent, Sr., had been married twice. His first wife was Mary Burge, and to that union were born three sons: James, John, and Maurice; and a daughter, Mary. He took as his second wife, Mary Coddington, daughter of Governor William Coddington of Rhode Island. Only two chlidren were born to the second union: Thomas, who died in infancy, and William, Jr., the subject of this study. By 1735, James, John, and Maurice had died, leaving only William, and his half-sister, Mary. William's mother died at the age of eighty-three years and is supposed to lie buried in the old Hopewell (New Jersey) cemetery. In view of the family background, there is little wonder that young Trent, with the ambition he possessed, became rather famous in the trade, politics, and land speculation of his period.

Although there is a difference of opinion as to the exact date and place of his birth, all sources agree that Trent was a native of Pennsylvania. Since the parental home seems to have been in Philadelphia around 1715, it is highly probable that those who list that city as his birthplace are correct. The story of his life between 1715 and 1740 is somewhat clouded. No record has been uncovered to indicate the breadth or depth of his education. One thing seems certain: he must have had an excellent teacher in penmanship. Amid the mass of scribbling found in the original manuscript material of this period, the chirography of Trent appears as a welcome relief to the researcher.

Existing records bring Trent on the public stage in his middle and late twenties, in the insignificant character of a witness to some business transactions. He was at this time a resident of what was then Lancaster County, Pennsylvania, and his first land deals, which involved relatively small tracts, seem to have been made in that county in the year 1745. At least three deals were made in that year, but none involved more than four hundred acres of land. At this time a more important role was in the offing. On June 10, 1746, Governor George Thomas called the Pennsylvania Assembly together in a special session. To the surprised legislators he conveyed the news that His Majesty, the King of England, had decided to conquer Canada and desired the assistance of the American colonies. Governor Thomas asked the assembly to appropriate money to defray the expenses of Pennsylvania's quota of troops. He further suggested that provision for bounties be made in order to expedite the recruiting. After due deliberation, the assembly sent the governor a reply. The lawmakers indicated that as Quakers pledged to peace they found it difficult to subscribe money for warlike purposes, but that they would do so nevertheless. At the same time, however, they informed Thomas that as no extra funds were available beyond the exigencies of regular government, he should authorize the issuing of an additional amount of paper money to finance the proposed campaign. Thomas was opposed to this plan, but his chief concern at the moment was the raising of the troops, and he attacked that task with a will.

Pennsylvania was called upon to contribute four companies of one hundred men each. To lead each company Governor Thomas commissioned a captain. Trent received one of these commissions; the others who received similar appointments were John Deimer, John Shannon, and Samuel Perry. This was Trent's first military commission. Each captain was ordered to enlist only able-bodied men, not over forty-five years of age, of good stature, and free from any fault that might make them unfit for marching. Only Protestants and those willing to take the oath of war were to be accepted. Each man was to be paid one dollar upon enlisting, and to that was to be added a bounty of three pistoles in gold. (A pistole was worth about three and a half to four dollars.) The captains were given the responsibility of finding quarters for their respective companies. They were cautioned to keep within the King's daily subsistence limit, which was six pence sterling for each soldier. The complete record of Captain Trent's company shows the name, place of birth, age, date of enlistment, and occupation of every man. It offers an interesting study of a typical colonial fighting unit.

As soon as the Pennsylvania levies were made up, the companies marched to New York, where they went into winter quarters in the neighborhood of Albany. Their troubles were not limited to the French and the Indians. In order to get the troops under way, Governor Thomas had advanced over £400 of his own money, and soon after their departure from his province, he asked the assembly for reimbursement. To strengthen his plea he cited the fact that other provinces were paying similar expenses for their troops, and indicated that he therefore could not hope to receive help from the Crown. He prophesied more monetary troubles for the assembly at the same time that he presented his own request for repayment. Only the week before, he said, he had received a letter from Governor George Clinton of New York informing him that the Pennsylvania troops stationed there had threatened a general desertion unless they were supplied with blankets as the troops from the other provinces had been supplied. Governor Clinton had stated that he had already secured 150 blankets for them on the credit of Pennsylvania, but that he could not secure any more. Two days after Thomas had made his requisition, one James Claxton, an innkeeper at Frankfort, petitioned the Pennsylvania Assembly for some £78 due him for feeding Captain Trent's company. The innkeeper said that Trent had issued him an order on the Governor, but that the executive had refused to honor it. The ardent pleading of Governor Thomas melted the hearts of the stolid, peace-loving Quakers, and they ordered the treasurer to pay him £450. Claxton was not so fortunate. He had to wait years before he was paid.

The troubles over funds and supplies continued. Captain Trent took it upon himself to write to Governor Thomas. Among other things, he informed the governor that he and the other Pennsylvania officers had "made bold" to draw some bills on Thomas for blankets to keep their men from freezing. He said that there had been sixty or seventy desertions from the Pennsylvania ranks since the troops had arrived at Albany, although only one man had deserted from his company. He claimed that fear of perishing from the cold had caused the desertions. Three weeks later another distress call was sent to the home province. This letter was signed by all four captains and informed Thomas that their supplies of bread and rum would not last much longer, and that their meat would be gone by January. They warned the governor that it would be impossible for them to hold their men together unless they received supplies. A letter of almost the same content was dispatched to Governor Clinton. Not wishing to call a special session of the assembly, Governor Thomas authorized the commanding officer at Albany to supply the needs of the Pennsylvania troops. When the assembly met in regular session in January, the governor informed the members of his orders issued on behalf of the troops, and reminded the assembly that since the Crown had shown no disposition to care for the provincial troops, it was up to Pensylvania to continue to care for her own. The assembly replied very shortly. They asked that the Pennsylvania soldiers be called home, as their period of usefulness had evidently expired, and the burden of maintaining them was too great. But many months were to pass before the order to disband was issued.

During their stay in New York, Captain Trent and his men seem to have had but one direct skirmish with the enemy. That occurred in the month of April, 1747, while Trent, Lieutenant Proctor, and forty men were returning from an escort to Saratoga. They were ambushed by a party of sixty French soldiers and Indians. Trent ordered his men to cover behind a bank and some trees and was able to hold out until reinforcements came to his rescue. He lost some of his light baggage containing letters from Saratoga; nine of his men were killed, nine were wounded, and six were taken as prisoners.

By June, troubles within the companies were causing the officers more worry than fear of the enemy had ever caused them. In a letter signed by the four Pennsylvania captains, Governor Clinton was told that a great many of the Pennsylvanians had deserted, and that there was a considerable disturbance among the remainder of the troops. The officers blamed most of the trouble on the New York German population. They said that since "a great part of our Companys consist of Germans who can converse in the language of those vile people they have had the greater influence over them." The New Yorkers, they charged, had told the Pennsylvanians that the last soldiers enlisted for Canadian service had been cheated out of all or part of their pay, and that the men in this expedition would probably receive the same treatment. The Easterners had further asserted that Governor Clinton had sent up enough money to pay the soldiers all that was due them, but that the officers had paid the soldiers only a part and had pocketed the remainder themselves. Finally, the Pennsylvania colonials had been told that Governor Clinton intended to make them soldiers for life. The captains informed Clinton that despite the disorder, their men had always obeyed commands and had been willing to fulfill the duties assigned. In this letter, the officers also indicated anxiety to get about the service that they were supposed to perform and that they hoped "in a short time [to] be enabled to do."

The King of England had other plans, however. In the European countries involved, interest in the war had reached such a state of lethargy by 1747 that both sides seemed ready for a truce. France became so indifferent to her promises that she concluded the conflict early in 1748 without consulting her ally, Spain. In view of this attitude in Europe, there is little wonder that the British Crown lost its desire to pursue the struggle in the American colonies.

After the Pennsylvania troops had languished in a New York army camp for several months longer, the royal order was given to set aside the "intended" expedition against Canada "for the present." Provincial governors were told to ask their assemblies to raise money to pay off the discharged soldiers; then they were to send the vouchers to the home government for final payment by Parliament. Everything was to be done as cheaply as possible. Late in the fall of 1747 Captain Trent and his fellow officers, together with their men, were mustered out of the Pennsylvania service, although the quarrel over payment for their services raged on for many months between the assembly and the council.

Following his retirement from army service in 1747, Trent resumed his activities in land speculation. His operations were the forerunners of similar and much larger deals, which were to mark him as one of the largest real estate plungers of the colonial period. It is interesting to note that in his first experiences in land dealing, he usually had one or more partners, and that at this period in his business life, he had already begun the practice of putting up one tract of land as security for a loan to obtain new working capital. Another field, however—that of trade in the Indian country—was beginning to beckon at this time, and the call was not ignored.

Prior to the middle of the eighteenth century, the region immediately west of the Appalachian Mountains had been of very little concern to either France or England. Neither country had made any particular claim to, or use of, the lands located between the mountains and the Great Miami River, then known as the Rock River. When the right of France was questioned, she argued that the region was hers on the basis of discovery by La Salle in 1679. She clung to that pretension tenaciously. But no documents were produced to support her stand; modern scholarship, therefore, is prone to discount the French contention. On the other hand, Professor Theodore C. Pease, in amassing evidence to back the English claim to priority in the territory, states as authentic facts that "Thomas Batts and Robert Fallam found their way over the mountains to the headwaters of the New River in 1671. . . . That within a decade English traders swarmed in the valleys of the Tennessee and the Cumberland, that by 1700 they had reached the mouths of the Tennessee and the Arkansas." The English either were unaware of these excellent proofs or felt that they were unnecessary. Instead, they usually cited the clause in the Treaty of Utrecht, made at the conclusion of Queen Anne's War in 1713, in which the French had recognized English sovereignty over the Iroquois, or Six Nations, Indians. Since the Six Nations were the overlords of the Indian tribes inhabiting the region in question, the English felt that they had a right to trade with the vassal peoples. The matter threatened to reach a crisis with the conclusion of King George's War in 1748. A provision of the Treaty of Aix-la-Chapelle provided for the creation of a commission to settle the boundary between the English and the French in North America. The commission proved to be exceedingly slow in action, and neither country was willing to wait for its findings.

The French had established trading posts in the upper Mississippi Valley many decades before this time; but all those posts were located west of the Great Miami River. One of the commonest routes taken by Frenchmen traveling north and south between Louisiana and Canada was that which connected the Ohio River, or "Beautiful River" (as the French called the stream of the Allegheny and the Ohio), with the

Great Lakes, by way of the Wabash and Maumee rivers to Lake Erie. The portage between the headwaters of the last two rivers was not long. There were communication lines farther west, too, connecting with the Mississippi, but it should be noted that no records exist to show that the Allegheny-Ohio route was ever used as a regular means of transportation between Canada and Louisiana.

French relations with the Indians in the back country are usually painted as fairly agreeable, but the picture is not entirely accurate. As early as 1727 a serious rebellion of the Fox Indians in the upper Mississippi and lake region had threatened to sever communications between the French colonies in North America. The period from 1727 to 1748, although notable for French enterprise in the expansion of the fur trade, was also marked by certain signs of incipient decay in the political domination of New France. Both Canada and Louisiana were liabilities to the French government from a budgetary point of view. That fact in itself may partially explain the Indian unrest that again became apparent. An additional cause of discontent was the neglect of the Indians occasioned by King George's War. The Indian was no longer independent; on the contrary, he was very dependent on his trade with the white man. Failure to supply his necessary wants could not be easily excused. From his standpoint, insult was added to injury at this time by the adoption of a new trading policy by the French. This system provided that in the future the trading posts in New France were to be sold to the highest bidder. While this plan tended to replenish the depleted colonial treasury, it automatically created a government monopoly over the Indian trade and resulted in the levying of extravagant prices on the goods that the Indians had to buy. The alteration of policy proved to be a costly mistake. The Indians immediately objected to the rise in prices, and the embarrassed French traders could do little to appease their resentment. They themselves were placed in an unfair competitive position. The relative freedom of the English Indian trader, coupled with the higher quality of his goods and their lower price, spelled doom for the French trader.

It was to this rich field of Indian trade in the western country, at what seemed to be a propitious time for English ventures, that Trent now turned his attention. His assistance to the colonies of Virginia and Pennsylvania at an Indian conference in Lancaster in 1748 may have acted as an incentive to him in this decision.

The events leading up to the 1748 conference began with the encroachments of the white men on the Indians' domain. Settlers from Pennsylvania, Maryland, and Virginia had appropriated land around the headwaters of the Potomac River and west of the Allegheny Ridge that belonged to the Six Nations Indians. The Indians had made several reasonable requests for compensation. But the requests had gone unheeded, and in 1742, Canasatego, the great chief of the Onondaga Indians (a tribe of the Six Nations), had threatened hostilities. That threat, along with the French War and the need for keeping the Indians friendly, had caused the provincial governors to arrange for an Indian conference, which had been held in Lancaster in 1744. There the Six Nations Indians with much oratory had refuted the claims of Virginia to the territory in question and reminded the provincial representatives that the Iroquois had won that land by right of conquest. The Indians had said that the land was theirs, and that if the white men wanted a title to it, the right would have to be secured from the Six Nations. But after much feasting, drinking, and bestowing of presents, the Indians had been induced to make concessions of territory to all three provinces. Virginia apparently got the best bargain, as the Indians promised to recognize the King's right to all lands that were, or should be, in the colony of Virginia. That was just the opening that certain enterprising Virginians wanted. In 1748 the famous Ohio Company was formed, and before the autumn of 1749 it had secured a large tract of land west of the mountains.

The Indian trade, dominated for the most part by Pennsylvanians previous to this time, was now threatened by Virginia. The Quaker province bestirred itself to meet the competition. Thus the Indian conference at which Trent was present was held at Lancaster in 1748—this time with the Twightwees, as the English called the Indians of the Miami Confederacy. There the Pennsylvania officials were made aware of the fact that their traders were often unscrupulous in dealing with the Indians. It was made clear, also, that the western Indians preferred to deal with the English traders, rather than with the French, because the English gave them much better bargains. Acting on the knowledge gained before and at the treaty, President Anthony Palmer of the Pennsylvania Council ordered prosecution of the traders guilty of carrying rum to the Indians. In addition, he pointed out the value of developing the friendship of other western tribes, now favorably disposed toward Pennsylvania, as a wedge that might be used in disrupting the connections between French Canada and Louisiana. Both Pennsylvania and Virginia sent presents at this time to the Indians residing on the Ohio River and the region to the west of it. Conrad Weiser, Indian agent and interpreter for Pennsylvania, handled most of the presents, but Trent assisted in the task. The council later thought Trent's charges for this service somewhat excessive. Up to 1748 Weiser had been able to conduct most of the Indian negotiations alone, but after that year, Trent, Andrew Montour, and George Croghan were often hired to assist. It is a pertinent fact that under this expanded Indian policy, the province of Pennsylvania spent as much money on Indian affairs in the years from 1748 to 1752 as it had spent on such business in the preceding thirty years.

As has been suggested, the observations made by Trent in this first Indian service probably opened his eyes to the possibilities in the Indian trade. But before he entered that trade in earnest he accepted a civil office in a frontier county. When Cumberland County was created in 1749, partially through the efforts of Trent and James Silvers, Governor James Hamilton appointed Trent to the position of justice of the peace. The year 1750 found him holding the same appointment. These years were eventful ones in his life, and the relatively quiet post of justice must not have held much of an attraction. It was in 1749 that Trent seems to have entered into a trading partnership with the amiable Irishman, George Croghan, although the two men had been associated in land speculation even earlier. The business associations that started between Trent and Croghan before 1750 grew into a mutual friendship that survived until Croghan's death in 1782. That the two were brothers-in-law is the claim made by most writers on this period; nevertheless, a careful search has failed to reveal any convincing evidence of blood or "in-law" relationship between them. Trent also became affiliated with another company in 1749. Its personnel included Croghan, Robert Callender, and Michael Teaffe. As if those two businesses were not enough to keep one man's energies occupied, Trent engaged as well in small private trading operations. Indian traders in general were looked upon as a low, mean, unscrupulous lot, but men like Trent, Croghan, and their immediate associates were exceptions to this general rule.

That Captain Trent was a versatile character cannot be doubted. Despite his activities as justice and as Indian trader, during the year 1750 he extended his real estate holdings in Cumberland County by the acquisition of three tracts of land totaling seven hundred acres. Moreover, his land titles were not always secured without bickering and litigation, which absorbed considerable time.

Regardless of his activities in eastern and central Pennsylvania, Trent's main interest was on the frontier. Early in 1750 the French had news of a reported uprising of the western Indians against their rule. The Indians as far west as the Osage and the Missouri tribes were supposed to have been affected. George Croghan was believed by the French to have been one of the instigators of the plot and to have used as his tool the great Miami chieftain known as La Demoiselle.

In July of the same year Trent wrote to Richard Peters, secretary of the provincial council, in Philadelphia, stating that there was trouble in the Ohio country. Two traders had gone from a place about three hundred miles west of Logstown (Ambridge, Pennsylvania) to the Twightwee or Miami country to trade for skins and had not returned. Some time later their horses were found, as well as their saddles with the buckles cut off, but the men were gone. The Ottawa Indians were blamed for the act. Trent said he believed the story to be true and then suggested an Indian policy. He argued that since the "Indians must be at War with some Body," it would be a good idea to make peace "now" between "our" Indians and the Carolina tribes and then set both against the French Indians. It seems that this suggestion was intended for official ears. To judge by later developments, it had the desired effect.

The spring of 1751 brought more bad news from the frontier. Trent, again writing to Peters, stated that one of "our men" had just come from the Allegheny for provisions with the information that the winter just past had been one of the hardest known "in them parts." Food had become so scarce that a peck of corn sold for five shillings. The Indians had marketed their own supply until it had become so depleted that they feared they would suffer before the next crop was harvested. Many horses had perished. Trent expressed the opinion that his company had probably also suffered heavy losses as a result of nature's harshness. Three traders, believed to be Trent company men, were reported taken by the French Indians. By far the worst news brought by this emissary was the rumor that as soon as spring opened, the French and their Indian allies intended to destroy the English traders in the Twightwee country. Moreover, Trent informed Peters that he understood that there were "several Hundred" families who planned to cross over the mountains soon, and that those already over did not intend to remove themselves.

About a month after Trent wrote to Peters, Governor Hamilton sent George Croghan to the Ohio region with a present for the western Indians. Croghan was secretly instructed to sound out the leading chiefs on the possibilities of building a fort on the Ohio to protect both the Indians and the traders. He carried out that order and received a favorable reply from the Iroquois chief, or Half King, and the leading men of the Delaware and Shawnee tribes. The Indians said that the building of a trading house in their midst had been agreed upon between them and the Six Nations, as a result of Céloron's trip down the Ohio in 1749. Before Croghan departed for the East again, the Indians held a council and agreed on a message to the Pennsylvania governor. In it they asked Pennsylvania to build a strong house at the forks of the Monongahela River for the protection of the Indians and the English traders. When Croghan carried his account back to Philadelphia he was insulted and told that the Indians could not possibly have meant what he reported. Conrad Weiser, likewise, sneered at the report and declared that it could not be true. Pennsylvania's leaders lived to regret this attitude, when it was too late to make any move without a large expenditure of money and effort.

In 1751 Captain Trent was elected to the Pennsylvania Assembly from Cumberland County, together with Daniel Williams. He was not to stay in the employ of his native province for many months, however, as the Indian service of the province of Virginia called him.

The friendship between the English and the Twightwee, or Miami, Indians, which had been sealed by the Lancaster Treaty of 1748, was distasteful to the French. Following the treaty, English traders by the dozens had literally flocked to the Ohio region. The town of Pickawillanee (Piqua, Ohio) had been founded by the Miami Indians, who had deserted the French post on the Maumee River, and had become an important trading center. A number of log cabins had been built in which to store the goods handled by the traders. Business flourished for the English; but the situation boded ill for the French. Trouble between the Miami Confederacy and the French had been brewing for several years. As early as 1747 the Miami had begun to withdraw from the French interest. In that year an uprising of the western Indians against the French, known as the Conspiracy of Nicholas, had occurred. The Miami had contributed their share of damage by destroying Fort Miami (Fort Wayne, Indiana) at the confluence of the St. Joseph and St. Mary's rivers. French power in the West had been seriously threatened.

That episode, added to the news that the English Ohio Company had been formed in the East, had led to definite action on the part of the French officials in Canada. Céloron had been dispatched on his famous journey down the Ohio Valley. In the summer of 1749 he had visited Pickawillanee, but almost all the English traders had been warned in advance and had left. Regardless of his doubts and suspicions, Céloron had displayed a kindly exterior and bestowed presents upon the Twightwee tribes; but at the same time he had asked them to abandon Pickawillanee at once and return to their old location on the Maumee, where the French post was established. They had promised to do so the next spring, but the Frenchman had reason to doubt their promise. The presence of the full fighting force of the Miami warriors, however, must have tempered his conduct. Attachment for the English had continued despite the gifts, and the request of the English traders for permission to build fortifications, which had been regularly refused theretofore, had been granted in the autumn of 1750. A fort had been constructed at Pickawillanee, which, when completed, was surrounded by a high stockade of split logs with three gateways. About that time the town of Pickawillanee contained four hundred Indian families and was the residence of La Demoiselle, the principal chieftain of the Miami Confederacy.

Although in 1752 the outlook for the English was promising west of the Ohio River, there were signs of trouble between that river and the mountains. The Delaware and Shawnee Indians living around the forks were becoming restive. They were tributaries of the Six Nations and tended to keep in reasonably close touch with the Onondaga Council in New York through such Iroquoian leaders as Tanacharison, the Half King, who lived with them. As the white settlers began to trek westward over the mountains looking for homes, the resentment of the Indians was aroused. Rumors that the Six Nations and their tributaries felt that they had been imposed upon at Lancaster in 1744 reached the ears of Governor Robert Dinwiddie of Virginia. At any time such a report might have caused concern; but in 1752 the causes for worry were greatly enhanced. Dinwiddie was a partner in the Ohio Company and as such had reason to fear the effects of the threatened French aggression on the Indians and the trans-Allegheny lands. Therefore, he moved quickly and in April commissioned Joshua Fry, Lunsford Lomax, and James Patten to pay a visit to the Ohio and western Indians. The emissaries were instructed to secure from the Indians, if possible, a confirmation of the 1744 treaty at Lancaster, in return for which the Indians were to receive a large present, which the Virginians took with them. The last of May found the commissioners negotiating with the Delawares at Shannopin's Town, a short distance above the forks of the Ohio. In a few days the three men were at Logstown, where the main Indian conference was to be held. It was at that important gathering that the affairs of Virginia and Captain William Trent, who was then in the western country, became interwoven.

CHAPTER II

In the Service of Virginia

The first week in June, 1752, was spent more or less unsuccessfully by the commissioners to the western Indians. On June 9 they called the Half King and some other chiefs to a private conference and showed them the Lancaster capitulations. On the next day the conference was resumed. The commissioners reminded the chieftains of the present given them by the English King in 1748 and informed them that the King had sent another large present, which was in Logstown ready for delivery. A kindly request that the Indians confirm the Lancaster Treaty followed; but the chiefs proved obstinate. They said that they were aware of the 1744 document, but understood that the territory involved did not include any land west of the mountains. They told the Virginians that they wanted them to build a strong house or fort at the forks very soon, since the Pennsylvania governor had refused a similar request. They made it clear, however, that they only meant to give the English land on which to build a fort, and not land on which to settle. That suggestion did not please the commissioners. They stated that it was too difficult to support a garrison so far from the settlements. The Half King replied that he was aware of the obstacles, but that the English need have no worries on that score. Regardless of the Half King's answer, the commissioners drew up an agreement confirming the Lancaster deed and embodying the promise that the Indians would not molest the Virginia settlements on the southeast side of the Ohio River. Then Andrew Montour was called. Montour, a half-breed with the standing of a sachem among the Indians, was asked to converse privately with his brethren in order to change their minds. The half-breed's arguments, whether liquid or oral, seem to have been effective. The document was presented to the Six Nations Indians on June 13 and signed by them. About twice as many white men as Indians signed the treaty. Captain Trent's name headed the list, followed by the names of such other outstanding frontier characters as George Croghan, Thomas McKee, Michael Teaffe, and Christopher Gist.

While these citizens of Pennsylvania were witnessing an agreement that threatened the power and prestige of their province on the Ohio, their chief executive was fuming at the obstacles facing him. At the very moment that the Logstown Treaty was being negotiated, Governor

14

Hamilton was unburdening his heart in a letter to Governor Clinton of New York. He told Clinton that he was mortified by the conduct of the Pennsylvania Assembly. Because of the religious scruples of its Quaker members, he felt that no matter how great the necessity, he would be powerless to send assistance to the Indian allies of the English. By hook or crook, the diplomacy of Dinwiddie at the moment was one step ahead of the diplomacy of Hamilton.

So far as Virginia was concerned, the Logstown Conference was not a complete success, for the Twightwee, or Miami, Indians were not present at the treaty making, although they had been expected. Since a part of the present was intended for this tribe, the Virginia commissioners decided to hire a trustworthy agent to take it to the Miami country, and Captain Trent was entrusted with the assignment. In his letter of instructions from the Virginia commissioners, Trent was detailed to go to the "Picks Town" (Pickawillanee), there to deliver a special part of the present to the "Pianguisha" (Piankashaw) King. The remainder of the gift was to be divided as the chief men of the Twightwees saw fit. In addition, Trent was instructed to promote the interests of the English and to assure the Indians of the great friendship of the government of Virginia and of the King of England.

There is no record of Trent's private thoughts as he accepted this commission in the interests of Virginia; but it would have been interesting to have read his mind at that time. The success of the mission upon which he was about to embark might change the whole future for the Pennsylvania traders. It is highly probable that he accepted the assignment because he wanted to see some sort of activity, in preference to the inertia displayed by his home province. Before the incidents of his eventful journey are chronicled, however, the main story, of which they are only a part, should be recounted.

The visit of Céloron to the Miami country in 1749, which had led to the unfulfilled promise of the Miami to return to their old home on the Maumee, had caused that tribe considerable worry. They had had every reason to fear a French attack. As a result they had asked the Indians residing near the forks of the Ohio River if they might not be granted a dwelling place on that stream. George Croghan and Andrew Montour had planned to call a council of the Six Nations Indians living near Logstown so that a reply might be given to the request of the Twightwees. But developments had come too fast, and no migration of the Twightwees to the east took place. It seems, however, that Céloron's journey had not fooled the Indians on the Ohio, either. Despite his suave language and his presents, the natives mistrusted his motives. Croghan asked the Indians around Logstown what they thought the real intentions of the French were. The Indians replied that they believed the French when they said they intended to drive out the English traders and take over the trade themselves. But that was not all. The Indians said they had every reason to believe that the planting by Céloron of metal plates in the streams, indicating French ownership of the territory, was a sign that the French intended to steal their land. They announced their intention of proceeding to the Onondaga Council to find out what could be done to check the threat.

In the meantime Céloron and the other French officers had carried their disagreeable reports back to Canada. The Governor-general, La Jonquière, ordered Coulon de Villiers to relieve Captain Charles de Reymond at the Miami fort. Villiers was supposed to have great influence among the Miami, and it was hoped that he would be able to curb any further defections to the English. Céloron, who had been placed in command at Detroit, was detailed in 1751 to lead a force of French and Indians against La Demoiselle's village at Pickawillanee. The Indian allies did not appear, however, and Céloron therefore failed to carry out his instructions. La Jonquière, already facing recall himself for engaging in the fur trade and practicing nepotism, was deeply disappointed and bitterly rebuked Céloron for his failure. In a letter to the French minister in September, 1751, he informed his superior that he was doing his best to break the influence of the English among the Indians and had partly succeeded. He mentioned the fact that he had held a council with some of the western Indians on July 5, at which he had asked them to strike a blow against the rebellious Indians along the Ohio, and he stated that "they promised me they would send a band of their young men as soon as they should reach their village." About a week later, in another letter to the minister, he reported that the English were continuing their intrigues with La Demoiselle and other chiefs in an effort to bring about an attack on the French. He admitted that "the English have won the confidence of the nations of the Ouabache [Wabash]."

To combat these activities of the English and their Indian allies, La Jonquière evolved a plan. A force of four hundred was to proceed from Canada to the Miami country, where the troops were to spend the winter. They were to be joined the following spring by an additional five or six hundred men, and the combined force would wage an early campaign against the recalcitrant tribes. Before his plan could be carried out, La Jonquière asked to be recalled. The complaints made against him at court had hurt his pride, and, not wishing to be removed, he submitted his resignation. But fate intervened. His request had not been acted upon when he became ill and died at Quebec on March 17, 1752. The Marquis Duquesne was chosen to succeed him; but since Duquesne was not able to reach Canada before July, the second Baron de Longueuil administered the affairs of New France.

Longueuil knew that his appointment was temporary, and he therefore did not attempt to inaugurate a new policy, but indicated that he intended to carry out the plans formulated by La Jonquière before his death. He said it was his hope that the completion of La Jonquière's strategy would restore the Ohio and western Indians to the French and oust the English from among them. He also expressed the fervent wish that the commissioners would soon round out their work and settle the boundary question between England and France in America. Longueuil's report to the French minister of April 21, 1752, is an interesting document. He noted that the Indians on the Ohio River were all friendly to the English, "for whom alone they work," and that not a party of Indians went to the Ohio River region "but leaves some there to increase the rebel forces." Evidently the English were having reasonable success at that time in their program of proselyting. The temporary governor-general set forth numerous facts of interest about the western Indians. He stated that the Wea, the Piankashaw, and the Miami formed one nation or confederacy. A rumor, he said, had reached the French that the Piankashaw, the Illinois, and the Osage Indians were going to assemble and make a general attack on the French. So far, at least a dozen Frenchmen had been slain in the region north of the Ohio; according to his information, most of the murders had been perpetrated by the Miami. Expected spring news from that area would bring a report of more deaths, he was sure. The real responsibility for the killings he placed at the feet of the English, whose closest ally appeared to be La Demoiselle. Longueuil feared that the general conspiracy then brewing against the French might even end in the capture of Toronto. As if those troubles were not enough to wrinkle the brow and tax the brain of his superior, the governor added more bad news. He said that the crops had failed all through the territory from the Ohio River to the lakes, and that a food shortage was imminent. He was certain that Detroit would suffer a famine. In addition, he stated that the dreaded smallpox was ravaging the entire frontier, killing friend and foe alike. Few administrators of that day or this would have envied the Marquis Duquesne the task that he was about to assume.

Duquesne's instructions were about as explicit as such directions could be, when the factors of distance and the vagueness of colonial reports are taken into consideration. Some definite changes in plans of action were made. Hitherto, it had been the policy of the French to set one Indian tribe, or group of tribes, against another tribe or group of tribes. In view of the general English threat, that policy was altered. Duquesne was instructed to avoid a war with the Indians, although he was expected to carry out the minister's orders. La Jonquière's plan, which Longueuil had intended to put into execution, was to be scrapped. The minister admitted to Duquesne that by the Treaty of Utrecht the English might claim the right to trade with the Indians; but he stated that the French were not bound to allow such trade to be transacted on French soil. He argued that the Ohio River and all its tributaries were incontestably French on the basis of La Salle's discoveries. The English pretensions to trading rights there, on the basis of sovereignty over the Iroquois Indians, he entirely disallowed. He informed Duquesne that it was highly important that the English activities in that territory be stopped. Failure in this matter would very likely mean severance of communications between Canada and Louisiana. The governor-general was instructed to drive out the English traders found there, seize their goods, and destroy their posts. He was just as carefully warned to make the French Indians understand that the French held nothing against them, and that the rebellious ones would not be driven from the Ohio. They might engage in trade with the English, if they wished, but such trade would have to be carried on in the English country. It was the minister's belief that if the English were driven out, and the French trading posts were thereafter kept well stocked and carefully managed, there would be little likelihood that the Indians would travel great distances merely to trade with the English. He informed Duquesne that if those goals could be achieved, peace and French influence would surely be restored in the troubled area. The strategy to be used in carrying out the orders was left to the ingenious mind of the new governor to develop. But before Duquesne arrived in Quebec, the Miami settlement at Pickawillanee had been attacked by a band of Indians from the upper lakes region, and the episode in which Captain Trent figured had already transpired.

Totally ignorant of what had happened to the Twightwees and their town of Pickawillanee on the very day that he and Andrew Montour set their faces westward, Trent recorded as the opening entry in his journal for June 21, 1752, "We left the Logstown." After four days of travel he and Montour met a white man who had departed from Pickawillanee about two weeks earlier. The traveler stated that the French Indians had visited the "Pict" town and had succeeded in getting twenty-five families of the Twightwee Indians to go back with them to the

French. That was not a pleasant message, but the bearers of gifts moved onward. Two days later they met a Mingo Indian by the name of Powell. He told them that he had left Detroit twenty days earlier and that ten days before he had left that post, a force of three hundred French and Indians had set out from Detroit to persuade the Twightwees to return to the French side. Thus the signs of trouble grew as the ambassadors pressed westward. On June 29, as they arrived at the Mingo village called Muskingum, on the banks of the Tuscarawas River, they met some white men from Hockhocken who bore the bad news of the fall of Pickawillanee. These messengers stated that all the white men at the town had been killed—a report that, according to later information, proved slightly inaccurate.

Not exactly the "timid soul" that he was later labeled by the young and inexperienced Washington, Trent pushed on in the face of the threatened danger. A few days later, at Hockhocken, he and Montour met William Ives. The latter had passed by Pickawillanee in the night, and he reported that the houses of the white men were on fire, and that the fort was deserted. He had heard one rifle shot accompanied by some shouts, but nothing more. The next day his story was confirmed at the village of Meguck. Since Pickawillanee was apparently deserted, Trent and his companion decided to change their course somewhat and visit the Lower Shawnee Town, located near the mouth of the Scioto River. There they expected to learn the details of the attack on the Twightwee town. Three days later they came in sight of the village and were greeted by the Indians with the usual yelling, shouting, and firing of guns, typical of an Indian welcome. After being kindly received, Trent and Montour were conducted to the long council house, where they were well fed and where the Shawnee asked them for news. The villagers were disappointed when their visitors begged to be excused from talking to them until the next day. There were two men in the town whom Trent and Montour wished to see before they talked with any others. They were Thomas Burney and Andrew McBryer.

When Pickawillanee was attacked, Burney and McBryer were the only white men to escape. They told Trent and Montour that on the forenoon of June 21, 240 Wisconsin Indians, led by Charles de Langlade and another Frenchman, had surprised the Twightwees while most of their warriors were out hunting and the remainder were at work in the cornfields. The attack was so sudden that the whites had the greatest difficulty in getting inside the fort. Three white men, who could not reach the fort, locked themselves in one of the houses. Later they were captured by the attackers without firing a shot, despite the fact that they could have put up a stiff resistance. The house they occupied was well stocked with guns and ammunition, and although they were encouraged to fight by those in the fort, they refused to do so. As soon as the three were taken, they told the French and their Indians that there were only about twenty men and boys in the fort, including the white men. That news gave an added impetus to the attack, and a smart fire was directed at the fort until the afternoon. At that time the French force agreed to raise the siege if the Twightwees would surrender the Englishmen in the fort. After a council of war, it was agreed by the besieged that since there were so few of them the best plan would be to surrender. Another factor in the decision to surrender was the lack of water; the well located inside the fort was dry at that season of the year.

After hiding McBryer and Burney, the Twightwees surrendered the other white men. Regardless of the understanding that the whites would not be injured, the French Indians, as soon as they got their prisoners outside the fort, stabbed one of the Englishmen, who had been wounded in the stomach, scalped him, cut out his heart, and ate it. That rite was performed on the assumption that to eat a captive's heart gave special strength to the diner. The Indian allies of the French were notorious for such cannibalistic habits, which were especially prevalent among the Ottawa, who were known to kill, roast, and eat their English captives. Little wonder that both the English and the more tractable Miami Indians feared the attacks of the northern savages. The five remaining English captives, along with £3,000 in plunder belonging to the English traders, were carried to Canada; McBryer and Burney remained hidden, and later escaped. But La Demoiselle, the principal chief of the Twightwees, who happened to be one of the small band captured in the fort, did not fare so well. For some time he had been known among the English by the pet name of "Old Britain," because of his close attachment to the English interest. On this occasion, that relationship proved to be his undoing. When the French Indians found him they killed him, and then boiled and ate him. After that feast there was no longer any doubt as to which side the Miami chief was on!

Governor Duquesne seemed well pleased with the five English prisoners and with the report that Langlade brought back with him from the Twightwee country. In his own report to the French minister, Duquesne said, "I trust that this blow added to the complete pillage suffered by the English on this occasion, will discourage them from trading on our lands." Then he made an impassioned plea that a pension of two hundred livres yearly be given to Langlade for his splendid service. It is not known whether Langlade received his annuity, but the task of Trent and Montour in the Miami country had without question become much more complex as a result of his foray.

The morning after Trent and Montour arrived in the Shawnee town, they were visited by some Six Nations Indians who asked Trent to accompany them in an effort to collect the scattered Twightwees. Trent replied that he and Montour would fulfill the request. Then the Six Nations and Shawnee Indians retired with the Englishmen to the long house for a council meeting. There, with much palaver and the use of many strings of black and white wampum, mutual reassurances of the continued existence of the alliance with the Twightwees were exchanged. Trent hoped to start on the proposed journey in a day or so, but he was disappointed. Five days passed before a small party of twenty men and boys could be gathered together for the trip, whereas Trent had expected at least one hundred. The cause of the delay was not hard to find; a quantity of liquor had been brought into the town, and most of the Indians were drunk. By July 20, however, the group was within a few miles of Pickawillanee. Scouts, who had been sent out to reconnoiter, reported that the town seemed to be abandoned, although two French flags were flying. The English and Indian party then proceeded into the town, lowered the French colors, and raised the Union Jack. Scouts were sent out to try to track the Twightwees and discover in which direction they had fled. When the scouts returned with their report, dusk was falling, and preparations were made to spend the night in the deserted fort. Water was carried inside the walls. Two of the three gates were closed, and, as darkness settled, everything was in readiness for rest, when suddenly three guns were discharged not far distant. Four scouts were sent out along the French road leading north, the direction from which the sounds had come, but no one was located. The scare was sufficient, however, to keep the entire party awake all night, guns ready for action.

In the morning another scouting party scoured the flanks of the French road, but did not find any people. At noon the group was reorganized and set off down the near-by creek to trail the fleeing Indians. They had traversed about ten miles when camp was made in order to hunt meat. That was necessary since their daily food supply depended on what they killed along the way. Then the journey was resumed. Trent noted that the weather was the hottest the natives in that region had ever known. Many Indian dogs dropped dead in the woods while hunting. The runs and creeks were so dry that the men "were almost perished for want of water." Finally they returned to the Lower Shawnee Town, to find that several of the hunted Twightwee people were already there. Among them were Old Britain's wife; his son Assapausa, sometimes called the young Piankashaw King; the Turtle; and a number of women and children. Apparently most of the Miami had fled in the direction of the Wabash. Trent had a chat with the young Piankashaw King and his party, but the main conference was delayed for several days.

By the time the Shawnee arrived at the decision to call a conference, there were many guests in the village. Besides Trent and the other Englishmen, there were Indians present from the tribes of the Six Nations, the Delawares, and the Twightwees; even the Cherokee from the South had six representatives there. The negotiations had scarcely started when Trent received an affront. A Shawnee raised a French flag as the emblem under which business was to be transacted. The act appears to have been an innocent one, but Trent quickly reacted. He rose to his feet and announced to the assembled group that he was there to transact the King's business, but refused to do it under a French flag. Then he turned on his heel and started to leave the council, closely followed by Montour. A quick-witted Cherokee chief, by the name of Blue Shadow, immediately sensed the difficulty. In a flash he jumped to his feet, grabbed the banner, and threw it as far as he could. Trent then resumed his place and, as soon as the usual preliminaries were over, began making speeches to the Twightwee Indians. After practically a month of delay, the business for which Virginia had hired him was about to be transacted.

Trent told the Twightwees that their brothers, the Delawares, had asked the English to remember the treaties made with the Delaware, Six Nations, Shawnee, Twightwee, and Wyandot Indians, and that the Delawares desired the Twightwees to renew the friendship already made. Moreover, the Delawares had requested that the Six Nations and the English place their hands upon the heads of the Twightwees to keep the French from hurting them, with the advice that the Twightwees should not listen to what the French told them. Trent then informed the refugees that the King of England, their father, had sent a large present of goods to Logstown to be divided among his children; that because the Twightwees had been absent from the Logstown meeting, the King had sent them a part of the present. The English, Trent said, joined with the Six Nations in advising the Miami tribes to stand fast by the English friendship. He further assured the Indians of the friendship of the government of Virginia. The speech was concluded and sealed in the usual Indian fashion by the delivery of a belt of wampum.

The Twightwees responded with a speech of friendship, which they sealed by presenting Trent with a fine beaver blanket with a green spot in the middle. This design was intended to represent spring in its bloom, or, in this instance, a renewal of the existing friendship between the English and the Indians. To the Six Nations the Twightwees directed their next harangue. They commented on the sorrow they felt for having given up the English traders in their fort to the French, even though it had seemed the best thing to do. It was their wish, they said, that all their Indian brothers should speak to the English so that the English would not desert them. They wanted the white men to pity their women and children and to continue to send their traders among them.

To this earnest plea the Six Nations replied in a reassuring fashion. The Twightwees were reminded of the high esteem in which the Six Nations and the English held them, and were warned to hold fast to that friendship. No trust was to be placed in the lies told them by the French. After a number of additional expressions of mutual friendship between the Six Nations and the Twightwees, the Six Nations Indians presented Trent with a twist of tobacco, which he was asked to carry back to the Half King with the facts about this conference on the banks of the Scioto. The Half King was invited to visit the Twightwees to see what could be done to help them. Pledges of friendship for the Twightwees were then made by the Shawnee, who also announced that they had gone against the French. All nations were asked to assist them in the latter move. The next speaker to appear before the council was a woman. She was the wife of Old Britain, and she called upon all the allies of the Twightwees to pity her lonely widowhood and her son, whose care she then gave into the hands of the English, the Six Nations, the Shawnee, and the Delawares. Her request was sealed by the delivery of a string of wampum. Immediately the Delawares produced a feathered pipe and a beaver blanket from the Ouiatenon, or Wea, Indians (a tribe of the Miami dwelling on the Wabash), along with a friendly and conciliatory speech. Then came the turn of the six Cherokee warriors to speak.

It was to the Shawnee that the Cherokee especially directed their discourse. They had come to make peace with the Six Nations and their allies. Therefore, they gave the council a pouch of tobacco to smoke, with the suggestion that while it was being smoked the council members should think of the Cherokee tribe and pity its condition. The reason for seeking the special attention soon became obvious. As the Cherokee speech continued, it was stated that these six delegates had come north to inform the council that in about two months, fourteen hundred of their number would be at the Shawnee Town to take up their residence among the Indians north of the Ohio. Their reason for wanting to migrate was laid at the feet of the English. They said that the English blamed them for killing their traders and for that reason would not supply them with powder and lead. Without such supplies they could not hunt and were therefore obliged to migrate. They knew that many traders had been killed, but the Cherokee were not guilty of the acts; the blame should rest on the French and their Indians. Then the warriors begged the Six Nations and the Delawares to intercede with the English, so that the English might take pity on the Cherokee women and children and give them protection. They concluded their speech with the presentation of a string of white wampum.

The council finally adjourned, and Trent went about the task of distributing the Virginia present to the Twightwees. A scarlet cloak was given to Old Britain's son, as well as a hat, a jacket, a shirt, and stockings. Old Britain's widow also received an outfit of clothing. Those specific gifts having been bestowed, Trent gave the remainder of the presents to Assapausa, the Turtle, and two other warriors of the Twightwee nation for distribution among their people in whatever manner they saw fit. He succeeded in persuading an Indian trader to lend his services and his horses to transport the present wherever the Indians wished to have it carried. Trent was then ready to leave the Shawnee village. Just before he and Montour departed, a messenger arrived from the Six Nations with an order for the Indians in that region to keep themselves together, since an army from Canada had arrived on the lakes.

When Trent and Montour returned to Logstown, Montour was given the task of redelivering the Shawnee council speeches to the head men of the Six Nations residing there. This was done in order that these Indians might in turn relay the speeches to the head council at Onondaga. Sometime between October 6 and November 6, Trent arrived in Williamsburg and made his report to Governor Dinwiddie.

Shortly thereafter, Trent made his first attempt at large-scale speculation in land. The Ohio Company and Virginia activities had evidently convinced him that success on the frontier was more likely to crown the efforts of Virginia than those of Pennsylvania. Thus, on November 6, 1752, with nine others, not named, he petitioned the government of Virginia for a grant of two hundred thousand acres. The grant was to be located on the Ohio River and waters thereof, beginning at the boundary of the grant to the Ohio Company, although not to interfere with it in any way. This first venture came to nought, but the virus of large-scale land speculation was thereby planted in Trent's blood.

On December 10, 1752, not long after Trent had returned from Picka-willanee, Governor Dinwiddie wrote a letter to the Board of Trade in which he indicated the deep concern with which he viewed conditions in the Ohio region. In this long and detailed epistle, the governor attempted to enlighten his superiors on the exact state of affairs in the back country, so that they might realize the necessity for quick action. He announced Trent's return from the Ohio and said that he was sending a copy of the trader's journal, which would speak for itself. The part the French were supposed to have been playing on the frontier was also set forth. Their habit of offering the Indians one hundred crowns for every white scalp was deprecated. Dinwiddie pointed to the fact that as a result of the robberies committed by the French at the expense of the English traders, the King's subjects were demanding protection from him and the power to make reprisals. He said that he had not granted the traders such rights, but wished that the Board would give him some advice on how to act in the future. Since Governor Dinwiddie was really stating the position of the governors of several of the English colonies, it is only fair to point out that the French, in their hostile actions against the traders, were merely retaliating for similar treatment accorded them by the English.

Evidence in support of the theory that the boundary dispute between Pennsylvania and Virginia began with the formation and aggressive policy of the Ohio company is found in Dinwiddie's statement that Pennsylvania disputed the right of Virginia to the Ohio. The governor also noted that after the arrival of Trent, Thomas Burney had come from the Twightwee Indians to Williamsburg with a string of wampum, a French scalp, and a calumet pipe, in addition to a written message, seeking Virginia's assistance. In response to the request, Dinwiddie had sent Burney back to the Miami tribe with wampum and a promise that in the spring he would send the Twightwees and their Six Nations allies a large present of guns, ammunition, and clothing. In explaining his act to the Board of Trade, Dinwiddie imparted the knowledge that the western Indians were powerful and therefore worth keeping on the English side. There was no time more propitious than the present, continued the wily governor—who, it must be remembered, was a partner in the Ohio Company—for the British colonies (Virginia?) to draw close to the Indians and encourage the settling of the interior parts of the country. He reminded his superiors that it would take a great many presents to accomplish this purpose, but he thought any expenditure authorized would be quickly counterbalanced by the returns from the new settlements that were bound to appear. Humbly, he proposed a plan: the Board should take £1,000 from the quit rents of the colony and invest the sum in Indian goods. He naively suggested John Hanbury, London merchant, as the proper person to handle the order and stated that he was sending Hanbury a list of the goods most useful in Indian dealings. Here the reader must be made aware that Hanbury was also a proprietor in the Ohio Company. The Virginia governor was apparently getting his private and public business slightly ensnarled.

Dinwiddie disclosed to the Board of Trade that he had already sent word to the Indians that he would meet them at Cheningue (Logstown) in the spring. A personal appearance, he understood, drew the deepest respect from the red men. To spur the English officials to action, he informed them of the rumor that the French were planning to build forts down the Ohio Valley to the Mississippi. He said that the Twightwee tribes intended to fall on the French and drive them out, and that this move, if successful, would open much additional land to English settlement. To help accomplish that end, he implored his superiors to support the building of English forts on the Ohio as the Indians had requested. He pointed out that since the Indians had opened an eighty-mile road between the headwaters of the Potomac and a tributary of the Ohio River, transportation to the region would be made easier.

That the Board of Trade was likely to approve Dinwiddie's December letter was indicated to him on January 17, when he received a favorable answer to an earlier dispatch. Nothing was done for several months, however, about arranging a conference or sending presents to the Indians.

In the meantime, Pennsylvania had also been officially informed of the attack on Pickawillanee. The same messenger, Thomas Burney, carried the news to the governor of the Quaker colony. Burney arrived at Carlisle on August 29, and from there his presence was announced to the governor by Robert Callender, a leading Indian trader and justice of Cumberland County. Callender indicated that Burney carried a message from the Twightwee Indians and was willing to appear before the officials of the province for a hearing, if desired. In their written message to Governor Hamilton, the Twightwees, after expressing condolences for the English traders who had been taken by the French, asked for advice on how to proceed against the enemy in the future. They said that since their great leader, the Piankashaw King, had been killed and eaten before their very eyes, they felt like a lost people. They feared that their brothers, the English, would desert them, and they were therefore making this special appeal to their Brother "Onas," as the Pennsylvania governor was called. Although Hamilton was interested and asked Burney to come to Philadelphia, the usual delays ensued. The year 1753 arrived before the assemblies of Pennsylvania and Virginia were ready to appropriate money for presents to the western Indians. By that time the French were already encroaching on the borders of Pennsylvania. The task of holding the Ohio Indian allies loyal to the English cause had become an almost insurmountable one.

CHAPTER III

Virginia Service Resumed

Governor Duquesne arrived at his post in July, 1752, and immediately began to study the situation that faced him. Very shortly he decided that if the English were to be kept out of the region west of the mountains, as his instructions indicated, it would be well to enlist nature on his side; he resolved, therefore, to build a string of forts southward from Canada along the Ohio River and its tributaries. That strategy, he thought, would effectively confine the English colonies to the seaboard. Thus at one blow the valuable fur trade with the western Indians would be restored, and the safety of the communication line between Canada and Louisiana would be assured. Before this elaborate plan could be put into effect, however, much difficult preliminary work had to be done. Conditions in Canada were chaotic. Many commandants at the various trading posts were engaged in the Indian traffic in one way or another and were careless about their duties as officials. The colonial officers were reluctant to accept active service in the field; and soldiers in general were insubordinate and disrespectful toward their superiors. In this relaxed atmosphere, desertions were common.

The new governor-general was not easily discouraged. He set about the task of rebuilding the army and strengthening the morale of the people with a will and determination that were bound to bring results. By the time he had completed his reorganization, he had created a colonial militia service of thirteen hundred men ready to march on short notice; and the number of habitants capable of bearing arms in a crisis was increased from a mere handful to thirteen thousand. As the work of organizing the expedition for the occupation of the upper Ohio Valley progressed, Duquesne was on hand at Montreal to see that everything went well. The army that was created there increased in size day by day. Many of the Canadian Indians—who had recently been courting the favor of the English—impressed with the growing numbers under the French flag, hastened to reassert their vows of fidelity to the French governor. In fear and trembling they told Duquesne that they were aware of his power and asked him to have pity on their wives and children. Even the proud and haughty Iroquois were impressed. As the commander of the expedition, the Chevalier de Marin, moved toward Lake Erie, the Iroquois sent out their messengers to inquire of him whether he was marching with the "hatchet uplifted" or whether he came in peace. Marin replied that he marched in peace so long as he encountered no opposition to his will.

Originally, Duquesne had intended to land his troops and build a fort at the portage called Chatacouit (Portland, New York), but at the last minute a much safer and more spacious harbor was discovered, which the French named Presque Isle (Erie, Pennsylvania). There, before the end of the first week in August, 1753, Marin completed the first of the proposed line of French forts. By the time it was finished, the vanguard of Marin's force had completed the opening of a twenty-mile carriage road soutward to French Creek, called by the French, Riviere au Boeuf. At that point a second fort called Le Boeuf (Waterford) was built before the summer ended. From Le Boeuf, Marin sent a detachment of fifty men south to Venango (Franklin), at the mouth of French Creek, to make preparations for a third fort. The French were not well received there by the Indians, although some members of the Delaware, Shawnee, and Seneca tribes had been helpful in carrying out the earlier operations immediately south of Presque Isle. This third fort could not be completed that fall, however, because the water in French Creek was too low to allow transportation of the needed supplies (It was completed in April, 1754, and called Fort Machault). In the autumn Marin detailed three hundred men to garrison the two forts already constructed, and the remainder of the army was ordered to return to Canada for the winter. Duquesne was highly elated at the success of his efforts, even though he had had to use force in order to obtain the necessary food supplies from the farmers. Concerning the efficiency and co-operation of his officers, including Marin and Le Mercier, the engineer, he could not speak too highly. Therefore, in view of Marin's ability, it was a great shock to Duquesne to learn of the death of the old campaigner in October, in the wilds of northwestern Pennsylvania. Duquesne considered his loss irreparable.

As the forces of France were being maneuvered into position for the approaching duel, her opponents were not idle. The spirit of inertia shown by the provincial assemblies in the matter of caring for the Indians was not equally manifest among the colonial governors, the members of the Ohio Company, or the Indian traders. With thousands of pounds invested, the fear of losing not only the profit, but the principal as well, galvanized these hardy and fearless frontier adventurers, and their backers, into action.

In February, 1753, Captain Trent, along with Thomas Cresap and several other traders, began to check conditions on the Ohio. There they found over a dozen Frenchmen building houses at Logstown, ostensibly for trading purposes. But there was every reason to suspect that the builders had other plans in mind. Alarmed, the traders notified Governor Dinwiddie of the French activities and of the report that some of the Twightwees had gone over to the side of the French. The governor was very much concerned. In his reply, he attributed the Twightwee desertion to the fact that Burney had not returned immediately to those Indians with the message that Virginia would send them a large present in the spring. As for the French, he hoped that the housebuilders at Logstown were traders only, and that there was no large army in the lakes region. It was a source of wonder to him where any French army on the lakes could be getting rations, since he had been informed by various dispatches that food was very scarce in Canada. He asserted that the running of the boundary line between Pennsylvania and Virginia was a necessary prerequisite to the establishment of order west of the mountains. The Indians had given the English full right to settle the lands east of the Ohio River, he said, and he therefore felt that some method had to be found to keep the French out. He expressed his pleasure that some of the Cherokee were planning to remove to the Lower Shawnee Town, but in view of that prospective move, he was concerned at the news that the warriors of the Six Nations had gone to make war on the southern Indians. He told Trent and Cresap that he was sorry that they had not been able to inform him earlier of the designs of the Iroquois, for it was his plan to keep the northern and southern Indians in a "confirmed State of Peace, which will be of great Service to the British Colonies on the Con't." In closing, he said, "I wish You Health, and when anything occurs of Consequence in regard to the Ind's, Y'r advis'g me there of will much Oblige."

Two months later Trent informed Governor Hamilton of Pennsylvania of the state of affairs on the frontier, which in that short interval had become much more alarming. Writing from Virginia on April 10, he told the governor that he had just received a letter from George Croghan stating that fifty Ottawa and Connewango (Seneca) Indians, one Low Dutchman, named "Philip Philips," and one Six Nations Indian, who was the captain of the party, had met some English traders at a place called Kentucky on "this side" of the "Allegheny River," about 150 miles from the Lower Shawnee Town. There the Indians had taken eight prisoners, five of whom were in the service of Trent and Croghan and the others in that of another trader, Lazarus Lowrey. Trent reported that he and Croghan had also lost goods valued at more than £300. He recounted likewise that three of John Finley's men had been killed in the Pict country, and that it was feared that Finley had also been captured. Moreover, a band of Wyandot Indians, accompanied by one Frenchman, had robbed Michael Teaffe's traders, near the lakes, of five horseloads of skins and had taken several of the traders as prisoners. Croghan, with some other white men and some Indians, was coming eastward through the woods, trying to avoid the enemy. The remainder of the English traders were coming up the river in a body, but it was a question whether they would escape. Three hundred Ottawa were expected at the Lower Shawnee Town daily, and another party of French and Indians was said to be moving in the same direction.

So far as the English traders were concerned, the Indian country had become untenable; they were setting out eastward for the settlements as fast as it was possible to travel. French strategy was working out as planned. The plight of the Indian allies of the English may easily be imagined. Deserted by their pale-faced brothers, they knew not where to turn. Describing the confusion prevailing among the Indians, Trent declared, "There is no knowing who to trust. I expect they will all Join the French, except the Delawares, as they expect no assistance from the English." He added that he intended to start at once for the Allegheny with provisions for "our People, that are Coming through the Woods and up the River."

When Trent's reports reached Philadelphia, the governor sent them on to the Pennsylvania Assembly. Only by such vivid portrayals could he hope to arouse the sympathies of the legislators. But evidence that higher authorities were becoming concerned about the trans-Allegheny conditions is to be found in the correspondence of the provincial executive. Early in May, Hamilton wrote to Dinwiddie concerning the backwoods difficulties. He mentioned Trent's correspondence and said that he was of the opinion that the Indians on the frontier would not be able to remain independent much longer. The proprietaries, he said, had instructed him to work with the colony of Virginia in the building of a fort on the lands granted to the Ohio Company. He then asked Dinwiddie if Virginia intended to build such a fort. The Pennsylvanian was very careful to remind Dinwiddie that any fort-building operations were not to be allowed to jeopardize Pennsylvania's claim to the region. Fuel was slowly but surely being added to a smoldering fire in the matter of the boundary question.

Two days later, Trent, in a letter ·from Pine Creek (Etna, Pennsylvania) to William Logan, Philadelphia merchant, announced some startling news: he and Croghan had just received a message from John

Fraser at Venango that a French army was coming down from Canada, with cannon, to build a fort at the forks of the Monongahela River. Trent recorded his surprise at the fact that the provincial governments were suffering "us dayly to be robed & Murdered without putting it in our power to do ourselves Justice." The French interpreter, he stated, had "plainly told" the Indians that the French intended striking the Pennsylvania and Virginia people. Trent supposed that Logan had heard of the recent trader robberies committed by the French Indians. Perhaps Logan was one of Trent's creditors, and Trent may have felt that the merchant's influence with the assembly might help to jar that body into action. Be that as it may, the losses faced by Trent were not a joking matter, and the trader's Scotch ire was thoroughly aroused. In no uncertain terms he expressed his feelings: "We are in hopes five or six hundred [Frenchmen] will come while we are here that we may have the pleasure of helping the Indians kill a few of them which would be some satisfaction."

Trent and Croghan had an important storehouse at this time near the mouth of Pine Creek, where they also had fenced fields of Indian corn and a number of large canoes and bateaux. At the time that the news from John Fraser reached the Englishmen, several other traders who had fled from points farther out in the Indian country, were also at Pine Creek. The traders thought it wise to inform the Half King of Fraser's message, and the chief was greatly perturbed. Daily, he said, he was expecting Scarouady (Monacatootha), the Oneida chief who had been detailed by the Six Nations to care for the Shawnee; upon his arrival, a council would be called. A few days later the chief arrived, and messengers were sent out to the surrounding Delawares and Shawnee, inviting them to a council meeting. But as those Indians were under the influence of the white man's "firewater," they did not appear. The Six Nations chiefs, therefore, with a handful of local Indians, held the proposed council with the white traders.

After Croghan had delivered a letter from Governor Clinton of New York and one from Sir William Johnson, British Indian agent for the northern tribes, Trent presented four strings of wampum to the chiefs with a message from Governor Dinwiddie. He stated that the Virginia governor looked upon the Indians as the owners of the Ohio lands, and that if the French attempted to drive them off, Virginia would supply them with arms and ammunition to defend themselves. But both traders and governors were most interested in the answer to one question: Did the Indians really intend to oppose the French or not? The welfare of the traders, present and future, depended on that answer, as did also the prospects for future peace on the frontiers. When the question was broached, the Indians refused an immediate reply. They, too, were well aware of the gravity of the situation they were facing. After an all-night council, which lasted until two o'clock the next day, the Half King, who was spokesman for the Six Nations Indians on the Ohio, declared that he was ready to give an answer. He indicated that if the French came peacefully they would be received in that manner as friends; but if they came as enemies they would be treated as such. It was his hope, he said, that the English would understand the position of the Indians and would send them arms and ammunition. He believed that if the English responded quickly, the Indians would be able to strike the French. The traders were promised safety among the Indians so long as the Indians were safe themselves. In a few days, the chief men of the Delaware and Shawnee tribes became sober enough to approve the Half King's statements.

On May 16 Trent and his group received another disconcerting message from John Fraser, stating that some Frenchmen had come to his trading post at Venango to trade some deer skins and furs. The Indians at the post had been informed that a body of Frenchmen would be at Venango soon with presents for them from the governor of Canada. These men were looked upon by Fraser and the Indians as spies. The English trader was considerably worried on his own account. In his isolated post there were certain advantages, but they were mostly economic in character and depended upon peacetime conditions for their exploitation. Fear of the possible consequences if he stayed on the upper reaches of the Allegheny too long caused him at this time to move his trading post from Venango to the mouth of Turtle Creek (North Braddock), not far from the forks of the Ohio, where he felt that his life and movable possessions would be safer from attack.

The late spring and summer of 1753 found Trent increasingly active. During the last week in May, he and several other traders appeared before the Pennsylvania Assembly to be questioned regarding Indian affairs on the frontier. The day following his appearance, the colony of Pennsylvania ordered a condolence present of £200 to be given to the Twightwees. During the same month Governor Dinwiddie, as a result of the startling information he had received from the traders in the Ohio country, sent word to Trent that he desired his services to carry another present to the Indians on the Ohio. Immediately after receiving this message, Trent dispatched a messenger with a letter and some strips of wampum to the Ohio Indians. The emissary was instructed to inform the Indians that Trent would be there in twenty days with a speech and some arms and ammunition for them. But the letter and the wampum were stolen from the messenger, which meant that he was forced to proceed on an important errand without the proper credentials. He reported back to Trent that in one of the Indian towns he had met a certain Colonel Russel who had claimed that he had been sent by the Virginia governor to invite the Indians to a treaty making to be held at Winchester. Russel had said that he had also been instructed to inquire of the Indians what the French movements were on the Ohio. When Trent's messenger had told the Indians that Trent was coming and that the trader had requested a guard of young men for his safe conduct, in case the Indians feared trouble, Colonel Russel had declared that it was all a "Lye"; that Trent was not coming in twenty days with powder and ammunition.

When this news reached Trent, he was thoroughly disgusted. He wrote to Dinwiddie from the north branch of the Potomac that he would proceed with the present at once, and that he expected to be with the Indians in another week. The present would have been delivered earlier, he said, except for delays encountered in getting the goods from Winchester and in replacing some horses that he had lost on the Potomac. He promised Dinwiddie a full and detailed account of his journey as soon as it was completed. Then he indicated his feeling concerning the Colonel Russel episode:

> But you must excuse Me Sir, if I decline transacting any further Business for the Government of Virginia, for I cannot help conceiving Myself much hurt by the Gentleman who undertook to send Colonel Russel (who at any time is but little better than a Madman) to interfere in a Business, which I had undertaken to transact for the Govr of Virginia at your Request.

Whatever damage was done to Trent's feelings was evidently repaired satisfactorily by Dinwiddie, however, for during the course of events the trader accepted subsequent commissions from the Virginia governor.

True to his agreement, Trent set out from the Potomac with the Virginia present for the Ohio Indians. Heavy rains and high waters delayed his progress somewhat, so that it was July 11 before he reached Logstown. There he spent a day in collecting news of the frontier and in conferring with the Half King. He learned that Scarouady and a party of warriors had been sent as spies among the French to gather information, and that they were expected back at Logstown in about four days. The Half King said that as soon as the spies returned, the chiefs would call all the Indians together, hear Trent's speech, and receive his present.

Two days after Trent's arrival at Logstown, an Indian runner came in from Lake Erie and stated that a French army of twelve hundred men had arrived on the lakes, in addition to canoe men and those who were detailed to carry provisions. Many more were supposed to be on the way. He said that the French had already built a strong fort (Presque Isle) and laid out a town, in which one hundred houses were completed, at the "side of Lake Erie," where several cannon had already arrived. But even more disturbing was this Indian's assertion that the French had chosen yet another site for a fort and town, and that a second French army was on its way up the Mississippi and had constructed two posts as it moved north. Finally, the messenger reported that the French claimed all the lands west of the Allegheny Mountains, having taken possession "three Years ago" by sinking iron plates at the mouths of several creeks and putting up tin plates on the trees.

On July 16 the Half King told Trent that one of his warriors had returned from the French army with the news that the French commander was going to proceed down the Allegheny and expected to take possession of the country along the way. The Frenchman had informed the Indian that the French intended to ask the English what they were doing at the forks of the Ohio and order them to leave, and that if the English "did not go, they wou'd catch them by the Hair & beat them, & throw them over the Hill." The Indian had reported that the French planned at this time to build forts as far down the Ohio as the mouth of Beaver Creek. There the plan was to wait for some Frenchmen who were coming down the Scioto River, before making any further moves. After delivering this news, the Half King, in the presence of Trent and some Indians, including several of the pro-French Delawares, made a speech in which he said that the French had poisoned a number of Indians with liquor, and that they would have killed him, too, except that he had refused to drink.

The next day two Frenchmen from the army on the lakes visited Shannopin's Town (on the site of the present Lawrenceville section of Pittsburgh). There they conversed with the Half King, who spent much of his time in that Delaware village. They explained that the French were going to divide the territory with the English; that there was a great silver mine, as well as several powder mines, in the region, which they now intended to take; that they expected to have a "hard Pull by the Hair with the English, but they wou'd have them"; and that the Allegheny Hill was to be the boundary line between the English and the French possessions. All waters that flowed into the Ohio were theirs. Trent tried to calm the fears of the chief by telling him that there were no powder mines. He also questioned the sincerity of the statement about dividing the lands, since the French were advancing with an army.

At the end of the third week in July other Indian runners came to Logstown from the lake region with more disquieting news. The French had begun another fort and town (Fort Le Boeuf) south of Lake Erie, and the French interpreter had employed some Delawares to repair Fraser's trading house at Venango, where the interpreter expected to live. The runners said that the French intended to build a third fort at Venango and, as soon as it was finished, to move on south to the forks of the Ohio, where a fourth structure would be erected. A fifth fort was planned for the mouth of Beaver Creek. After the completion of these projects, the French builders intended to join the forces moving up the Ohio River and attack the Shawnee and Twightwee Indians.

The similarity of all the reports was enough to cause Trent a great deal of concern. Activities of the French Indian spies in and about the town during the ensuing week did not help to allay his growing suspicions. Andrew Montour's brother, Lewis, came to town on August 4 and talked of the great numbers of Frenchmen south of Presque Isle. He said that they would move down toward Logstown just as soon as the river rose. Trent recorded in his journal that he was suspicious of Montour because the latter was a Frenchman at heart. The next day the head man of the Connewango Indians arrived and said that his people had received Trent's invitation to come to a conference, but that the French would not permit them to attend because it was feared that the tribe would join the English.

Not until August 7 did Chief Scarouady and his party of Six Nations Indians return from their trip to the French army. They verified all the previous reports about the French forts and French operations in general. Here and there they had gathered new and interesting details to add to facts already known. They mentioned the existence of a small lake near Fort Le Boeuf, with which the French intended to connect French Creek by means of a canal that they had already started digging. The idea was to control the flow of the water from the lake into French Creek by a gate, so that any time they wished to navigate the creek it would be easy to raise the level of the water by lifting the gate. The French commander had told Scarouady that the French army when together numbered ten thousand men, and that it was going to march southward to drive the English out and take possession of all the lands west of the Allegheny Hill. At each fort the governor of Canada would deposit powder, lead, and guns for his children, the Indians. So far, only eight hundred Frenchmen had arrived in northwestern Pennsylvania, according to Scarouady's estimate. Nevertheless, they were as busy as beavers, opening up a road, transporting supplies, and constructing buildings. The Indians observed that the French were almost dead from working seven days of every week, and he therefore believed that one hundred "brisk young Men wou'd kill a Thousand of them." He reported the presence of but eight cannon, although he said that more were on the way. Fort Presque Isle was described as a very strong fort protected by a ditch, a high earthen wall, and four bastions; while Fort Le Boeuf had only palisades for its protection.

Finally, on August 10, the Indians gathered together and informed Trent that they were ready to listen to what he had to say. It was an imposing group. Among those present were the Six Nations chiefs, Half King and Scarouady, with a band of their own warriors; the Delaware chiefs, Shingas and the Beaver, with many of their warriors; the Shawnee chieftains, Nuchecomer and the Young King, with a number of their followers; a Wyandot chief; the young Twightwee King and the Turtle, with several others who acted as deputies from the various Miami tribes. Trent told the assembled Indians that he had been sent to them by the governor of Virginia to brighten the chain of friendship; that the governor would build a trading house on the plot of ground that they had offered the Virginia commissioners the previous spring; and that the trading house would serve as a "nursery for you" and at the same time be a place of refuge for the Indians and their families. He then delivered to them the formal speech sent by Governor Dinwiddie. In that discourse they were informed that through Trent, Dinwiddie had learned of their plight and of their request for arms and ammunition. At that point Trent waxed eloquent in delivering the governor's message: "Is the heroick Spirit of your Ancestors lost? Will the Six Nations, who were formerly a Terror to the French, suffer themselves to become their Slaves?"

Dinwiddie urged the Indians to drive out the French and keep them from building forts in the Indian country. He warned them that once the French had a string of forts built, they would tell the Six Nations what to do, and the Indians would cease to be a people. It was much easier to stop the invaders now. He promised the chiefs that as soon as the trading house was built at the forks of the Ohio, a quantity of powder, lead, and other supplies would be kept there for Indian emergencies.

After presenting another of the many strings of wampum used in the conference, Trent reviewed the atrocities committed by the French against the various tribes during the previous year or two, and asked the Indians if they intended to sit idly by while the French took all their land. He recommended that the Six Nations make peace with the Cherokee, the Chickasaw, and the Creeks, as they had done with the Catawba. He also suggested that they use their influence to bring peace between the Wyandots and the Cherokee, so that the northern Indians would be able to make a solid front against the French. The Six Nations were urged to remain sober so that they would be able to keep out spies, and to do their best to stop the killing of the southern Indians, as well as the English, at the suggestion of the French. After this speech, Trent delivered an invitation to the assembled chiefs to accompany the Twightwee nation to Winchester for a special conference with the governor of Virginia or one of his council. There, he said, Governor Dinwiddie would have a small present for the Twightwees. The Winchester conference would begin on August 20. With that announcement and the delivery of a final string of wampum, Trent concluded the council meeting.

After delivering his speeches, Trent proceeded to the quarters of the Half King, where the chiefs were gathered, for some private conversation. To a query concerning what he thought the French treatment of the Indians would be, the doughty captain replied that the French would enslave the Indians just as the English had enslaved the negroes. Nothing could have sounded more distasteful to the free sons of the forest. The chiefs said that while some of them proceeded to Winchester for the treaty making, others would go and warn the French to get off their land. Then the Half King arose and said, "Now let our Women hold their Tongues, they must not concern themselves about our Business, for we are now Warriors."

The day after the Indian council on the Ohio, Trent sent a message to Dinwiddie telling of his success with the Indians and of their promise to attend the proposed conference at Winchester. He said that he was assured that the Indians would not leave their country at this time, were it not for their expectation of seeing the governor. After setting forth most of the information that he had acquired regarding the movements of the French on the south side of the lakes, he wrote:

Eyes of all the Indians are fixed upon you—you have it now in your Power, with a small Expense to save this whole Country for his Majesty, but if this Opportunity is missed it will never be in the Power of the English to recover it but by a great Expense & the united Force of all the Colonies.

Only time could tell how startlingly true this prophecy of Trent's was to be! Despite the fact that the trader had noted that the Delaware Indians were pro-French, he did not believe that they were beyond redemption by the English, for in closing his letter to Dinwiddie he stated: "Now is our Time, if We manage well all the Indians may be brought to join against the French, otherwise they will join the French against the English."

On the night of August 16 a Mohawk Indian came to Logstown from Venango with some bad news. He said that a party of seventy-five French soldiers, commanded by a captain, had arrived at Venango and had taken an English trader by the name of Trotter, and his helper, prisoner, and had confiscated all his goods. He also stated that the French had pursued John Fraser and another Englishman for eight miles down the river, but that the men had escaped. According to the Mohawk, forty large canoes filled with provisions had arrived at Presque Isle during the previous week; five cannon had been transported to Fort Le Boeuf; and a great body of Indians was assembled at Niagara ready to start on an expedition to the southward.

Trent was anxious to conclude his business on the Ohio and return to Virginia, but the Indians could not be hurried in making their decisions. Nor did the red men believe in all work and no play. Forced to wait for a final reply from the Shawnee and the Delawares, Trent disgustedly wrote that he would stay until they "finish their Dance which is likely to hold these five or six Day's; they seem to think of Nothing else but their dancing." While Trent was still killing time, Fraser sent him a French deserter who said that the French had eight hundred soldiers and sixteen hundred militia collected. Trent was inclined to doubt the statement of the Frenchman and said that he believed the fellow "is a great Liar." By August 23 the Delawares and the Shawnee had finished their celebrating and had their decision ready. They told the Six Nations, with two strings of wampum, that they looked upon them as their rulers and were ready to fight the French when the Six Nations ordered them to do so. At the conclusion of their speech, the Delawares gave the Six Nations another string of wampum, with the ominous black beads of war predominating.

Now that the Iroquois were assured of the support of their powerful allies, they were ready to make a concluding commitment to Trent before he returned to Virginia. Therefore, on the following day, the Half King and Scarouady informed him that they had decided to warn the French to leave the Indian lands, and that if the French refused, they would attack them. Any further comments they said would be reserved for the conference at Winchester. Had the English authorities but realized it, this was the apex toward which they had been working for years.

The majority of the Indians north of the Ohio River and south of the lakes were so incensed against the French that they were ready to strike on short notice, provided they received the necessary supplies and support from the English. But the rod of the red man's anger was allowed to cool without being shaped to the English purpose; and the result was that the nadir of despair and disappointment was reached by those Indians who had pledged themselves to defend the British cause.

There was considerable activity around the forks of the Ohio on August 25, 1753. Captain Trent was on the "Point," viewing the ground on which Virginia proposed to start building a fort in less than a month. The Indians were making preparations to accompany Trent and Andrew Montour to Winchester, with the exception of one band of Six Nations warriors that had been delegated to accompany the Half King to the French forts to order the French out of the country. By the evening of August 26 there was silence at the mouth of the Monongahela River. Practically every Indian had gone. The Half King had led his band north; Trent and Montour had taken nearly all the remaining Indians, and one French deserter, along with them as they headed east over the mountains toward Virginia.

During the very same week that Trent was leading his Indian party toward Winchester, an event of far-reaching significance was transpiring in London. The Earl of Holdernesse was drawing up a series of instructions to be sent to the colonial governors in America. This communication was started from Whitehall in the last week of August, 1753; its primary importance to Governor Dinwiddie lay in its official endorsement of certain steps that the Virginia governor feared would be necessary. The governors were instructed to investigate charges that foreign (French) troops and their Indian allies were encroaching on English territory. Should any such interlopers be found, they were to be asked to retire peacefully. If they refused to remove themselves, "you are then to draw forth the armed Force of the Province, and to use your best endeavors, to repell force by force." Added to that bold command, which if carried out actually meant war, was a clear and specific qualifying clause: armed force was not to be used except "within the undoubted limits of his Majesty's dominions." The only difficulty with this order was the fact that no definite boundary had as yet been established between the English and the French possessions in America. But that condition was not to deter the duelists. In closing, Holdernesse admonished the colonial governors to assist each other and to keep up a close and "exact" correspondence. If danger threatened they were to appeal to their respective assemblies to grant supplies for defense.

It was September 4 before Trent and his party arrived at Winchester for the conference that had originally been scheduled to open on August 20. Andrew Montour had been sent on ahead to notify the Virginia officials of the imminent arrival of their sylvan guests. Therefore, when the delegates came into view they were greeted with salutes and cheering, to which were added, when the Indians reached their destination, presents of wampum, wine, and rum. After they had rested, the Indians were regaled with speeches and treated by the Virginia commissioners to a sumptuous supper of roast beef. On the morrow the long delayed treaty making was to begin.

Apparently Captain Trent was married shortly after his arrival in Virginia. He took as his wife a young woman by the name of Sarah Wilkins, who may have been the daughter of an Indian trader of that name. The pair established their residence for a time on the Potomac River opposite the mouth of Wills Creek, in the colony of Virginia. It was there that their first child, William, Junior, was born on May 28, 1754.

CHAPTER IV

Accepts a Virginia Military Commission

The Indian conference opened in the courthouse at Winchester, Virginia, on September 11, 1753. Two of the expected principals were not present. Since the highest ranking Indian on the Ohio, the Half King, was not with the party, Governor Dinwiddie did not think it proper to attend in person, and appointed commissioners to represent him. Colonel William Fairfax headed the Virginia delegation. Among the traders and Indians in attendance were such outstanding characters as Trent, Christopher Gist, George Croghan, Scarouady, and the Beaver. Andrew Montour served as interpreter. The Indians were not in a very good humor and declared that they had decided to withdraw the consent they had given at Logstown, earlier in the summer, to a settlement in their country; but they stated that they did want the English to build a strong house on the Ohio in which to store goods. Colonel Fairfax indicated that the temper of the Indians was such that he dared neither to discuss the question of settlement west of the mountains, nor to refer to the Lancaster deed, although he was careful not to mention this fact in his subsequent letter to the Pennsylvania governor.

The Virginia commissioners informed the Indians that they intended to build the suggested strong house, and again promised them protection against their enemies. They then gave a small part of the Old Dominion's present to the red men and told them that the remainder would be delivered to them at a later date by Trent, Gist, and Montour. This procedure was justified on the part of the English, because Virginia's present consisted mostly of guns and ammunition. That fact, coupled with the precarious state of affairs on the frontier, caused the officials to fear that they might be signing their own death warrants if they delivered the entire present at the treaty making. After the conclusion of the Winchester gathering, the Indians decided to follow the suggestion of Montour and visit the Pennsylvania officials before returning westward. The chiefs therefore asked Colonel Fairfax to write to the Pennsylvania governor and request him to meet them at Carlisle.

Governor Hamilton consented to a conference on Pennsylvania soil, but he refrained from attending in person, since Dinwiddie had not deemed the governor's presence necessary in his colony. The French activities in the upper Ohio Valley had apparently so excited the Pennsylvania Assembly that it had voted £800 for Indian services and had placed the funds at the disposal of the governor. Hamilton was therefore able to act immediately. He appointed Richard Peters, Benjamin Franklin, and Isaac Norris to represent him and the colony at Carlisle; their commissions bore the date of September 22, 1753. These men, thinking that the Indians would be waiting for them, hurried from Philadelphia with all dispatch and arrived at Carlisle on September 26. To their surprise, the Indians appeared there on the same day. Immediately the Pennsylvanians consulted George Croghan and Andrew Montour concerning the importance of these Indians and for advice on how to proceed in dealing with them. They then prepared to open the conference. But the Indians were not ready; they were not backward about telling the English officials that before any business could be done, the presents that Pennsylvania proposed to give them would have to be spread out before their eyes. Their request delayed the treaty making until the wagons arrived with the Indian goods. Thus it was the first of October before negotiations were started.

The Indians said that in their opinion the governor of Canada had invaded the Indian country because he had heard that the Virginia governor had asked permission to build a strong house on the Ohio. They asked that for the present Pennsylvania and Virginia cease settlement on the Indians' lands west of the mountains. They said that they would appoint Croghan to represent them in their relations with the English, and that Pennsylvania should appoint some official delegate from the colony to deal with Croghan on Indian affairs. It was their special request that the provincial representative so appointed be given power to warn people not to settle the Indians' lands; and if violations occurred he was to remove the settlers. In order to reduce friction with the French and provide for greater safety among the Pennsylvania traders, the Indians asked that most of the great number of traders scattered widely throughout the western country be called home. They requested that three groups, only, be allowed to remain. These three groups were to have their residences respectively at Logstown, at the mouth of the Kanawha River, and at the mouth of the Monongahela River. At those points the Indians promised to come and trade with the English and to be accountable for their safety. Virginia traders were to be handled similarly. The Indians complained that the English goods were too dear, and they believed that if only honest and sober traders were allowed to deal with them, the goods could be sold more cheaply. An impassioned plea was made that the colony of Pennsylvania stop its unscrupulous traders who brought only rum and flour and robbed the Indians while they were drunk. By these tactics, the chiefs pointed out, the whiskey traders got the furs and skins that should be used to pay debts owed to the reputable traders such as Trent and Croghan. Ruination was thus visited upon both the Indians and the honest traders.

To the requests of the chiefs the commissioners replied that they were sorry for the conditions that existed, and that on their return to Philadelphia they would lay the recommendations of the Indians before their government for action. It had originally been the intention of the commissioners to send the Pennsylvania present home with the Indians; but a letter that arrived from the Ohio during the conference caused them to change their minds. They told the Indians that the bulk of the present would be left with Croghan for delivery to them when conditions became more settled over the mountains. The letter in question was one written by the traders Robert Callender and Michael Teaffe, from Shawnee Cabins (Schellsburg, Pennsylvania), to William Buchanan, announcing the receipt of news from the forks of the Ohio. The message was that the French commander had told the Half King, on his recent visit, that the chief was an old woman; that all his people were on the French side, except himself; and that if he did not go home the French would put him in irons. The Half King had returned then to the forks of the Ohio and with tears in his eyes had asked the English traders to leave the Ohio lest they might be hurt.

This letter was read by the commissioners in the presence of the Indians, who showed great alarm; at the conclusion of the conference on October 4, they were anxious to start back over the mountains as soon as possible. As they returned home, almost empty handed, from two conferences with the white men, they must have had many misgivings. The mighty kings of the forest had been treated like children. Their precious presents, which they had actually been allowed to feast their eyes on, had been left in the hands of English traders, to be delivered at the discretion of the white men. Justified though the English may have been in protecting themselves, the real wonder is that they were able to hold as many Indians loyal as they did. But the slipshod methods of handling Indian affairs had proved unsatisfactory to the British Crown, and a new plan was being formulated.

The drawing up and the confirming of the Lancaster deed, followed by the settlement of the English west of the mountains, had caused the Six Nations Indians to become very restless, and numerous complaints had reached the ears of the British ministry. As a result of the discontent among the most powerful of the English Indian allies, royal instructions were sent to Governor Osborne of New York about the middle of September, 1753, asking him to try to give some sort of redress to the disgruntled natives. He was further instructed regarding a pending interview between the Six Nations Indians and the colonies of New York, Pennsylvania, Virginia, Maryland, New Hampshire, Massachusetts, and New Jersey, and was asked to inform the participating colonies of the meeting date. The Crown also recommended that a general treaty be made between the Indians and the colonies mentioned. Apparently the British authorities had at last taken cognizance of the jealousies and hatreds that were usually engendered by the making of separate provincial treaties with the Indians. But almost a year was to elapse before the proposed conference was called together at Albany.

By the end of October, Governor Dinwiddie had received the long-awaited letter from Holdernesse empowering him to make some definite move to oust the French from the upper Ohio Valley. Accordingly, on October 31, he wrote a letter to the French commandant on the Ohio, stating that it was well known that the lands on the Ohio River, in the western part of Virginia, were the property of Great Britain. He indicated his surprise at the French for building forts and settling on English territory, and politely asked them to withdraw. On the same day, after failing to get anyone else to accept the task, he commissioned the twenty-one-year-old Virginian, George Washington, to deliver his message.

Washington set out for the West at once. At Fredericksburg he engaged Jacob Van Braam to accompany him as French interpreter. From there the two men proceeded to Winchester, where horses and baggage were procured, and on November 14 they arrived at Wills Creek (Cumberland, Maryland). At that place Christopher Gist was engaged to guide the party, and four others were hired to act as servants. This last outpost of English civilization was left on November 15, and the party pushed westward over the mountains, through a region strange to the young Virginian. Because of excessive rains and heavy snows, it took a full week of traveling to reach John Fraser's trading post at the mouth of Turtle Creek on the Monongahela. There Washington learned the latest news regarding the French movements. Then, because the waters of the river were so badly swollen, he borrowed a canoe from Fraser and sent two of his men with the baggage down the Monongahela to meet him at the forks, where he planned to cross the Allegheny. Since he arrived at the rendezvous a little ahead of the canoe, he spent some time viewing the "Point," which Trent had tentatively chosen the previous August as a good location for the English fort. Washington recorded that the land was about twenty feet above the level of the water, flat and well-timbered, and very convenient for the construction of a fort. The rivers, he noted, were each about one-fourth of a mile wide; the Allegheny running quite swiftly, and the Monongahela deep and still without any perceptible fall. The Delaware chief, Shingas, lived about two miles down the river at the mouth of Chartier's Creek (McKees Rocks). The young Virginian was of the opinion that the junction of the Monongahela and the Allegheny rivers was a better location for a fort than the Delaware village site, which had been considered at one time by the Ohio Company as the spot for the proposed structure.

The baggage canoe finally appeared, and Washington proceeded with his party and some Delaware Indians to Logstown for a conference with the Six Nations chiefs. Upon his arrival he was conducted immediately to Chief Scarouady, as the Half King was not there. Through John Davison, his Indian interpreter, Washington announced to the chief that he was carrying a message to the French general from the governor of Virginia and had been ordered to acquaint the sachems of the Six Nations with his intention. The Indians announced that they would send for the Half King in the morning.

At the very time that the young Virginia emissary was on his way toward the Ohio, some peculiar news, supposedly from the frontier, was being announced to the Pennsylvania Executive Council in Philadelphia. Governor Hamilton informed the council that Lewis Montour had recently come from the Ohio with a message from the Half King and other leading chiefs. The document called upon the colonies of Pennsylvania and Virginia to join quickly with the six Nations against the French. It stated further that the Indians agreed to give to the English all the lands on the east side of the Ohio River as restitution for the losses of the English traders. And, finally, the colonies were urged to come quickly and build two forts on the Ohio to protect the Indians. Five Indian traders of the Mitchell and Campbell families claimed to have witnessed the drawing up of the paper.

Hamilton, after consulting with the Carlisle Treaty commissioners and with the council, and after conducting an examination of Montour, was of the opinion that the message either was spurious or had been made by the Indians while they were intoxicated. More doubt was cast on the authenticity of the Indian requests and grant when it was learned that Lewis Montour was a pro-French Indian. One of the Campbells was also suspected of being pro-French, while the Mitchells were reputedly traders of little character. Hamilton therefore decided to communicate with Dinwiddie before taking any action, and he advised the withholding of the Indian goods held by Croghan until Virginia was ready to deliver the Indian present that had been placed in the care of Trent, Gist, and Andrew Montour.

At Logstown, Washington was having little success in his efforts to get started on his way to the French forts. On November 25 several French deserters came to the town. They said that they were part of a body of one hundred men who had been sent from New Orleans with eight canoeloads of supplies for Kuskuski (near the site of New Castle, Pennsylvania). There they were supposed to meet a similar number of men from the upper Ohio Valley to help them carry the stores and provisions up the river. Since the second group had not appeared, they had deserted.

In the afternoon of the same day the Half King arrived in the settlement. Washington called him to his tent in order to get more information about the French and to ask him for a bodyguard. The Half King told the Virginian about his stern reception by the French; also that he had asked the French to return to Canada, since the lands on which they had built their forts belonged to the Indians. The Indians, he had told them, lived on the lands between the French and the English and intended to keep both people at arm's length. After stating that the Indians intended to side with the nation that agreed with them, he had withdrawn. Apparently his words had been intended as a hint to both the English and the French. This warrior had evidently earned his rating as a chief and sachem of the Six Nations! But his speech had only served to exasperate the indomitable Marin, the old French commandant. In anger he had roared at the Half King:

> I am not afraid of Flies, or Musquitos, for *Indians* are such as those. I tell you, down the River I will go, and will build upon it, according to my command. If the River was block'd up, I have forces sufficient to burst it open and tread under my Feet all that Stand in Opposition, together with their Alliances; for my Force is as the Sand upon the Sea Shore.

Thus, from the Half King's story Washington had a glimpse of what he might expect from the French when he delivered Dinwiddie's letter.

After an irritating delay of several days, the young Virginian and his party started on their journey. At the last minute a change in plans reduced the guard of Indians to three chiefs and an able hunting warrior. One of the chiefs was the Half King. On December 4 the men arrived at Venango, where they saw the French flag waving from Fraser's old trading house. Washington stopped at the house, which was occupied by three French officers. One of them was the influential

Indian interpreter, Captain Chabert de Joncaire, who, because of his Seneca Indian adoption and his power over the natives, had been left behind at Venango to prepare the way, both diplomatically and physically, for an early advance southward in the spring. Joncaire received the English messenger courteously, but told him that he would have to deliver his letter to the commandant at Fort Le Boeuf. Having accepted an invitation to dine with the French officers, Washington was soon able to hear the French plans with his own ears. Captain Joncaire's reticence decreased in proportion to the wine he consumed, until finally, in an unguarded moment, he blurted out with an oath that the French intended "to take Possession of the *Ohio.*" The expedition, he declared, was intended to stop the movement westward of the English settlers, and, although the French were aware that the English could raise two men for every one of theirs, they had nothing to fear, since the English were too slow to act.

The day after Washington's arrival at Venango, Governor Hamilton, in Philadelphia, decided to get some first-hand information from the frontier. He used as his excuse for sending an agent to the Ohio, the occasion of the return of two recently imprisoned young Shawnee Indians to their people. John Patten was the man chosen to accompany the warriors. To Patten was given a message for the Half King and the other Six Nations chiefs on the Ohio, announcing the delivery of the two Shawnee from a Carolina prison, and urging the northern Indians to keep the peace that had been established with the southern Indians. But Hamilton also gave a list of secret instructions to Patten. He asked him to learn all he could about the location, plans, and strength of the French; to discover the name of the commander; and to note the distance of the forts from Shannopin's Town, as well as the distance from the latter place to Carlisle. The governor also wanted data collected on all the Ohio Indians, in order to estimate their numbers and discover which tribes intended to help the English, and which the French. Patten was to observe which traders were carrying whiskey to the Indians, and the amount being carried. Lest Virginia might steal a march on Pennsylvania, Hamilton wanted his agent to ascertain the amount of arms and ammunition that had been sent to the Indians by the Virginia government; also, to discover what use had been made of such presents. He was to learn, too, whether any Indian councils had been held, and whether any plans had been drawn up for the defense of the Indians against the French the next summer. On his return toward Philadelphia, Patten was to visit George Croghan's residence, where he was prudently to examine the Indian present stored there by the Carlisle Treaty commissioners and find out what Croghan planned to do with it. Finally, he was to inquire of Croghan whether any orders had come from Virginia for the delivery of the Indian goods left with Trent, Gist, and Montour. Patten was expressly instructed not to let anyone know that he was interested in anything more than the safe delivery of the two Shawnee. In case of sickness or danger, he was to destroy his secret instructions, as well as any records that he had made of his journey.

Patten, who was able to utilize the assistance of Andrew Montour and George Croghan in his duties on the Ohio, found no occasion for destroying his records and brought his findings safely back to Hamilton. Croghan, who had also been gathering information on the frontier, presented the governor with an interesting journal and some other documents. Possibly his most valuable contribution was a message signed by the Half King and six other chiefs. In it the chiefs admitted that the Lewis Montour paper was accurate to the extent that the Indians wanted the English to hurry assistance to the Ohio tribes, but declared that the section of the report stating that the Indians would trade their lands east of the Ohio for the traders' debts had evidently been added by the traders. They specifically said they knew nothing of such a promise. The chiefs did repeat, however, that they wished that both the Pennsylvanians and the Virginians would send men out to the Ohio, and that each province would build and occupy a strong house for the protection of the Indians against the French. About that time Trent must have been negotiating with the Ohio Company to fulfill just such a plan. In the meantime, Virginia's emissary was making what progress he could among the French and their forts.

It was December 7 before Washington was able to break camp north of Venango and move on toward Fort Le Boeuf. After a grueling journey of more than three days through rain, snow, and swamps, his party arrived at its destination. There followed an extended delay, during which the young surveyor collected all sorts of information about the French fort, its defenses, and the number of boats and canoes available. Then the French commandant, Legardeur de St. Pierre, indicated that he was ready to receive the English ambassador. The day after they had examined the English note, the French officers held a council of war, and St. Pierre drew up a written refusal to Dinwiddie's claims and requests. The commandant then delivered to Washington, in much the same formal terms as those contained in his message to the governor, his refusal to retire from what he considered French territory.

Nothing remained for Washington to do but to return to Williamsburg. With the greatest courtesy the French stocked the canoes of the

Englishmen and their Indian guides with food and wine for their homeward journey, and on December 16 the party started southward in their borrowed French canoes. From the very first contact with the French, Washington had experienced difficulty in holding his Indian companions loyal to him. Every wile known to the shrewd Europeans, from liquor to valuable presents, was used to inveigle the Indians to join the French cause, and, although none of them deserted, they were restless. Because of the weakened condition of the horses, Washington and Gist decided to abandon the animals at Venango. From there the sturdy Virginian, dressed in Indian walking clothes, set out for home on foot. After narrowly escaping death, first at the hands of a hostile Indian, and then in the treacherous, icy current of the Allegheny River, he arrived at John Fraser's trading house on Turtle Creek toward the end of the last week in December. It was not possible to leave Fraser's post until New Year's Day, since the trader's horses, which Washington and Gist wished to borrow, were out grazing and had to be hunted. The next day the two men arrived at Gist's New Settlement (Mount Braddock, Pennsylvania), where Washington purchased a horse and riding equipment. Four days later, as he rode eastward over the mountains, he met Trent traveling westward with an Ohio Company caravan of seventeen horses loaded with supplies and tools for the building of a storehouse at Redstone Creek (Brownsville) and a fort at the forks of the Ohio. The next day he met several families moving westward to settle on the frontier. In a little more than a week after that, the future Father of His Country delivered St. Pierre's letter and his own report to Governor Dinwiddie in Virginia.

Dinwiddie was not credulous enough to believe that the French would retire on receiving his note, but he thought that its presentation would serve as a basis for any future negotiations on the transmontane question. Therefore, on receipt of Washington's report, he took what he considered to be appropriate action. Trent, well known to Dinwiddie by January, 1754, was given a captain's commission to head the first English military detachment ever to be sent to the forks of the Ohio. In the official document the governor said:

> I do hereby constitute and appoint You Wm. Trent Esq'r to be Com'd'r of such and so many of his My's Subjects not exceeding 100 Men as You can immediately raise and enlist, and with s'd Comp'a and the Assistance of our good and faithful Friends and Allies and Ind's of the Six Nat's and such others as are in Amity with them and Us, to keep Possession of His M'y's Lands on the Ohio and the Waters thereof and to dislodge and drive away, and

in case of refusal and resistance to kill and destroy or take Prisoners all and every Person and Persons not Subjects of the King of G.B. who now are or shall hereafter come to settle and take Possess'n of any Lands on said River Ohio, or on any of the Branches or Waters thereof. And I do hereby require the s'd Men who shall so enlist themselves and every —— of them to obey You as their Com'd'r and Capt'n &c. and You are to constitute such and so many Officers under You as the Service shall require, not exceeding 1 Capt. and 1 Lieut't.

With the commission Dinwiddie enclosed a letter to Trent in which he told the trader that according to Washington's report the French intended to build forts and take possession of the Ohio country, and that, if possible, they must be prevented from doing so. It was for that reason that he was commissioning Trent and authorizing him to raise men in Augusta County and the exterior settlements of Virginia. Trent's company was to be in the pay of the colony of Virginia, "agreeable to the Assembly." The governor instructed him to march his men to the Ohio, where a fort was to be erected, and informed him that Major Washington had also been commissioned to raise one hundred men and was to join him there. Upon his arrival at the place appointed, Trent was "to protect and assist them in finishing the Fort" and to guard against French attempts to oust the builders. It was Dinwiddie's opinion that the woodsmen enlisted by Trent would be supplied with guns; other stores and provisions were to be supplied by Major John Carlisle of Alexandria, who had been appointed commissary of stores and provisions for the Ohio expedition. The governor also mentioned his hope that the trader's influence with the Indians could be used to good account. Furthermore, he trusted that the House of Burgesses at the next session would make it possible for him to send four hundred more men to Trent's assistance in the spring. He had written to the other colonial governors for help, he said, and hoped that they would respond. Of a recent shipment of cannon, he had ordered ten to be taken to Alexandria; from there they were to be transported over the mountains to the fort at the mouth of the Monongahela. He was aware that it would be difficult to send regular supplies to Trent's men, but advised Trent of Washington's statement that John Fraser could supply an abundance of bear and venison, and asked the captain to write to Fraser requesting him to provide whatever meat he could. Near the end of his letter Dinwiddie wrote, "You see the Confidence and good Opinion I have of Y'r Capacity and Diligence w'ch I hope You will Exert on this Occasion."

At the time that Trent received his commission and instructions from the Virginia governor, he was, as has been indicated, in the employ of the Ohio Company. He had been designated the factor of the company, and when the message from Dinwiddie arrived, he was engaged in building a strong, square, log storehouse at Redstone Creek. This structure, which was nearing completion, was primarily intended as a storehouse for goods that were later to be shipped by water down the Monongahela to its junction with the Allegheny, where the fort was to be built. It had, however, been equipped with loopholes and was deemed strong enough to withstand a short siege. As soon as Trent received his orders he dispatched messengers throughout the country to collect the scattered traders for his company. These men constituted practically his sole source of recruits, since only a few families were settled west of the mountains, and the more thickly populated settlements were over fifty miles to the eastward. Word was also sent to the friendly Indians. When the Half King and Scarouady learned of Trent's orders, they pleaded with him to hurry and build a fort at the mouth of the Monongahela; their assistance was promised just as soon as they could collect their people. Trent then started for the forks of the Ohio with a crew of only thirty-three men, and on his way enlisted Edward Ward as ensign of his company. On their arrival at the forks, the Englishmen were greeted by a band of Indians representing the different tribes of the region. After Trent had made a speech to the assemblage, he delivered a present to the Indians from the Virginia government. His friend and business partner, George Croghan, assisted him in completing this transaction.

Ground was then cleared, and Trent proceeded to lay out the dimensions of the fort. After some logs had been squared, it was thought fitting to have the Indians participate in starting the structure. They were more than willing. Happy to see evidence of action on the part of the English, the great Half King himself laid the first log, with the declaration that the fort "belong'd to the English," and that anyone who attempted to halt the building of it would face an Indian war. So far as can be ascertained, no formal name of any kind was ever given to this fort, which, although never completed, was the first English structure to be started within the limits of what is today the city of Pittsburgh. Dinwiddie's intention, however, had been to call the post Fort Prince George.[1]

---

[1] After a careful search the author has found no real evidence to support the claim that this embryo fort was christened Prince George. Governor Dinwiddie had that name in mind, but no record has been found to indicate that he instructed Trent to apply it or that Trent ever did. See Virginia Historical Society *Collections*, III, 343-345. Letter, Governor Dinwiddie to Horace Walpole, September 23, 1754.

Trent was forced to feed the attending Indians as well as his men, almost exclusively from his commissarial supplies. Thus before many weeks had passed, the supplies became so low that, despite the extreme cold and snow, the captain made a trip east over the mountains and brought fresh provisions back to the mouth of the Monongahela on pack horses. The Indian hunters around the forks disappointed the fort-builders in the matter of providing meat. Those living nearest to the junction of the rivers were Delawares, who were pro-French in their sympathies. Trent had brought goods along to trade for the meat he expected to purchase, and presented good bargains, but the Delawares were not very much interested. Wild turkeys were especially desired by the English. The extravagant sum of seven shillings and six pence was offered to the Indians for each bird brought in; nevertheless, few were presented for sale. John Fraser, at Turtle Creek, proved no more reliable than the Indians. Perhaps he did supply some meat, but no record has been found to prove it. Trent had actually commissioned Fraser a lieutenant of his company, but the honor was of so little consequence to the trader that he stipulated certain conditions before he would accept it. Trent had to promise him that it would not be necessary for him to reside at the fort, and that he would not have to visit it more than once each week if he did not wish to. In view of the uncertainty and danger existing on the upper Ohio at this time, it is difficult to understand the apparent lack of interest on Fraser's part, or Trent's willingness to issue a commission on such terms.

When Governor Dinwiddie appointed Major Carlisle as commissary for this expedition, he was fully aware that armies travel on their stomachs. For, despite his belief that Fraser and the Indians would supply plenty of meat, he cautioned Carlisle, "But You must take Care to have a Sufficiency for Maj'r W. and Ct. T. that there may be no Delay to their prosecuting the Orders they have frome me." That very danger was now approaching reality. The paucity of meat forced the English to rely almost solely on the supplies of flour and Indian meal, which were all too quickly depleted. A short while after the men had been reduced to a diet of Indian corn without salt, Christopher Gist came into camp with the news that Major Washington's detachment might be expected in a few days. For a brief time the spirits of the recruits were rejuvenated, but not for long. Day after day passed without any sign of Washington. The men were getting weaker from want of sufficient food, coupled with their hard work in the spring sunshine. Even the ardor of the Indians had cooled, because of the lack of dispatch in the movement of Virginia troops to the Ohio. The Half

King earnestly urged Trent to go east again in order to hurry out the troops and provisions, and, the captain finally decided to do so.

The celerity with which French orders were given and executed in Canada during these months stands out in bold contrast to the dilatory motions of the English. On January 15, 1754, five hundred militia and regulars set out from Quebec for the Ohio country under the command of Captain Claude Pierre de Contrecoeur, who had succeeded St. Pierre. At Montreal they were joined by three hundred additional militiamen. From that point the army, equipped with provisions for two months, set out on February 3 with the express purpose of conquering the Ohio Valley. The squeaking of sleds, laden with supplies, mingled with the ringing of hundreds of skates, as the sturdy sons of New and Old France advanced steadily westward over the ice of Lake Ontario. Niagara was reached by the last week in February, and one hundred men were left to strengthen that garrison. From there the remainder of the army pushed on as fast as possible toward Presque Isle, Le Boeuf, and Venango, and arrived at the latter post on April 4. There, under the superintendence of Captain Chabert de Joncaire, Fort Machault was erected, the third of the series of fortifications planned by the French. By the middle of April everything was in readiness for the French advance down the Beautiful River. Canoes and bateaux were loaded with hundreds of French soldiers and their Indian allies, who had joined them as they proceeded along the lakes and down French Creek. Thus the epochal journey began.

After Trent had left for Virginia to procure the needed supplies, Gist appeared at the forks and asked Ensign Ward to send some men with him to get certain provisions that he said were at the Redstone storehouse. Ward did as he was requested. (He later learned, however, that there were no supplies at Redstone.) About April 13 he received the first news that the French were about to start down the Allegheny River. Although it was in the dead of night, the startled ensign, accompanied by two or three other Englishmen and an Indian, immediately set out for Turtle Creek to consult Fraser. The newly commissioned lieutenant, after listening to Ward's story, said that he was sure the French intended to come, but what could be done about it? The following morning Ward held a consultation with the Half King, who advised the officer to begin at once the erection of a stockade around the uncompleted fort. Ward, not wishing to be insubordinate, consulted Fraser again and asked him if he would not come to the fort, but the lieutenant replied that he had "a Shilling to loose for a Penny he should gain by his Commission at that time, and that he had Business which he could not settle under Six Days with his Partner." In disgust, Ward said that he would order the building of the stockade himself and would hold out against the French to the last, so that the Indians could not say the English were cowards. He put his men to work, and before the French appeared, the last gate in the stockade had been completed.

It was on the evening of April 16, 1754, that the advancing French and Indian army quietly made camp somewhere near Shannopin's Town along the Allegheny River. Before retiring for the night, the commandant, Contrecoeur, wrote out the summons that he intended to deliver to the English on the morrow. Ensign Ward was so apparently unaware that the French were near until April 17, when he first observed them moving southward on the river about two miles above the fort. They approached until they were but a short distance from the stockade, when they disembarked. They then formed into military columns and marched to a point just out of gunshot from the fortification, where they halted. Contrecoeur then sent a subordinate officer, Captain Le Mercier, and two Indian interpreters to Ward with the summons that had been written the previous evening. This occurred at about two o'clock in the afternoon, and the inexperienced and almost helpless Ward was allowed but one hour in which to deliver his answer to the French in writing. He read Contrecoeur's summons, which ordered the English to retire in peace from the territory claimed by the French, at once and without delay. The French commandant refused to wait for any message that the English might wish to get from their governor. Protection was promised if the fort was surrendered quickly. Ward, in consternation, used half of the hour allotted to him in conferring with the Half King, since Lieutenant Fraser was at Turtle Creek, and Captain Trent had not yet returned from Virginia. The Half King advised him to stall for time and to use the argument that as he was not an officer of rank, he would have to wait for the arrival of Trent before he could reply. Ward, therefore, accompanied by the Half King and two English interpreters, proceeded to the French army for an audience with Contrecoeur, and presented the arguments suggested by the Half King. But Contrecoeur was adamant. The English would either move out at once or be removed by force!

Ward, bewildered and frightened, looked about him. He estimated that there were at least one thousand men in the French force, and in addition to their side arms, he understood that they possessed some cannon. His force numbered forty-one men, thirty-three of whom were soldiers. There was no alternative. He agreed to capitulate, with the understanding that he was to march out of the fort with all possessions by twelve o'clock noon of April 18. The night of April 17 he camped with a party of Six Nations Indians within three hundred yards of the fort. Contrecoeur asked him to come and dine with him that evening. The ensign obliged. There apparently was more than good manners involved in the gesture of the Frenchman, since his guest was subjected to a polite cross-examination on English colonial affairs. Ward said that he was ignorant of such matters and could be of no service. Then Contrecoeur offered him whatever price he cared to ask if he would consent to sell some of his carpenter tools; but the proud Englishman refused, with the statement that "he loved his King and Country too well to part with any of them." There was a considerable demonstration against the French the following day by the Half King, but the French paid no attention. Ensign Ward and his men marched away as agreed, with all the honors of war, carrying their tools and equipment with them as they headed eastward. The French had captured the forks of the Ohio River without so much as firing a gun or shedding a drop of blood.

Responsibility for the failure of the English to hold the Ohio Valley in the spring of 1754 is hard to place. Conclusions are likely to vary with each individual examination of the facts. It seems fair, however, to distribute the blame among the various human and physical elements involved. Governor Dinwiddie appears to have applied himself conscientiously to the task of trying to secure the territory for the English. Shortly after sending Trent his commission, the governor had issued a proclamation designed to facilitate the onerous job of raising a company of men on a raw and sparsely populated frontier. His order set aside one hundred thousand acres of land contiguous to the fort at the mouth of the Monongahela River, and another tract of one hundred thousand acres on or near the Ohio River, as bonuses for the soldiers who would enlist for service in the building of forts on the Ohio and the protecting of English property there. The land was to be apportioned according to the suggestions of the officers, and the division was to take place immediately after the performance of the service. Less than a month later, when Trent and Cresap had warned Dinwiddie of the reported activities of the French up the Allegheny River and the need for more troops, the governor had immediately ordered Washington to take what soldiers he had enlisted and proceed at once to the forks of the Ohio, with wagons and provisions. He had promised Washington that he would send Colonel Joshua Fry to the same point as soon as possible, and mentioned his hope that the expected Cherokee and Catawba Indians from the South had already arrived at the forks. In closing, he had cautioned young Washington to avoid an ambush by the enemy. A similar order for a quick march had been sent to Colonel Fry.

Dinwiddie was irked by the failure of the other colonies to send assistance. On March 21 he took Governor Hamilton to task for the lethargy shown by the Pennsylvania Assembly. In his letter he also mentioned the request of the Crown that New York and Carolina send soldiers to serve under his command in the Ohio region, and stated that he planned to send those companies to reinforce Trent as soon as they arrived. Two forts, he said, were to be built on the Ohio the following summer. If his own assembly had voted money the previous November, the fort then in progress would have been finished already, but the troubles he was experiencing with his legislative body were the worst he had ever been called on to face. Four days after dispatching this letter, Dinwiddie wrote to Governor Sharpe of Maryland in a similar vein, lamenting the fact that the Maryland Assembly had refused to send any troops for service over the mountains. Two weeks later he again wrote to Sharpe and enclosed a letter from Governor Glen of South Carolina calling for a general meeting of all the colonial governors to be held somewhere in Virginia about the middle of June. Dinwiddie's reasons for opposing this conference were logical: the French were expected down the Allegheny River daily, and the business of dealing with them could not be delayed; also, the governor of New York expected to meet the Six Nations in a conference at Albany in June, and he himself expected to meet the northern and southern Indians at Winchester on May 20.

In the meantime, Captain Trent had arrived from the Ohio, seeking supplies. When Trent reached his own domicile, near Wills Creek, there was no news from Washington's troops, and no provisions were on the way. He therefore collected a supply of provisions himself, with the intention of starting back over the mountains to join his company; but the day before he had planned to start, he received a letter from Washington, asking him not to leave until the latter arrived. Before any further moves could be made, word arrived that the French had captured the embryo fort. Thus Dinwiddie's efforts went for nought. Possibly too much criticism should not be heaped on the other colonies for failure to co-operate, since to some of them the problem must have seemed one that concerned Virginia alone.

Perhaps it would not be far wrong to lay most of the blame for the defection of the western Indians and the early defeats of the English in the French and Indian War at the feet of the British officials in London. Before 1748, when the Privy Council had acted favorably on the Ohio Company petition, no imperial colonial policy, applicable to the American colonies, had been formulated. All questions involving the fur trade, Indian affairs, and land settlement had been left to the various colonial governments for solution. The resulting hodgepodge was not a policy and had ended in wholesale robbery of and injustice to the Indians, which in turn had led to their suspicion and desertion of the English. In the race between the English and the French for the Ohio Valley, which was launched by 1749, the French had the advantage at first. For, although there was some disaffection among their Indians, the generosity and the dispatch with which the French officials handled the delicate Indian problems were in sharp contrast to the muddling of similar questions by the English. The same lack of a colonial policy on the part of the Crown gave full play to the rivalries and jealousies existing among the colonies. Thus, when French aggression appeared on the frontier, it was practically impossible for the English to achieve unity of action in defensive operations. The feeble attempts of the British officials to solve the pressing Indian problems on the eve of the conflict ended largely in failure. Hence before the war had been many years under way, the Crown was forced to send large numbers of regular troops to fight colonial battles, since colonial levies and supplies were not forthcoming.

To return to the events following Ward's surrender, Colonel Washington, after receiving the discouraging news, called a council of war at Wills Creek. He did not wish to advance over the mountains with his small force, but the ever loyal Half King and his Indians strongly urged him to do so. Therefore, it was decided to advance as far west as the storehouse on Redstone Creek and there await further orders. On the same day, Captain Trent's men from the forks of the Ohio arrived in Washington's camp in a bad humor. They had been enlisted as militia, and according to Washington, "the officers having imprudently promised them two shillings per day, they now refuse to serve for less pay." That was the beginning of trouble for Trent. A few days later, Dinwiddie wrote to Colonel Fry that he had been advised that Trent and Fraser had been long absent from duty at the forks of the Ohio before the French appeared. The colonel was instructed to inquire into their conduct at a court-martial and to mete out whatever punishment seemed appropriate.

The Virginia troops moved slowly over the mountains, but all did not go well, and Trent was blamed. Washington wrote from Little Meadows (near Grantsville, Maryland) that he had only 160 effective men with him,

> since Captain Trent's have left us, who I discharg'd from this De-
> tach't, and order'd them to wait your Honour's Com'ds at Captain

Trent's for I found them rather injurious to the other Men, than Serviceable to the Exp'n, till they could be upon the same Estalish't with us, and come under the rigor of the Martial Law.

Trent was also accused of retarding Washington's advance westward by failing to make good his promise to Washington and Carlisle that he would secure a train of pack horses for transporting the army supplies. Not accustomed to taking the kind of orders that the young colonel gave him, Trent disbanded his men, and Washington complained to Dinwiddie from the Great Crossing of the Youghiogheny that they had "now left the new Store and dispers'd, contrary to my positive orders." Less than two weeks after this difficulty, Washington met Trent and received an explanation as to why the captain wanted higher pay than that prescribed by the regular militia scale. Trent said that the officers on the Canadian expedition had been allowed British pay while they were in that service, and he considered his commission in the same light. It was shortly after this conversation that evidences of Washington's youth and inexperience came to the surface when he wrote that "Captain Trent's behaviour has been very tardy, and has convinced the world of what they before suspected, his great timidity." It is not known whether the captain was court-martialed or not, but the false accusation made against him at this time by Dinwiddie, probably as a result of Washington's report, ended in a lawsuit, which Trent won some time later. Trent and Croghan naturally resented the interference and losses that they sustained when Washington impressed their horses on his ill-fated expedition over the mountains in June. Judging from subsequent events, the idle charges made against Trent in 1754 had little, if any, effect on his prestige.

CHAPTER V

FINANCIAL TROUBLES, PENNSYLVANIA AND ROYAL SERVICE

The failure of the English to hold the Ohio country made it possible for the French to drive the English traders completely out of the Ohio and Lake Erie region by the autumn of 1754. Since the Indians were too practical not to recognize a *fait accompli,* virtually the whole native population swung over to the French side. There were a few exceptions, but not many. For the Indian traders—especially Trent and Croghan —these conditions spelled calamity. To the losses from goods confiscated by the French and the Indians were added the accounts for goods bought by the Indians on credit, all of which were made worthless as a result of the hostilities.

At the end of the summer of 1754 Trent and Croghan found themselves between the Scylla of their unredeemable losses on the frontier and the Charybdis of their creditors demanding payment for the lost goods in the East. One of these creditors estimated that the partners owed at least £10,000 in old debts. Edward Shippen, a Philadelphia merchant, wanted his money and complained to Thomas Penn that Trent and Croghan claimed that they could not use their pack horses for private business, since the Virginia government was using them in military service. He noted that the traders had promised to dispose of their horses in the fall and divide the proceeds among their creditors; but up to the time he wrote his letter no additional information had been sent, and not "one farthing" had been received by way of payment on the debt. The merchant calculated that if the partners sold 150 horses, each creditor would receive only about £5, but he thought that that would have been better than nothing. There was little that could be done to remedy the situation at the moment. Very few Indians had time for hunting, and those who did hunt were more inclined to trade with the French than with the English. Nevertheless, Trent took advantage of every opportunity for Indian trade around Fort Cumberland, small though the transactions were.

The year 1755 found Trent and his family residing at the mouth of Conococheague Creek (near Williamsport, Maryland). That year Trent became a captain in the provincial service of Pennsylvania. His joining the military forces neither eliminated nor hid his financial troubles. In the spring, Richard Hockley, agent of the Penns, and a partner of Trent and Croghan in a business venture, became worried lest he be forced to pay a debt charged to the triple partnership, which was in reality a debt of his partners alone. The goods had been purchased of Edward Shippen, who had recently removed to Lancaster and who now presented Hockley with a bill for £700. Little wonder that Hockley was perturbed, for he was easily accessible to the arm of the law, while Trent and Croghan were farther distant, usually on the move, and thus more difficult to apprehend. Still another, and larger, obligation was presented to the firm of Trent, Croghan and Hockley for liquidation —a matter of £900 owed to John Carson of Paxtang Township. Hockley's contention that he was not accountable for either debt was evidently accurate, because Trent and Croghan, at Wills Creek, drew up and signed certificates clearing him of any responsibilities for payment.

At the time that General Braddock suffered his fateful defeat on the Monongahela, Trent apparently was east of the mountains, for on July 16 he wrote to Governor Robert Hunter Morris, who had succeeded Hamilton, telling him of the event and stating that the defeated army was making a good retreat and that as he did not anticipate any danger in the East for the time being, he was preparing to depart the next day for Fort Cumberland. But placid conditions among the settlers of Cumberland County did not prevail for long after the crushing defeat of the English in the Ohio Valley. Murderous bands of Indians, sometimes accompanied by Frenchmen or half-breeds, roamed up and down the periphery of the settled regions, visiting death and destruction on the people and property in their paths. Settlers not killed were often taken as prisoners. By the first week in October, Trent was writing that he expected his home soon to be the frontier, so thorough was the destruction of the savages and so sudden the flight eastward of those who were fortunate enough to escape the tomahawk. On October 4 he wrote to Colonel Burd stating that he had talked with an express headed toward Annapolis, who had told him that about forty people had been killed around Fort Cumberland, and that one whole family had been burned to death in a house. The following morning, he said, another express had stopped at his domicile with the news that forty-two people had been buried near the mouth of Patterson's Creek after the last Indian foray. The express had been on his way to try to raise the militia. He had said that the settlers around the mouth of the creek were afraid to investigate conditions farther up the creek, although they feared that the people in that region had been massacred. In closing, Trent recorded his disgust with the authorities for permitting such outrages and expressed the belief that it was time for all men to provide for the safety of their families.

To Trent's worry over the matter of protecting his home was added the old and ever-recurring problem of the partnership debts. In order to avoid incarceration or serious inconvenience from arrest, he and Croghan hit upon the idea of having their creditors sign a petition asking the Pennsylvania Assembly to pass a special bankruptcy act freeing them from arrest, or molestation by their creditors for a period of time. Both he and Croghan were sufficiently respected to be able to procure a number of signatures to the document, and during the last week of November, 1755, it was presented to the assembly. It stated that the creditors of the traders were so widely scattered that it was impossible to get them all to sign a general letter of license, which was the usual custom in such cases of bankruptcy, and that the petitioners therefore requested that a special act, covering the same general principle, be enacted by the assembly. It was pointed out that the traders' losses were not due to their own failures, but rather to the defection of the Indian allies of the English and the conquest of the frontier regions by the French. The sad plight of the traders was described, and the fact was emphasized that in order to avoid arrest they were forced to stay in dangerous locations near the mountains—especially Croghan, whose residence was at Aughwick (Shirleysburg, Pennsylvania)—and that under those conditions no opportunities to recoup their losses could be utilized. The petition was signed by Jeremiah Warder, Samuel Neave, William and David M'Ilvaine, Buckridge Sims, Benjamin and Samuel Showmaker, James Wallace, James Benezet, Thomas Campbell, William West, Adam Hoops, John Potter, and, for the late firm of Levy and Company, by David Franks and Joseph Morris.

This request was favorably received, and a bill was passed providing for the relief of Trent and Croghan for a period of ten years. On November 28 the bill was presented to Governor Morris for his approval. A slight delay ensued: the petition supposedly contained the names of all the "principal" creditors, but according to Richard Hockley, his signature had not been sought by Trent and Croghan, although he had been one of their partners and was also one of their chief creditors. He suggested an amendment to the bankruptcy bill, which was accepted by the assembly, and on December 2 the governor affixed his signature. The passage of this act, which was in effect for several years, greatly relieved the minds of the two traders.

For some reason, purposeful or otherwise, a copy of this particular bill was not delivered to the clerk of the Privy Council in London for some years after its passage. When it was finally received and presented to the council for its consideration, it was immediately thrown out. In no uncertain terms the British officials expressed their criticism of such legislation and its method of passage. They criticized the bill on the grounds that it was unfair, since not all the affected creditors had signed it, and that it was passed improperly, having been read twice in one forenoon, and never committed, but passed in the afternoon of the same day. It was their final opinion that an act "so unjust and partial in its nature" would be a "precedent of the most dangerous consequence in the Colonies," and its repeal was ordered.

While Trent and Croghan were trying to free themselves from their financial entanglements, the Indian dangers were assuming greater and greater proportions. On December 1, Edward Shippen wrote from Lancaster to James Hamilton that an Indian alarm had been broadcast through that town one night at eleven o'clock, with the result that three hundred men had turned out for defense. The irony of the situation was that two-thirds of the men had no guns, since they were too poor to buy any. Shippen said that one fort was being built, but that the people wanted two. Toward the end of January, 1756, Trent, writing from his home, possibly to Washington or another military official, stated that he had succeeded in hiring some Indians for express and spy work among the Twightwees and around Fort Duquesne, if they were wanted. He indicated that he had been to a conference with Governor Morris and some other colonial officials on January 19, but that no Indians, except those staying at Croghan's, had been present. He reported that Sir William Johnson, in charge of British relations with the northern Indians, planned to call a conference of the Six Nations soon, in order to find out why they were allowing the Delawares and the Shawnee to kill the English. According to Trent's information, a treaty between the southern Indians and the governors of Pennsylvania, Virginia, Maryland, and the Carolinas was also scheduled. Pennsylvania, he said, had raised three hundred men in Cumberland County, who were engaged in building four forts at strategic points in the district, about twenty miles apart. Each fort was to be garrisoned with seventy-five men. In a postscript Trent asked the recipient of his letter to send him the balance due on an old account, if he had not already done so.

Within the next few weeks the Indian raids came closer to the large Pennsylvania towns. Writing to Richard Peters from Carlisle about the middle of February, Trent said that two lads had been taken or killed near Widow Cox's, just under Parnell's Knob, a few days before, and that another lad, who had gone from McDowell's Mill to investigate the episode, had never returned, although his horse had come back. The Indians in that section had burned the settlers' buildings and shot down their cattle. A party of redskins was also reported to have attacked some of the inhabitants along the Susquehanna. Fresh Indian tracks had been discovered the day before in a valley near Carlisle. Trent stated that all the people between Carlisle and the mountains to the west had fled from their homes. Some of the fleeing settlers had taken refuge in the county seat, while others had sought safety in the little forts. He announced the fact that the inhabitants of Shippensburg were deserting the town with what possessions they were able to carry. Everyone, he wrote, was thinking of flight to the eastward unless the government immediately found some effective method of securing the frontier, and he predicted that if present conditions continued, there would "not be one Inhabitant in this Valley one Month longer." He remarked that he and several others were trying to bolster the spirits of the people and had proposed going after the marauders on the morrow, but he was dubious as to whether enough men would appear to make the sortie possible. Concern was expressed because the people refused to stir until danger threatened them personally; then they became much excited. A fort in the town was what the trader felt was needed. The absence of one made it seem probable that Carlisle would be deserted if the Indians killed any people close to the town. Trent's anger had been aroused, and he was not backward in describing his feelings: "I was of opinion the Forts as they were built would be of no Service I was laughed at first but now the Inhabitants here are convinced of it." He had called for the militia, he said, but at the time he penned his letter, no reply had been received.

The fact that Trent was writing from Carlisle would seem to indicate that he, too, had removed from his former abode in the danger zone to the county seat. In addition to his military connection with the colonial government, Trent also held at this time the civil office of justice of the peace of Cumberland County. During the summer of 1756 he and Croghan, in order to be relieved of debt-heckling by Richard Hockley, signed over to Hockley their power of attorney to collect any sums granted by the Crown as a result of the traders' Indian losses. This sort of conniving to ease financial pressure was to become a frequent ruse in future dealings with their creditors. As the Indian danger grew around Carlisle, Trent evidently moved his family farther eastward to Lancaster, where, on October 20, his second child, Ann, was born.

With the fall of the Quakers from political control in Pennsylvania in 1756, there came a change in the handling of military and Indian affairs. Sixty thousand pounds were voted for military use and placed in the hands of a commission; land bounties were offered to men who would enlist; and a schedule of monetary rewards was set up for those who brought in Indian scalps. The formal declaration of war between France and England tended to heighten the interest among the American colonials; and the spring and summer of 1757 saw increased efforts on the part of the English in Pennsylvania to come to some peaceful agreement with the various Indian tribes. Captain Trent participated in the ensuing conferences.

An Indian council was scheduled to meet at Lancaster toward the middle of May, 1757. As it was highly desirable that Tedyuskung, an influential Delaware chief, be there, Trent was delegated to accompany two chiefs of the Six Nations to Bethlehem to meet him and escort him to Lancaster. But the Delaware sachem had not arrived at Bethlehem, and Trent, accompanied by some Indians, set out for the Lancaster conference. The difficulty in securing Delaware representation at the conference seems to have been caused by the fear on the part of that tribe that it would be blamed for some of the recent murders of white people. At last it seemed necessary to proceed with the Indian conversations without waiting for Tedyuskung. When the authorities were casting about for someone to take the minutes of the conference, George Croghan suggested that there be but one secretary and nominated Captain Trent for the position. The officials agreed, and Trent prepared for his task. An attempt to open the conference on May 11 failed, and the actual negotiations were not started until the following day. Those present included William Denny, who had succeeded Morris as governor of Pennsylvania; the governor's council; a committee from the House of Representatives; a delegation of Indians, consisting mostly of Six Nations chiefs, with a few from other tribes; Secretary Trent; and Interpreter Weiser.

After a great amount of palaver over various affairs, from land claims to French opposition, the officials concluded the conference on May 22—not, however, without having first arranged the most conciliatory invitation to the absent Tedyuskung to be present at the next meeting with the Indians. Just a few days later Trent wrote to Timothy Horsfield at Bethlehem, asking him to furnish supplies to Hugh Crawford who would soon be passing through that town with a number of Delaware Indians bearing Governor Denny's message to Tedyuskung. Trent said that he considered the restoration of amicable relations with the Delawares and the Shawnee "to be of the greatest Consequence to this Government." In a postscript he stated that the Six Nations Indians in attendance at the Lancaster meeting, just concluded, had been inclined to use all their influence to bring about an "accomodation between us & the Delawares & Shawnees had they come to this Meeting," but that since those tribes had not seen fit to come, the Six Nations had strongly recommended to Trent and the other officials that they "send again for them and the Senacas."

Captain Trent was engaged in various wartime activities during the early summer of 1757. From Lancaster he went to Fort Cumberland and was there during the time when a successful attack by the enemy was expected daily. The location of the fort was considered poor, and for that reason its invulnerability was doubted. In June, Trent was at Winchester attending a conference with the southern Indians. While there he received the news that a number of Cherokee, operating as spies around Fort Duquesne, had seen an army of French and Indians leave the fort and start eastward toward the English settlements. The French army was supposed to have been two thousand strong, and by June 16 it was believed to have reached the Little Meadows. This intelligence had a tendency to create a panic among the settlements east of the mountains. After taking stock of the forces near-by, Trent estimated that Virginia did not have more than 230 soldiers around Winchester, although Colonel Washington was preparing to raise the militia. He counted about eighty Indians in the vicinity, in addition to the English soldiers.

Fortunately for the English, the report concerning the French army moving eastward proved to be a false alarm. The Cherokee had been to the Monongahela, but the officer who originated the story had not had an interpreter when he talked to the Indians, and consequently their report was garbled. Scouts sent over the mountains brought back the news that no French army was moving east of the fort. The English population breathed a sigh of relief. Had the French actually appeared, however, a fair-sized force from Pennsylvania would have been able to join the Virginians against them. When Colonel John Stanwix, in command of five companies of Royal Americans at Carlisle, had heard the rumor of the French advance, he had planned to go to Shippensburg, and then south toward the Potomac River. He was to have been accompanied by 250 men of Colonel Armstrong's battalion, which would have brought the total force to 600 men. In the event of success in the expected attack on Fort Cumberland, Stanwix had planned to make a determined stand at Winchester. But luckily no problem of that kind had to be faced at the moment.

The Pennsylvania authorities busied themselves in the midsummer of

1757 with the task of getting the Delawares and the Seneca to a conference, in order to try to sever their French connections and thus put a stop to the murderous raids on the frontier. On July 7 Governor Denny informed Sir William Johnson's deputy that Tedyuskung had consented to attend a conference and expected to bring with him a large delegation of Seneca. After a number of delays, Tedyuskung, accompanied by over 150 Delawares and nearly 120 Seneca (in both groups the women and children far outnumbered the men), appeared at Easton on July 21 to begin negotiations. Preliminary conversations consumed the first four days. In those talks Tedyuskung made the unusual demand that he be given a separate clerk to take down the minutes. Denny did his best to dissuade the chief, but was unsuccessful. Thus on July 25, when the formal public conference opened, it was decided that Captain Trent should take down the official minutes; but at his side sat Charles Thompson, the Quaker clerk of Tedyuskung. The respect and confidence reposed in Trent are amply attested by the fact of his being frequently accepted by both the English and the Indian officials to fill responsible positions at these important councils. Present at this gathering were Governor Denny, his official council, the speaker of the assembly, a group of four provincial commissioners, a number of Quakers— whom Denny had tried to keep away—several interpreters, and Tedyuskung, who represented ten different tribes of Indians and was attended by several chiefs of the nations he represented. During the course of the meeting the Indians were successful in getting Pennsylvania to grant their request for a trading post in the Wyoming Valley. But the land question that came up for discussion was referred to the superintendent of Indian affairs, Sir William Johnson, for settlement. After almost two weeks of somewhat ruffled parleying, the Easton treaty making came to an end on Sunday, August 7.

For the next few months Trent was probably engaged in routine military and private duties in the neighborhood of Carlisle and Lancaster; no outstanding activities marked his career during this period. In January of the new year, an interesting incident occurred. A few years earlier Washington had been very quick to criticize Trent for his lack of promptness in attending to official matters; but now the tables were somewhat turned. Washington still owed Trent over £165, and Trent, desiring payment, sent his bill to George Mason for collection.

Trent was still a justice in Cumberland County in the winter of 1757-58, but his private and military affairs often carried him far out of his legal jurisdiction. During the first week of March he was at Winchester, but on March 14 he left that place for Lancaster, where, on his arrival, he penned a long epistle on Indian affairs and trade to his good friend, George Croghan. In this letter he gave it as his opinion that so far as the Cherokee Indians were concerned, the colony of Virginia was using her old tactics of making promises that she did not fulfill; some documents in support of his beliefs were enclosed for Croghan's perusal. His great concern in the matter was based on the fear of losing the support of the southern Indians against the French. He said that there had been a total of about eighty-five Cherokee around Winchester at the time of his departure from there. Several parties had made attempts to harass the French stragglers around Fort Duquesne during the winter, but their efforts had been largely nullified by the heavy snows. Captain Abraham Bosomworth, he reported, had left Lancaster about two weeks earlier for Williamsburg, and it had been said that he had gone to meet a large band of Cherokee Indians who were coming north to assist the English against the French. Trent informed Croghan of the rumor that some western Indians had gone to Philadelphia with some belts of wampum, and he understood that there were hopes of restoring trade with the Indians. Of considerable interest to both Trent and Croghan was the story that had been told Trent by Colonel Burd that some gentlemen of Burd's acquaintance were willing to advance £20,000 toward the promotion of the Indian trade, if it could be restored. Trent, however, had not been able to learn the name of the prospective promoters.

Some months later Trent experienced difficulty in controlling some of the Cherokee Indians operating around Fort Loudon, Pennsylvania. Near the end of the first week in June a party of these Indians came to him at the fort and asked for some presents, stating that they intended to go home. The captain told them that Colonel Henry Bouquet would be there in a few days to hold a council with their chiefs, and that in the meantime he would give some presents to their younger men who had been at war and had not received any. To that proposal the Cherokee said no! If Trent would not consent to give them a large present to take home, they would rob all the English settlements that they found on their journey southward. In order to intimidate Trent, the Cherokee stated that the French were good people; that the Creek Indians were going to join the French and fight against the English, and that the Cherokee would do likewise. Trent attributed the trouble partially to the lack of a good interpreter, but primarily to the fact that the Cherokee had not been told what they were to receive before they went to war for the English. In a letter to Colonel Bouquet, he heartily recommended the early adoption of a plan whereby the Indians would know what their reward was to be before they entered the English service, and claimed that this method would be the one most likely to succeed in holding the Indians during the coming campaign. Just a few miles away Colonel Adam Stephen was encamped with some Virginians and about twenty-five Catawba, and Trent planned to consult Stephen on the matter and get his opinion.

When the Cherokee Indians failed in their attempt to frighten Trent by their threats, they tried other methods. After the captain had refused them presents, one Indian took off his shirt and threw it at him. Trent took it, jokingly thanked the warrior, and told him that he needed a shirt. The Indian said that Trent was to wash it and give it to Bouquet. That was the signal for several of the others, who brought their bundles and threw them at Trent's feet with the admonition that he was to give them to Bouquet, who, they said, "loved goods." The next day they declared that they would send several of their number to Winchester to warn the rest of their people to return home, as they would get nothing if they fought for the English. After consulting with Stephen and learning that the Cherokee had not received anything previously, Trent finally agreed to give them a present. That put the Indians in a better mood, and the captain thought they might consent to stay a few days longer. According to report, there were sixty-seven warriors at the fort at that time. Colonel Bouquet was urged to send some information as to when he might be expected at Fort Loudon, and to hurry the wagons out from Carlisle with the Indian goods that Captain Bosomworth had told Trent were on the way. On June 7 Trent informed Bouquet that two small bands of Cherokee Indians had just arrived from Fort Le Boeuf, where they had suffered some losses in skirmishes with the enemy. He reported that they had noted the presence of a large number of French Indians at that fort.

As the army of General John Forbes moved westward from Carlisle in the late summer of 1758, on its expedition to recapture the forks of the Ohio, precautions were taken to avoid a repetition of Braddock's ambush. Colonel Bouquet, serving as an able subordinate to Forbes, gave explicit orders to his officers. Captain Bosomworth, in command of the southern Indians attached to the English army, was to march with all the Indians under him on September 4 to join Colonel John Dagworthy in covering the head of the advancing army. Bosomworth was instructed to send out, continually, small scouting parties to reconnoiter the enemy and bring back all available information. Should the assistance of the Indians be required for any enterprise, he was to march with them, following whatever orders were issued to him by the commanding officer of the moment. Since the Delawares and other Indians settled on the Ohio were inclined toward making peace with the English, Bouquet warned the captain to prevent any of his southern Indians from crossing the Ohio to disturb them, until he should receive further orders. To avoid the possibility of misunderstanding and accident, Bosomworth was to see that all Indians on leaving camp were in possession of their identification badges. He was also to repeat to them the prearranged signals. All assistants, interpreters, and others employed with the Indians were placed under his command.

Among the officers chosen by Bosomworth to assist him in handling the Indian allies was Captain Trent. On September 3 Trent received his appointment at the army camp at Raystown (Bedford, Pennsylvania):

> I do appoint you one of my Assistants in Conducting & regulating the Indians going to War & you are hereby directed and required to obey such orders as you shall from time to time receive from me or in my absence any other Command y offi r at the Post and to use your best endeavours in Keeping the Indians under proper Regulations and preventing any abuse being Committed by making sale of their Goods wasting their Provisions Ammuition, &c. for which you are to receive 12/ [shillings] Pennsylv a & [per] day & this shall be your sufficient Warrant.

Trent accepted his commission and started out over the Allegheny Mountains, in an effort to keep the van of the English army free from ambush. The end of the third week in September found him and his Indian companions as far west as Loyal Hannon (Ligonier, Pennsylvania). On September 22, with one white man and twenty-five Indians, he set forth from that post to scout the French around Venango. The party had not advanced more than five miles before the Indians discovered some fresh tracks of the enemy and decided to change their plans and follow those tracks early the next morning. The following day the men traveled along a warriors' path toward Fort Duquesne and finally arrived at Turtle Creek. Trent reported that the ground was in good shape for travel between Loyal Hannon and Turtle Creek, and he thought "the Road very practicable to be made for the Conveying of Artillery." Most of the way, he said, the warriors' path led through an open woods. At the creek the Indians held a council. This consultation was decided upon after they had located a Royal American soldier who supposedly had got lost from them the day before. It was the belief of the Indians that he had turned spy and had gone to Fort Duquesne to warn the French of their approach. Therefore, twelve of the most active Indians now decided to proceed toward Fort Duquesne in order to take a prisoner or distress the enemy in any way possible. The remainder of the band returned with Trent to Loyal Hannon.

General Forbes, despite his sick and weakened condition, was at Raystown as early as the first week in October. He was reported in good spirits and determined to advance as far that autumn as his force and his provisions would permit. The English army was described as being in good condition physically and mentally, with the exception of the Virginians. They were chagrined that a new road was being opened through Pennsylvania, eliminating the use of Braddock's old road. It was said that "Colonel Washington has been a good deal Sanguine & Obstinate upon the Occasion"; but the presence of General Forbes helped to relieve the tension.

Before the end of the month, Forbes temporarily gave up hope of reaching the Ohio that fall and made plans to garrison the various posts and send the remainder of his force east for the winter. But he had underestimated the efficiency and perseverance of his immediate subordinate, Colonel Bouquet. That intrepid campaigner, burdened with a double load of responsibility because of the illness of Forbes, rose to the occasion and with superb leadership pushed on westward. The determination of the general to accompany his men, even though he had to be carried much of the way on a litter, undoubtedly contributed greatly to their morale. This tenacity of purpose, in the face of great obstacles, resulted in the arrival of the English army at the Monongahela River on November 24. On learning of the proximity of the enemy, the French became so alarmed and confused that they blew up their magazine, set fire to Fort Duquesne, as well as to the surrounding cabins, and took flight as quickly as possible. The following day the brave little army of Forbes and Bouquet reoccupied the strategic forks of the Ohio, in exactly the same manner as the French had acquired it —without firing a shot! Trent, who had played a significant role both in its loss and its recovery, found his task completed for the moment and turned his face to the eastward.

General Forbes, in a letter dated November 27, informed William Pitt, England's efficient prime minister, that he had christened the reconquered post "Pittsbourgh," in Pitt's honor. On December 3 Forbes set out for Philadelphia where he died on March 11. Colonel Bouquet left Pittsburgh a few days after the departure of General Forbes, leaving Colonel Hugh Mercer to command the temporary works which were thrown up at the forks of the Ohio by January, 1759. The English had found it advisable to construct defenses of some sort immediately, since the French still entertained the ideas of driving the English back over the mountains, in spite of their failure to hold Fort Duquesne.

CHAPTER VI

ASSISTANT DEPUTY INDIAN AGENT OF THE CROWN AT FORT PITT, 1759

It was in Philadelphia on April 3, 1759, that George Croghan received orders from Brigadier General John Stanwix (who had been placed in command of the army following the death of Forbes) to hold himself in readiness to proceed to the forks of the Ohio River as Sir William Johnson's deputy. (Croghan appointed his good friend, Trent, as his assistant.) There he was to transact business with the western Indians and generally to promote the English interests among them. About three weeks later Stanwix gave Croghan an order to purchase, on behalf of the Crown, a large quantity of goods suitable for presentation to the Indians, and on April 26 he directed him to transport the goods to the Ohio.

Everything being in readiness, the journey from Philadelphia to Pittsburgh was started on the following day. An express from Ligonier, met on the road to Lancaster, brought a discouraging message: the French and Indians had killed over thirty men along the road east of Ligonier since March 20! This was ominous news indeed, for that road had to be traversed; besides, the party was escorting a prize that any band of French and Indians would fight hard to capture. When the group arrived in Carlisle, approximately a week was spent in purchasing and outfitting forty pack horses to carry the goods on westward. Then the caravan proceeded. Fort Bedford was reached on May 18 without mishap, but farther than that it was not deemed wise to go without an escort. Colonel Adam Stephen of the Virginia troops, in command at that post, was willing to furnish an escort, but explained that only twenty of his three hundred men were in camp. The remainder of his force had been sent in two different sections as escorts for provisions for Fort Ligonier and Pittsburgh; the garrisons at both of those posts, he said, were in a starving condition. On the advice of the colonel, it was decided to wait for the return of the troops from the West.

While waiting at the Bedford post, there was an opportunity to hear the reports brought in from the mountains. An express arrived from Ligonier on May 24 with the message that Captain Bullit and his command of 110 men had been attacked three miles east of Ligonier as they were escorting twelve wagonloads of provisions toward the fort. Thirty-six men had been lost in the engagement, and several had been wounded. All the horses had been stolen, and five of the wagons burned; the other seven wagons had been saved only by the sudden appearance of reinforcements from Fort Ligonier. Two days later another runner brought in a similar report. Captain Morgan with fifty men, engaged in escorting a string of loaded pack horses to the forks, had been attacked on his return eastward with the unburdened horses and had lost seven men. He had put up a good fight, however, and as a result had been able to save the horses from seizure. The reports of these unfortunate events caused the Indian agents to take immediate action. Captain Andrew Montour, accompanied by three Indians, was ordered to proceed through the woods to Pittsburgh to invite all the Indians of the various tribes near there to meet at that post. Montour was further instructed to inform the Indians that if any of them wished to enter the service of the English Crown, they might come eastward and join the party on the road and help escort it to the forks.

The Indian agents, convoyed by Colonel Stephen and approximately three hundred men, left Fort Bedford on June 8. Five days later the pack horses and their large escort were met near Fort Ligonier by Montour and a band of thirty Six Nations and Delaware warriors. The French and their Indian allies evidently feared the outcome of a battle with so large a force, and the caravan arrived safely at the forks on June 18. There one hundred Indians were waiting for a conference. They were joined later in the day by forty Delawares and Shawnee under the chief, Delaware George.

Little time was lost in preparing for the first Indian conversations. The English were determined to make the best of their second opportunity to promote good fellowship with the natives. On the evening of his arrival, Croghan called all the Indians together and, after the usual preliminary talk, gave them a beef, a bag of flour, and a keg of rum for a feast. The next morning a meeting of about 165 warriors of the Six Nations, Shawnee, Delaware, and Ottawa tribes was called. With the aid of a belt of wampum Croghan explained his business and asked them to send runners home to invite their respective chiefs to come to the forks as soon as possible to ratify the peace. The Indians promised to comply with the request, but said that it would take about fifteen days to get their people collected. Since practically all the Indians were naked, Colonel Mercer permitted some two hundred of them to be clothed, including sixteen women and eighteen children. Fourteen Wyandots and eight Shawnee appeared at the forks on June 21; they had heard of the agents' presence there and had decided to come to the post, instead of going to join the French. Croghan bribed them in order to win them over to the English side, and on their departure they promised to join the English service when called.

That same night two Indian spies came in from Venango. They reported that there were about one hundred and thirty French and eighty Indians at that post. In the presence of the spies, the French commandant had made a speech to the Indians and urged them all to attack the English convoys on the Forbes road. To that suggestion the Indians were said to have agreed. The French officer had also told them that there was a large French army at Niagara, which was going to march south and kill all the English. The spies doubted the truth of the Niagara story, since two Wyandot Indians who had recently come from Niagara had told them that there were only four hundred French at Niagara, thirty at the portage, one hundred at Presque Isle, and sixty at Fort Le Boeuf, and that there was no evidence of preparation for a southward move at any of the posts. Nevertheless, a report of the news was sent to General Stanwix. Two other Indian spies were sent to Venango to learn all they could about the French, their supplies, and their movements. A special message was dispatched to the warrior allies of the French, asking them to retire to their towns immediately. The Indian agents were of the opinion that the Indians would comply when they learned how well the Indians were being treated by the English at Pittsburgh. Twenty-two Wyandots arrived in the evening of June 22 with twelve horses loaded with skins and furs, which they wished to trade. They had two of their principal men with them, and said they were pleased that the English were in possession of the post again. The next day the visitors brought their pelts to barter. Croghan noted in his journal that the provincial store at the forks had such an "ill sorted" supply of goods that he had to buy part of the Indians' furs and skins with the King's goods. The Delaware chief, Shingas, came into the Indian camp on June 25 with the good news that the Beaver was on his way to Pittsburgh with a great number of the chiefs from nine different nations with him, including some from over the lakes. All nine nations, he said, had agreed to renew their ancient friendship with the English. The policy of clothing the new Indian arrivals from the stock of presents was continued.

The day following the appearance of Shingas, the two spies sent to Venango returned. They said that there were not over two hundred French and Indians at the fort; that they were short of provisions; and that they had no cannon. Fifty bark canoes were supposed to have been constructed a few miles above Venango, but the spies thought these were intended for transportation only to the mouth of Kiskiminetas Creek, where they would be anchored while the warriors attacked the English forces along the communication line. The messengers stated that the French Indians were aware of the approaching treaty at Pittsburgh and had declared that they would leave the French as soon as the treaty was concluded. That same evening two messengers arrived from the Seneca country. They brought news for all the Indian tribes on the Ohio River to the effect that the Six Nations were under arms and had sent a war belt to Sir William Johnson, saying that they were ready to join him in an attack on Fort Niagara. The Indians on the Ohio were ordered to be ready to join the Six Nations on short notice in their effort to cut off all the French south of the lakes. As soon as this news was received, the Indians were called together and the message was relayed to them. They seemed pleased, and it was thought that if the English had had a good supply of provisions and some troops at the forks of the Ohio, it would have been possible to get most of the Indians living on the river to join them in the destruction of the French forts on the rivers and the lake.

It must not be surmised that all the Indians in the region about Pittsburgh were friendly. They were not, as one incident proved. While on sentry duty near the post, a soldier deserted his station long enough to go a short distance to a spring for a drink. Not having been trained in Gideon's army, he evidently drank with his head down, for he was killed and scalped by three Ottawa who were skulking about looking for an unwary victim. In the evening of the last day in June, ten Delawares arrived with the report that forty French soldiers and about three hundred Indians had left Venango to attack any English people who appeared on the road between Pittsburgh and Fort Ligonier. It was believed that for a time at least the high water in Kiskiminetas Creek would delay them.

During the first few days in July various groups of chiefs and warriors arrived at the forks, but the scheduled conference was again delayed. On July 5 Croghan recorded in his journal: "I called all the Indians togeather, bid them welcome, and condoled with them on Account of their People who dyed & were killed at War since I see them, which is agreeable to an Ancient Custom of theirs." On the following day he and Colonel Mercer held a private meeting with the Beaver and a number of the other chiefs and told them that General Stanwix was on his way to Pittsburgh to build a trading house, and that it was the wish of the officials that the Indian conference be postponed until he arrived, since the Indians had refused to go to Philadelphia. This request the Indians would not grant; they reminded the white men that it might be dangerous to delay the meeting. Therefore it was decided to proceed with the council.

During the days of the treaty making Captain Trent helped in the negotiations whenever he could, and at the same time continued his routine activities. On July 6 two more Indian spies were sent to Venango for information and five other Indians were sent to Fort Ligonier to serve as pilots through the woods to a small escort on its way to the forks of the Ohio with flour for the garrison. The next day some Indians asked what the prices of skins were, and, on being told, stated that the English used to pay them more. Then they asked that the governor change the price level.

By July 8 some of the chiefs were getting anxious to leave the Indian powwow, and, accompanied by the Beaver, they presented fourteen belts and two bunches of wampum, which they said were from nine of the nations represented there. The nine nations had expressed a wish that the Wyandots should treat for all of them at this meeting. It was agreed that the deputies should speak to these Indians in council the next day, so that they might start for home as soon as possible. Accordingly, on July 9, several speeches were made to the Indians, in the presence of a considerable number of officers and traders. King Beaver expressed his satisfaction with the requests made, and declared that the Indians would begin to perform their agreements. Thereupon he surrendered ten white prisoners, two of whom were his adopted mother and sister. On the following day, after clothing 375 Indians, private, and more valuable, gifts were given to the chiefs and principal warriors. After two days of consideration, the Wyandots expressed their satisfaction with the deputies' statements. They promised to go home and try to get their young men away from the French, and a promise was also made to return the few prisoners in their possession. The Delawares and the Shawnee then indicated their pleasure that peace had been restored with the English, and they likewise promised to return all the white prisoners in their custody. Thus on July 11 the Indian conference came to what appeared to be a successful conclusion.

Late in the afternoon of the day on which the treaty making ended, two Indians arrived from Presque Isle with the news that eight days before, a party of some seven hundred French and Indians had come to Presque Isle from Fort Detroit with a large supply of provisions, some cannon, and a number of horses to carry them to Beef River (French Creek). There, or at Venango, they expected to be joined by more Indians. When the whole force was collected they were supposed to move against Pittsburgh or Fort Ligonier. The spies said that when they had left, the French had been busily engaged in moving their supplies over the portage to Fort Le Boeuf. This report caused great consternation on the part of Colonel Mercer. The next morning he dispatched three hundred men, piloted by Captain Montour and thirty Indians, toward Fort Ligonier to meet and guard a provision train believed to be on the road toward the Ohio.

If there were any individuals at the forks of the Ohio who believed in the superstition that the thirteenth day of the month was unlucky, the information that filtered into the little post on July 13, 1759, must have made them sure of it. Delaware George came to Fort Pitt with the story that one of his warriors had come in from the lake region with a confirmation of the report that the French and their Indians were concentrating south of there. He had learned that French strategy called for the combined force to drop down the Allegheny River when ready, to a point four miles above Pittsburgh. From there the Indian allies were to scatter in all directions in order to cut off the communication lines, keep the Delawares from joining the English, and draw small parties out from the fort. In the meantime, the French intended to land their artillery and attack the English. Just after an Indian express had been sent in haste to give Fort Ligonier the evil news, another Indian runner came in with the pessimistic message that no escort had arrived there with provisions. Uneasy, indeed, must have been the sleep of those who tried to rest in the English post that night.

The next day two Indian spies were hurried up the river as far as Kittanning to see if the French were coming. In the evening of the same day two Six Nations spies appeared. They said that when they had arrived at Venango some days ago, there had been over one thousand French and Indians gathered at that place. The French commandant had accused the spies of being from Pittsburgh, but they had told him that they were from the Scioto country. Then the Frenchman had declared that he proposed to destroy the English in a few days, and that during the next three days he expected about six hundred Indians to join him. The spies reported that all but fifty Indians had arrived in the expected time, and that they had all been clothed and equipped for the forthcoming expedition as fast as they had arrived. With a large supply of goods available, the French were bestowing presents on the Indians with a free hand. The spies said that by the evening of July 11 all the red men had been outfitted, and that on the morning of July 12 the French commandant had called them all to a council meeting and told them that he intended to march on Pittsburgh the next day; he had then thrown down a war belt. At that point a Six Nations Indian had arisen and stated that the French father's action was too hasty. The Indian had thrown down some strings of wampum and had said that the Indians wished to consider the matter for a time before they acted. This had confused the Indians in general; and, before they could come to an agreement, two messengers had arrived with a packet of letters for the commandant. The officer had then told the Indians that the runners had brought news that a great English and Six Nations Indian army, under Sir William Johnson, was moving against Fort Niagara, and that he had orders to take them and hurry to that post. There was some doubt in the minds of the two spies as to whether all the Indians at Venango would follow the French north, although before the spies had departed, a number of warriors had already started in that direction. The spies also said that on July 13 some Indian scouts who had been watching the Forbes road had come to Venango with the report that an English army of one thousand men or more was east of the Allegheny Mountain, that it was moving westward, and that the English had with them a vast number of loaded pack horses and cattle. Thus in the short space of twenty-four hours the whole outlook at the forks of the Ohio was changed from one of pessimism to one of optimism. Sir William Johnson's move against Fort Niagara had relieved the ominous pressure against Pittsburgh, and the soldiers, at that post, as well as the Indians, breathed more easily.

With Mercer's permission, two Wyandot messengers were sent to Venango on July 16 to tell all the western Indians who were with the French there, that the English had come to carry on trade and commerce, and not war, and that a peace treaty had already been made with many of their brothers. The red men were invited to abandon the French, go home, and await a call from the English. The Indians at the forks joined in this message. Croghan added that he expected the Indians at Venango to heed his invitation, and that if they did so, their action would be ample proof to the English that they desired peace. At the time that this notice was sent to Venango, the Indians around Pittsburgh said that they hoped that General Stanwix would not bring any southern Indians with him to the Ohio.

Five days later the Wyandot emissaries returned with the report that the invitation had been received kindly by all the Indians except a brother of Tedyuskung's, who wanted war against the English. The messengers claimed that there were 100 French and over 450 Indians still at Venango. Also, that about 30 French and 300 Indians had set out to lay an ambush along the road between Fort Ligonier and Pittsburgh.

A short time later some Shawnee chieftains came into camp with the news that a "large body" of their people had been ready to start on a raid against Virginia, when two of their tribe, who had been at the Pittsburgh treaty making, had arrived with Croghan's message and his wampum. When they had received this communication, the Shawnee had decided to cancel the Virginia excursion.

More spies were sent out in order to keep in close touch with the movements of the French, and on July 29 some agreeable information was received. Two Indian spies returned from Venango with the account that most of the Indians had deserted the French, with the exception of thirty whom the French had hired to scout the English. The messengers stated that there were not over one hundred men at Venango, and that the French feared that the English would attack them. The twenty Wyandot warriors there had sent a belt of wampum to the Delaware chiefs asking them to come to Venango and chastise a Delaware who wished to keep on fighting when the Wyandots wanted to bury the hatchet. The next day two Shawnee Indians arrived with the report that some Cherokee had visited their nation and had told them that the English intended to cut off all the Indian nations. The Cherokee had said that in a short time they expected to be at war with the English. They had invited the Shawnee to join them, but the invitation had been refused.

At this time additional spies were dispatched to Venango, and some to Presque Isle, to watch the movements of the French and especially to learn what had become of the cannon intended for the attack on Pittsburgh. Information about the fate of Niagara was sought also. Two Wyandot scouts returned the next day from Venango and confirmed the previous report that there were only about one hundred Frenchmen and thirty Indians there. The French, they said, were sending bands of Indians out from time to time to attack the English stragglers along the road, in order to gather information. They declared that there were no cannon at Venango, and that the French had not been able to persuade more than fifty Indians to accompany them to Fort Niagara; the remainder had deserted the French cause and returned to their homes across the lakes. Regarding the conditions at Fort Niagara, the spies reported that the English and Indian army was only a day's march from the fort, and that, according to a French tale, over two thousand of the English force had been destroyed. Nevertheless, the English were said to be continuing the siege. Two more spies came in from Venango the following day with a repetition of the Niagara story. They also declared that a number of Indians were leaving the French at Venango and were coming to the forks as Croghan had requested.

Soon the reports from Fort Niagara underwent a decided change for the better. On August 4 two more spies returned from Venango and described the confusion that prevailed at that post. The excitement was caused by the news that the English army had appeared before Fort Niagara, had entrenched itself, and could not be dislodged. French losses were said to have been very heavy. It was reported that the French commandant at Niagara had sent a statement to Presque Isle that he would have to surrender before long. Since Sir William Johnson had threatened to cross the lakes with his Six Nations allies and take the French settlements at Fort Detroit (Detroit, Michigan), the commandant had further asked the officer in charge at Fort Presque Isle to send an express to Detroit with the order that all women and children were to flee with their effects to the head of the Scioto River. There they were to await a warning that the Six Nations warriors were crossing the lakes, and upon that signal were to move to the French settlement down the Mississippi. Another twenty-four hours brought from Presque Isle a confirmation of the foregoing message, with the additional observation that the fall of Fort Niagara was expected momentarily. Two days after receiving this news, a meeting of all the Indians was called at Pittsburgh.

Present at this short conference on August 7 were practically all the important English and Indian figures around the forks at that time. They included Colonel Hugh Mercer; a number of officers of the garrison; George Croghan, still deputy Indian agent for Sir William Johnson and Trent's immediate superior in Indian affairs; Captain Thomas McKee, another assistant of Croghan's; and Captain Andrew Montour, who acted as interpreter. The Indian chiefs and warriors represented a number of widely scattered tribes: Delaware, Shawnee, Wyandot, Twightwee, Ottawa, Chippewa, Kuskuski, and Potawatomi, When the Indians had congregated, they were told that they had been called together to talk among themselves, since one of the tribes had been instrumental in starting the war on the English. It was stated that despite the treaty, the English were still being murdered, and Croghan asked them to let him see them bury the hatchet and to promise to stop their killing. The English, he said, would consider their failure to do so a breach of the treaty. On the morning of August 8 the Indians said that they would meet in the afternoon and comply with his wish. The Beaver asked Croghan to open the council, which he did with a friendly speech and a belt of wampum. Then the Beaver made several speeches, after which a principal warrior of the Delawares arose and admitted that his people had started the trouble. They promised, however, to bury the hatchet deep in the ground. The western Indians then made a similar promise, and the conference ended.

Reports and rumors of various kinds drifted in to Pittsburgh during the next week. Colonel Bouquet, writing to Croghan from Fort Bedford, was worried about commissary problems. He informed Croghan that the number of Indians in the English service would have to be reduced as much as possible. It was his opinion that fewer Indians were needed under the improved conditions, and he thought that it would be impossible to build a magazine of provisions for the soldiers at Pittsburgh, if the idle Indians continued to eat all the food. He asserted that it was the French custom to give the Indians the same rations as the soldiers received, and he could see no reason why the English had to be slaves to the red men. He wished the English to be their friends and brothers, but not their slaves. In closing, he ordered the unemployed Indians to be called into a conference and disbanded. That was the beginning of an Indian policy of constriction on the part of the English that was to result in suspicion, discontent, and an eventual savage explosion on the frontier.

On August 12 Fort Pitt was visited by two Shawnee Indians who carried the information that the Cherokee were back among them again, trying to solicit their aid and that of all the other western Indians in a war against the English. They asked what they were to do. The Cherokee threat was somewhat nullified by the encouraging news received on the following day. In the forenoon, and again in the afternoon, Indian scouts reported that Fort Niagara had fallen on August 5 (actually it had fallen on July 24), and that the French had left the forts in northwestern Pennsylvania and were headed toward Detroit for succor, with their arms and equipment. Before deserting their posts they had given the Indians a great many presents and much clothing, with the comment that they expected to be again in possession of the Allegheny River before the next spring.

For almost a week nothing of significance transpired at Pittsburgh except the delivery of some letters from Sir William Johnson and the return of some prisoners. But on August 23 Croghan commented:

These three days I have been plagued with the Indians of all Nations on account of a report spread amongst them that we were [to] bring the Catabas on them, and that when we had settled a Peace with the French we were to cut off all the Western Indian Nations & give Part of the Country to the French.

To dispel their fears several meetings were held with the Indians and it was explained to them that the rumors were unfounded. Those words were seconded by the Mohawk Indians who had brought the messages from Sir William Johnson. They told the Indians at Pittsburgh that the

English were not on the Ohio of their own accord, but had been invited
by the Six Nations to build there, trade with the Indians, and establish
a lasting peace. Also, that the Six Nations intended to back the English,
and that the Indians from the West should return home to hunt and
to plant their crops. Then Croghan produced a copy of the draft of land
showing the dividing line between the Indians and the English, as it had
been drawn at the Easton Treaty. He announced that as soon as General
Stanwix arrived, the Indians would all be called together to confirm the
transactions and fulfill their engagements to the English. Within the
next week most of the Indians around the post dispersed, except a few
Shawnee and some Delawares.

On September 2 Stanwix arrived (construction of Fort Pitt was
soon started), and on the following day he held a council with the
remaining Indians. He told them that he had sent George Croghan to
treat with all of them, and that whatever had been done in July he would
confirm in the name of his Majesty. He reminded them that the English
would expect a punctual and full performance of every agreement made
by the deputies of the various nations. In reply, the Indians pledged
peace and assistance to the English, accompanying their promises with
strings of wampum and the smoking of peace pipes.

On September 6 Andrew Montour and a party of Indians were dispatched to view the ruins of the French forts at Venango, Le Boeuf,
and Presque Isle. About one week later Chief Crow, with twenty-six
Indians of the Six Nations, came to Fort Pitt and asked for clothing,
powder, and lead. He said that his band expected to settle at the mouth
of Beaver Creek. There was little Indian activity around the forks until
the middle of September, when some Wyandots and Delawares came
in to trade. Several of the group were from across the lakes. Before
starting to barter their pelts, they described the movements of the
French at Detroit. They reported that the soldiers there were building
a palisade around the fortification, which was to be filled with earth
breast high on the inside; when completed, the enclosure was expected
to be large enough to accommodate all the settlers around that post.
When the Wyandots finally began to trade, they objected to the high
prices (£6 10s) that the provincial agent at Pittsburgh charged for
hunting saddles.

Indian messengers brought the information on September 25 that a
party of sixty Indians, consisting of Delawares, Iroquois, Shawnee, and
Twightwees, had started out from the Scioto to make war on the Cherokee. In his journal Croghan recorded his hope that such forays would
tend to keep the Cherokee from attacking the Virginia frontier settle-

ments. The next day another Indian visitor announced that all the Indians south of the lakes were quiet and engaged in hunting. Four days later a group of Shawnee warriors charged that the French at Detroit were doing their best to get the Indians to join them in attacking the English convoys along the road between Fort Bedford and Fort Pitt. They stated that the French had sent to the Illinois country for men and Indian goods. But the news did not worry the English unduly; they felt that the chief interest of the Shawnee at the moment was to get the assistance of all the western Indians for a war that they were planning to start against the southern tribes. A week later a large party of Shawnee declared that they had refused to have dealings with the French at Detroit and were coming to Fort Pitt to renew their friendship with the English.

An old Wyandot friend of the traders came to Fort Pitt on October 10 with some reports that the Indian agents were inclined to believe. The messenger said that before he had left Fort Detroit, all the Indians from above the lakes, except one small tribe of two hundred, had returned the war hatchet to the French; that there were only about five hundred French in the settlement at Detroit; and that their provisions were low. It was the Wyandot's belief that the new stockade would not be very strong. He declared that the French commandant at Detroit had said that if the English from Fort Niagara or Fort Pitt made an attack, he would surrender.

Almost immediately after the receipt of this intelligence, Croghan was called into a private meeting with the Shawnee chiefs, who told him that all the Indians between the Ohio River and Lake Erie would soon be at open war with the southern Indians. Several parties, they said, had already started. The chiefs had refused to declare open war, however, until they had talked with Croghan. If the English would promise friendship and support, they would declare war at once and invite all the Indians from across the lakes to assist them. But Trent was not in a position at that time to pledge such complete support. It seems that the Shawnee were especially angry with the Cherokee and the Chickasaw for having killed a number of their people several months earlier. They were bent on revenge, and ever since that time had been seeking allies to help them in their proposed war.

The utter economic dependence of the native Indians on the caprice of the white men, English or French, was amply illustrated by a speech made at Fort Pitt on October 17 by a small band of Wyandots from near Fort Detroit. They charged that necessity had required them to make war on the English. Had they not joined the French they could not have kept alive; they said, "You know our Circumstances, & Know very well that no Indian Nation live now without being supported either by the English or French, we can not live as our Ancestors did before you came into our Country." In addition, they stated that the French at Detroit were fearful lest the English attack them, and that they were in great need of ammunition and provisions. There were supposed to be about eight hundred in the settlement, including both inhabitants and soldiers. According to the Indians, there were no cannon at the fort, which raised the suspicion that the French must have buried some in Pennsylvania before they evacuated their forts.

General Stanwix sent for Croghan on October 21 and asked him to tell the Indians of the several nations that Quebec had been taken by the English, and that he would hold a conference with them shortly. Croghan immediately ordered Montour to spread the good news. Montour reported that the Indians seemed happy at the announcement, but that they requested a gift of two kegs of rum so that they might make merry with the English! Their plea was granted, with the result that the conference, planned for October 22, had to be postponed for two days, because the Indians were too drunk to attend.

On October 24, however, Stanwix was able to meet the Indians in a general conference for the purpose of approving the earlier agreements made between them and the English. Most of the English officers who had attended the July meeting, with the addition of General Stanwix, were present at this conference, as well as many of the same Indians. Trent again acted in the capacity of an assistant to Croghan. This was a significant day in another respect for Trent. While he was engaged in his duties as assistant deputy Indian agent at Fort Pitt, his third child, Martha, was born in Lancaster.

The most important information brought to the fort in a number of days was the news carried by an Indian of the Ohio region that the French at Detroit had just received a supply of provisions and goods from the Illinois country, and that the garrison there had been reinforced by three hundred men from the same source. It was said that the French were sending out traders to all the Indians living both north and south of the lakes. A few days later several Ottawa Indians arrived from near Detroit with the statement that their people were divided; that some intended to stay with the French, and that the others were moving south of the lake to hunt and to prepare for planting the next spring. They said that the French had refused to supply them with powder and lead, with the comment that they were to go to the English for what they wanted. In the afternoon of the same day, thirty Shawnee called at Fort Pitt to express their approval of the late treaty making. Among other statements, they declared: "We return thanks to the great King of England for the care he has of us in Supporting a Trade amongst us, & Apointing People who we are acquainted with, to Transact the publick business, between him & us."

About two weeks after the report regarding the reinforcement of the French garrison at Fort Detroit had been received, there came a confirmation by two Six Nations Indians who had just been to that post. These messengers also stated that French officers were accompanying the Indian traders in order to carry on negotiations with the Indians. The French at Detroit, they reported, were telling the Indians that the English were going to build a large town at Fort Pitt, and that the next summer, when a great number of people had collected there, the English would begin to settle the country. The Indians had been promised that if they would attack the English along the Forbes road in the spring, the French would assist them, and they would thus be able to force the English to depart.

During the first week in December a meeting was held with a group of Ottawa in order to encourage them to affiliate with the English. After giving them a present of some clothing, Croghan promised them "that Strict Justice in Trade will be observed here to all Indian Nations that chuse to live in friendship with his Majesty's Subjects." As if to test the veracity of his statement, several Indian hunters came in to Fort Pitt to trade and brought with them "better than a 1000 Deer Skins." More than a week later some Shawnee from the mouth of the Scioto reported that all their people were out hunting, in the hope that they would be able to trade at Fort Pitt in the spring. On the last day of the year 1759, a Shawnee Indian delivered the intelligence that the French at Fort Detroit expected to retake Fort Niagara in the spring, so that they might clear the road to Montreal. It was their desire, he said, to get goods from the latter town in order to supply the needs of all their Indian children. Since the French pitied the Indians and knew that the English intended to take their lands from them, they had volunteered to help the natives if they wished to drive the English out. The Shawnee then asserted that the Indians north of the lakes had not yet decided whether they would assist the French in their spring campaign against Niagara.

CHAPTER VII

Assistant Deputy Indian Agent and Trader at Fort Pitt, 1760-1761

From about the middle to the last of January, 1760, additional reports concerning the French interests were conveyed to the Indian agents. On January 13 more than fifty Ottawa and Chippewa Indians came to Fort Pitt to trade. They said that they had permanently deserted the French cause and had come to settle and hunt south of the lakes. Two weeks later, an English prisoner, Charles Powers, who had spent six years among the Wyandots and the French at Fort Detroit, apprised Croghan of some interesting facts. He stated that every spring during his captivity, great numbers of Indians had come from across the lakes to make war on the English, and that sometimes there had been as many as seven hundred in one company. He said that all the Indian nations in whose custody he had been, with the exception of the Wyandots, were very cruel to their prisoners. Up to the previous autumn, according to his story, the Indians had been under the impression that the French had merely abandoned Fort Pitt and would ultimately be able to conquer all the English in America. The fall of Fort Niagara, however, had opened the eyes of the Indians; as a result of this display of English strength, the more sensible ones now favored a neutral policy. Powers reported that the chiefs of all the nations north of the lakes had much more affection for the French then for the English, because they feared that the English would settle their land. A detachment of men and two thousand beeves, he stated, were expected at Detroit in the spring from the Illinois country. He was not familiar with the purpose for which the reinforcements were to be used, but he declared that if the French were planning a spring campaign against the English, there were numbers of Indians north of the lakes who would join them. The French may have suspected this state of affairs, he said, for the commandant had sent a messenger to the Indians hunting south of the lakes, asking them to return to Fort Detroit as early as possible in the spring.

The month of February was relatively quiet at Fort Pitt, with no event more exciting than the occasional return of a few white prisoners, or the appearance of some Indians who wanted to trade. But on March 8 the tempo changed. Six Indians from the Six Nations council at Onondaga (New York) came with a message to all the Indians dwelling west of Fort Pitt. The council requested that all the warriors of those nations bury the bloody hatchet, unhang the war kettle, and return to their ancient employment of hunting and trading with the English. They were also told to turn their eyes to the rising sun, as they might expect a deputation from the council to visit them in the summer, with instructions for the future good of all nations.

On March 18 two Indian spies whom Croghan had sent to Fort Detroit, by order of General Stanwix, returned with their findings. They declared that the French commandant was in great fear that the English would attack him, either from Fort Pitt or from Fort Niagara. They said that the people were running short of provisions, because in the fall the officials at the fort had seized all the extra food supplies and had stored them in the fort, along with what had been received from the Illinois country. Up to the time of the spies' departure the stockade had been unfinished. They reported that the fort had no cannon, only two small swivels; each day the more valuable effects of the settlers were being moved inside the fortification for safety. Three hundred men, they declared, were expected from the Illinois country in the spring. Contrary to the story told by Powers, the spies insisted that the Indians living near the fort had flatly stated that they would not join the French against the English, even to defend the fort itself. Many of the Indians around Detroit, the messengers said, were scheduled to move to the south side of the lakes during the coming summer to plant corn and build towns. And finally, all the Indians along the Ohio River were determined to make war against the southern Indians in the spring.

Croghan, in command of a band of Indians, set out from Fort Pitt on March 21 to escort General Stanwix as far as Fort Bedford on his return journey to Philadelphia. Five days later the party arrived without mishap at the Raystown Branch of the Juniata River. The return trip to Fort Pitt, which had been left under the temporary command of Major Tulleken of the Royal American regiment, was completed on April 5, and Croghan found a great number of Indians collected at the fort for another conference. The policy of lavishing presents on the Indians was resumed, to judge by the notation, "500 Cloathed," in Croghan's journal. Aside from the Indian conference of April 6, nothing of outstanding importance was chronicled for that month.

About one hundred Delaware Indians, led by the Beaver, appeared at the fort on May 4 to trade and to return fourteen white prisoners. They asked that traders be permitted to visit their town to trade with them. They were given a present of four kegs of rum, since the generosity shown before the conference had practically exhausted the supply of other gifts. The following day nearly one hundred warriors of various nations arrived, in four different parties. After they had been supplied with fighting equipment, they departed to make war on the Cherokee. Some Wyandots appeared the next day. They delivered two prisoners and at the same time asked that English traders be sent to their town.

The many evidences of an increased interest in hunting and trading on the part of the Indians must have had their effect on Trent. He apparently could no longer tolerate the sight of others reaping extravagant profits from the Indian trade, while he received none. Therefore, on May 16, he entered into a business partnership with the Lancaster Jewish firm of Joseph Simon, David Franks and Levy Andrew Levy, for the purpose of carrying on a fur trade with the western Indians. The arrangement was supposed to continue for nine years. Since it was an agreement of the "adventure" type, in that it did not hinder the partners from engaging in other activities during the time it was in effect, Trent was able to pursue his duties with the English military forces for the time being.

On May 21 a Six Nations Indian who had lived for fourteen years among the Wyandots near Detroit came to Fort Pitt with some valuable intelligence. He reported that the people living about Fort Detroit were in distress. Only five of them had done any planting; the majority were afraid that the English might do the reaping. The commandant was sending out Indians toward Fort Niagara to capture a prisoner, if possible, so that the French might learn something of the English plans. The warrior stated that a little more than a month before he had left home, the Wyandots had been called to a great council with the Ottawa, Chippewa, Kickapoo, and Choctaw. At the gathering the Canadian Indians had complained bitterly about the losses they had sustained at the hands of the Six Nations the previous year at Fort Niagara. Since the Six Nations had done nothing to restore friendly relations with them, they had proposed, in revenge, to make a great "Push" against them and the English on the Ohio. They preferred peace with the English, they said, since the French could not supply them with Indian goods, but as the Six Nations and the English were so close together, it was impossible to strike one without involving the other. The informant said that the French at Fort Detroit had attempted to spread a rumor that Quebec had been retaken by the French with the loss of the entire British force. He thought that if a large English force went against Detroit, the Indians would stay neutral; but that if a small force appeared, they would probably help the French. Croghan considered the service of this trusted Indian so valuable that he paid him fifty dollars.

Reports and rumors of various sorts were always being circulated among the Indians, and those in charge of Indian relations had to be constantly alert in order to avoid trouble from these sources. Typical of frequent misrepresentations was the rumor carried to Croghan on June 11. Indians from several of the nations represented at Fort Pitt asked him if what had been told a Wyandot Indian by the commander of the Virginia troops was true: that ten thousand soldiers and great numbers of Catawba Indians were going to proceed against Fort Detroit, and that all the Indians native to the region around Fort Pitt were to sit still and smoke their pipes, lest they get hurt. The deputy told them that he had heard nothing of such a move. Thereafter, he endeavored by every means at his disposal to put a stop to such reports, since he felt they were dangerous.

Nearly a week later, additional information from Fort Detroit was received from a Wyandot Indian. He claimed that the French had received a letter dispatched from the head of the Wabash River, which said that a detachment of French soldiers with provisions and ammunition had arrived there on its way from the Mississippi to Detroit. The report had stated that that whole country was under arms and was marching up the river to attack Fort Pitt. Supposedly, the French were accompanied by the warriors of three Indian tribes. The commandant at Fort Detroit was to hold himself in readiness to march with his soldiers and all the Indians he could muster, as soon as he was called.

Further, the Wyandot related, the governor of Montreal had sent word to Fort Detroit that an army from the St. Lawrence was to reopen the road to that post, so that the Indian trade could be resumed. Serious bloodshed had been narrowly averted at Detroit by the intervention of the Wyandots, when the French commandant had refused to release to the Ottawa, Potawatomi, and Wyandots an imprisoned Mohawk messenger, who had been sent to Detroit from Fort Pitt in the spring. The Indians had outnumbered the French two to one, and the result might have proved disastrous had not the Wyandot plea for delay been heeded.

Toward the end of June, General Robert Monckton, who had succeeded Stanwix in command of the army in the West, arrived at Fort Pitt with reinforcements. On July 7, Croghan, with several assistants, probably including Trent, and some Indians, left the fort to escort Colonel Bouquet and a force of Royal American and Virginian troops who were being sent by Monckton to establish garrisons at the former French posts on the communication line to Lake Erie. (After the march to Presque Isle had been completed, Bouquet was to send a detachment on to Fort Niagara.) At the end of five days of travel, Venango was reached. Fort Machault was found to be in ruins, with the exception of a sawmill, which was in a state of bad repair. Leaving the English force at Venango, the Indian agents, with Chief Custaloga and the other Indians, set out on July 13 to visit Custaloga's town, situated about sixteen miles away, near French Creek. The village contained about 40 dwellings and 120 fighting men. Croghan's purpose was to collect all the Indians living in that vicinity and hold a conference with them, and on July 15 he was able to open the council. He told the assembled Indians that the English general had sent him to inform them that it was necessary to open communications between Fort Pitt and Presque Isle, and that the English intended to establish a post at the latter place. The Indians were asked to assist any troops that might pass through their locality. In return, they were guaranteed the protection of the Crown, so long as they behaved well toward the English. In another speech, the Indians were invited to come to Fort Pitt for a conference to renew their friendship with the English and to receive some presents sent them by the King of England. The Indians showed pleasure and promised to carry out the requests made in both speeches. Then the English delivered some goods to them which had been brought to clothe their women and children.

Immediately upon the conclusion of the conference the party was joined by Colonel Mercer. Together they marched two miles to a Six Nations village, where they encamped for the night. In the morning they made an early start, passed another Six Nations town, and moved on through fairly good country for seventeen miles. This journey brought them to the bank of French Creek, where they again made camp. Another early start and part of a day of travel through swampy country carried them a distance of thirteen miles to Fort Le Boeuf. About midforenoon of July 18 they arrived at Presque Isle, where they rejoined Bouquet's force. Croghan noted in his journal: "This days March was (two Miles open dry Woods near Prisqu' Isle, and one Mile at the other end excepted) a Continued Chestnut Bottom Swamp, near Nine Miles of which are laid with loggs, but much out of Repair."

Early the next morning two Indians were sent out to reconnoiter the surrounding woods. In the evening one of the scouts returned and said that he had talked with two Wyandots and two Chippewa, who belonged to a party of twenty spies sent out by the French at Fort Detroit to capture and return an English prisoner to the French. But the Indians had said that they had determined to do nothing hostile to the English, and had asked the scout to so inform the Indian agent. The scout was sent back at once to invite the Indians to visit the English; but since several of their band had already gone, they declined. They claimed that the only reason they had come on such an errand in the first place was that they feared the English would take Fort Detroit without letting them know about it.

On July 20 Croghan and his party started on the return trip to Fort Pitt. Two days later they were intercepted by two Indians from the Twightwee country. Croghan wrote in his diary: "These two Indians was sent by an Indian Spye who I have had in that Twightwees Town all the Spring." He had, therefore, good reason to trust their message. They reported that twenty days before, twenty-eight bateaux, loaded with provisions, had passed up their stream on the way to Fort Detroit. No soldiers, but about one hundred country people, had accompanied the bateaux. The French had told the Twightwees that three hundred men with seventy bateaux and twelve pieces of cannon were coming north shortly; and after them still another party of one hundred men was coming with a great number of bateaux. All were reported to be from New Orleans. French strategy called for the Louisiana forces to join with the Fort Detroit troops and move toward Fort Niagara to meet a French army coming from Montreal. After recapturing Fort Niagara, the French planned to advance against Fort Pitt and drive the English east over the mountains. Croghan's spy had sent the message that he would stay one month longer in the Twightwee town to see what happened, and then return to Fort Pitt. Following the receipt of this news, the party moved on toward Fort Pitt, where it arrived on July 25.

On August 3, General Monckton began the preliminaries of a conference with the deputies of the Twightwees, Potawatomi, and Kickapoo. Among other things the Indians promised never to break the peace with the English; asked to be forgiven for their past conduct; and made the request that traders be sent among them. The general tried to quiet their suspicions by telling them that the only reason the English had invaded their country was to establish free trade and communication. He also told them that he had presents for them.

From the Twightwee people came more news on September 2. A Delaware Indian spy reporting from that region said that a great Indian council had been held at which the Twightwee warriors had almost unanimously decided not to join the French. For the next two weeks little information was received, except a rumor that the French were to attack the English post at Presque Isle. Less than a week later this report was verified by four Ottawa who came directly from Fort Detroit to Fort Pitt. They stated also that the French had held a great council with their nation, at which the Ottawa were asked to assist in defending the fort against an expected English attack. The Ottawa had refused;

whereupon about one-third of the French at Fort Detroit had departed for Montreal to bolster the defenses there.

Montreal, however, was not able to withstand the English attacks. It was on October 1 that the English at Fort Pitt learned the joyous news of the fall of that important post. The event soon had its effect at the forks. Croghan's entry in his journal for the period from October 1 to October 20 states, "Not any thing happen'd Remarkable till Major [Robert] Rogers arrived who brought me Orders to Joyn His Majesty's Troops under his Command to go to D'Troit and assist in taking Possession of that Place it being included in the Capitulation of Montreal."

On October 21 Croghan departed from Fort Pitt to carry out the instructions given him. Four days later he joined Captain Donald Campbell at Venango, where he tarried for two days. Another four-day period was consumed in travel before Presque Isle was reached. From that point Captain Brewer of the Rangers, with a party of forty men, started overland on November 3 with a herd of bullocks. With that force Croghan sent fifteen Indians of different nations as guides, with instructions to tell any western Indians they encountered to pay Croghan a visit. On the following day Major Rogers and his detachment, with Croghan and some other officers, left Presque Isle for Detroit by boat. By mid-afternoon they made about ten leagues, with the assistance of sails. Their progress was halted the next day at noon when they encountered a party of thirty Ottawa. All went ashore to get acquainted. They soon re-embarked and, after moving a little farther along the lake, called a council with all the Indians.

At the conference the Indians were informed of the fall of Montreal and of the fact that Major Rogers and his force were on their way to take possession of Fort Detroit, Michilimackinac, and St. Joseph. They were told that the French inhabitants were to remain in possession of their property if they took an oath of fidelity to the English King. All Indian nations were guaranteed free trade with the English, as well as protection for their hunting grounds, so long as they adhered to the English cause. The Ottawa replied that they were glad to exchange the French for the English, since the latter could better supply their needs. They sought forgiveness for their hostility in the war and explained that they had been forced to join the French in order to get supplies. Several of their chief men planned to accompany the English to Detroit. Those who remained behind asked for some powder, lead, and flour, so that they might go hunting, and Major Rogers ordered Croghan to issue the requested supplies. During the next few days progress was slow. From November 7 to November 12 the boats had to seek a harbor to escape a heavy storm. There the Indians supplied fresh meat, while the army officers furnished flour and condiments.

At this time Trent was the recipient of a letter, which bore good news, even though belated. George Mercer, the author of the epistle, informed Trent that he had been present at the trial of Trent's suit against former Governor Dinwiddie of Virginia at Williamsburg. He wrote:

> I may assure You that all his malicious Attempts & Aspersions of your Character & Credit, were sufficiently cleared up both to the Court & Jury; the former were sensible of the ill Treatment your Character had suffered, & the latter so well satisfied of the Injury done you in both Respects, that they have brought you in a verdict for £800 besides your costs—I give you Joy of this Piece of real Justice.

Some months later the Virginia House of Burgesses made a decision as to the possible share of the judgment against Dinwiddie that should be assumed by the public; but that matter hardly concerned Trent as much as the vindication of his character, upon which young Washington and Governor Dinwiddie had heaped censure in 1754.

In the meanwhile Major Rogers' party was proceeding toward its destination. Messengers had been sent ahead to Fort Detroit with a flag of truce and with instructions to collect the Indians for a council at the portage between Sandusky Bay and Lake Erie. The scheduled conference was held at nine o'clock on the morning of November 22. At that meeting the Indians welcomed the English and requested that a free and open trade be carried on between the two peoples. They made a special request that their houses and property around the fort be saved from plundering. The English then told them of the conquest of all Canada. Major Rogers stated that he would take them along to Detroit and there deliver to them some speeches that had been sent by General Amherst, commander-in-chief of the British army.

On November 25 several messengers from Detroit brought the news that the French were angry with the Indians for meeting with the English and threatened to burn their towns. The French said that until they had orders from the governor of Canada they would not allow the English to come to Detroit. To quiet the fears of the Indians, the English promised them that any losses they suffered at the hands of the French would be made good by the English. The next morning a canoe with two interpreters and four Frenchmen appeared at the camp with some papers for Major Rogers. Soon thereafter, the English got under way again and shortly reached the mouth of the Detroit River. There the chiefs of the Wyandot, Ottawa, and Potawatomi Indians joined Rogers' party in its approach to Detroit. Six miles farther on, a French officer carrying a flag of truce was met. He was interviewed and delivered his message on a near-by island. After the conversation Captain Campbell was sent ahead, with a flag of truce, to give the French commandant orders to surrender. That night Campbell returned with the report that the English were politely requested to take possession of Fort Detroit and the country around it the next morning. At noon of November 29 the French surrendered the fort to the English, and the flag of France was lowered forever at Detroit.

During the next two days the French militia at the fort laid down their arms and took the oath of fidelity to the English Crown. The French garrison, accompanied by an English officer, was started toward Fort Pitt on December 2; with that group Croghan sent fifteen English prisoners whom he had just recovered from the Indians. On the following morning Croghan's duties as Indian agent were resumed. He was visited by the principal Indians dwelling around the post, who had some pointed comments to make. They told him that the French at Detroit had always supplied them with a smith to repair their guns and hatchets, and a doctor to attend their people when sick, and that the English would be expected to do the same. Since it was the beginning of their hunting season, they requested that the conferences with them be expedited as much as possible so that they might leave. Thus the Indian business around Fort Detroit was concluded by December 7. Forty-two English prisoners were delivered by the Indians at that time.

On the same day a small detachment of men was detailed to Fort Miami on the Maumee River to relieve the French garrison there. An interpreter was sent with the English troops, equipped with wampum and other necessities, and "with Instructions in what manner to speak to the Indians in those Parts." Major Rogers departed for Fort Michilimackinac on December 8. To conduct Indian affairs at that post, Croghan assigned Captain Montour and four Indians who were well acquainted with the natives and the country about the strait. Captain Donald Campbell, who was left in command at Fort Detroit, called the French inhabitants about the fort together on Decembeer 9 and 10 and read them some English law. In reply, they agreed to furnish provisions and firewood for the English troops and to do any other constructive work within their power. Croghan, carrying letters from Campbell, started for Fort Pitt on the evening of December 11. He left with the commander at Detroit all the wampum, silver trinkets, and other goods that had been carried there in the interests of the Indian service.

Croghan's description in his journal of the overland part of his journey through what are now Ohio and western Pennsylvania is of interest chiefly because of the contrast with present-day conditions. He recorded practically unimpeded travel through clear woods for many days. What a sight those vast stretches of virgin timber must have presented to the human eye! But he and his party were not interested in scenery. On January 7 they arrived at their destination.

Fort Pitt was now under the command of Colonel Bouquet, who had been left in charge on the departure of General Monckton in October. To judge from the journal entries, very little serious Indian business confronted the agents there during the first month of the year 1761. About the middle of the month a band of twelve Six Nations Indians, on their way to make war on their southern enemies, was outfitted with needed supplies and ammunition. On January 22 Major Rogers appeared at the fort; the weather had proved too inclement to permit his occupation of Fort Michilimackinac. Correspondence for January and February indicates that Trent made good use of his spare moments in the furtherance of his own private business interests. As soon as the English military took over the surrendered French posts, the doughty trader and his confreres prepared to take advantage of the beckoning business opportunities. Trent's interests were referred to by Colonel Bouquet in a letter to his superior: "Several Traders prepare themselves to carry goods to Detroit. I suppose that there is no Difficulty in granting them passes." (It appears that Trent left the service of the Crown about this time.)

The required permission was received, and apparently Trent and Alexander Lowrey set out for Sandusky and Fort Detroit to open Indian trading posts. George Croghan, in supreme charge of Indian relations in the western region, realized only too well the trouble that could come from a careless trading policy, and he wrote to Trent and Lowrey to remind them that he expected them to adhere strictly to the prices that he had drawn up for each type of commodity. The traders were asked to promote rigorous justice among the Indians in order to cultivate their good will. The next instruction must have been harder for Trent to follow. Although Croghan was fully aware that the granting of credit was the custom among Indian traders, he forbade the practice in order to avoid future disputes. On their arrival at Detroit, Trent and Lowrey were told to show Captain Campbell their invoices and prices of goods, so that he might explain them to the Indians. After being assigned a location, they were to proceed with their trade.

If Trent went to Detroit in person, his stay was brief. He must have been back at Fort Pitt by the last week of that month, for Colonel Bouquet, in commenting on the arrival of a French trader from Fort Miami, said: "The Savages in those Parts being destitute of all Kinds of nesessaries, I have engaged Trent & some other Suttlers to trust him with a Cargo, & he is to set out in a few days down the Ohio."

The renewal of the Indian trade brought varied difficulties. In addition to the trading licenses granted by the Pennsylvania authorities, the provincial agents, and the British commandant, there were those granted by Sir William Johnson's deputy Indian agent. The competition of the merchants with one another always created friction. Charges and countercharges were made as one group accused the other of violating the instructions laid down by the authorities in their efforts to control the Indian traffic. At one time the heat became so intense that seven of the traders wrote a complaint (with Trent's name heading the list of signatures) to Colonel Bouquet at Fort Pitt. They reminded Bouquet that the orders issued to the traders the previous summer by General Monckton, and later renewed by Bouquet, stated that no trader around Fort Pitt was to sell powder, lead, or spirituous liquors to the Indians without first getting a permit from the deputy agent of the Crown. The penalty for violating the order was the destruction of the trader's house and his expulsion from Fort Pitt. Just a few days before the letter was written, some of the traders had been refused a permit to sell liquor to the Indians. That in itself was bad enough, but when they later observed the provincial agent selling liquor to a Delaware Indian woman, they felt that things had gone too far. They requested Bouquet to bring the agent under the same rules that they had to obey, on the grounds that such unfair competition would ruin their trade.

Thirty Shawnee warriors and principal men called at Fort Pitt on March 1. They apologized for not having brought in the skins that they had promised in payment of their debt for supplies. They explained that difficulties had kept them from fulfilling their promises, but that they would pay their obligations yet. An admission was made that their young men, while drunk, were stealing horses, but they pledged themselves to try to stop the practice and to make atonement for the losses. The report that they were going to join the Cherokee was declared false, despite the fact that the Cherokee had requested them to do so. Croghan replied that he would acquaint the colonel with their speech and give them a reply on the morrow. When he met them on the following day, he charged them with failure to deliver their English prisoners as they had promised. He indicated his pleasure at their statement that they intended to fulfill their obligations, but pointedly informed them that promises would not be sufficient. If the English were to have any faith in the honesty and sincerity of the Indians, the prisoners would have to be released. Should the Cherokee persist in their unjust war against the English, then the English would go against them in force and crush them as they had the French. Croghan's speeches brought the assurance that the Shawnee would return home and lay the captain's messages before their people. They guaranteed that before the corn was in the ear the following summer, they would release all the English prisoners held by them.

On March 4 an Indian from the Lower Shawnee Town reported that fifty Wyandots who had stopped there on their way to make war on the Cherokee had been joined by fifty Shawnee. The next week a party of Six Nations Indians appeared with a request for ammunition for an expedition against the Cherokee. They were supplied and within twenty-four hours after their departure, seven large canoes loaded with Six Nations Indians from the upper Allegheny arrived. They surrendered two white prisoners and then made a speech. Among other things, they stated that they were on their way to make war against their natural enemies—the southern Indians—and that there would be many of their people passing Fort Pitt in the coming days. Many supplies would be needed, and they asked the English to provide these necessities, as had been done by both the English and the French before the war. The fact that the English were living on the path of the warriors was an added reason, they asserted, for granting the request; besides, their warriors were poor and had nothing with which to buy what they needed. In order to prevent any misunderstanding, the Indians implored the English not to be too harsh about their young warriors who committed misdeeds, since the red men had no laws to punish their evildoers as the English had.

Trader problems were becoming so pressing around the fort at this time that Colonel Bouquet wrote to General Monckton in disgust:

> This Place is Particularly infested with a number of Inhabitants the scum of the Neighbouring Provinces, who have no visibel means to live, except a Licence, I think it of bad consequence for the garrison, and I could wish the number of Traders was limited & obliged to give security for their Behaviour. A Dozen would be more than sufficient to drive the trade & supply the Garrison.

The last weeks in March and the first in April were replete with Indian activities. Indian bands containing from twenty-five to forty warriors passed by on their way southward, while news of the building of new Indian towns, and the requests for traders to be sent among them, came from other dark-skinned visitors. The presence of the Indians in large numbers, added to their thirst for the white man's firewater, made the task of prohibiting the sale of liquor to them an almost insurmountable one. Though a conscientious officer, Bouquet admitted,

"It has not been in my Power yet to put a stop to the villanous Practice of selling Rum to the Indians contrary to orders. The consequences where of have been fatal to them lately. Two Indians & a Squa having killed one another, & a fourth much wounded." To try to check the violations, a new order against selling liquor was issued on May 3. That the more sensible Indians approved of such limitations was proved by a speech of the Beaver on his visit to Fort Pitt several days after the issuance of the last command.

Not all Bouquet' s difficulties were caused by the traders; for, despite the promises of the Indian chiefs, the warriors continued to steal the traders' horses, as well as those belonging to the teams of the English garrison. At the time that Bouquet was writing to Monckton concerning these transgressions, Trent, who had lost ten horses in one of the raids, was out trying to apprehend the thieves. However, such efforts were usually futile.

Financial troubles demanded Trent's attention in the East for a time. During his absence reports were brought to Fort Pitt that the Six Nations had sent deputies to encourage the Indians around Detroit to commit hostile acts against the English traders. At first the stories were doubted, but subsequent confirmation tended to give them credence. On July 5 the Beaver and several other Delaware chiefs appeared at Fort Pitt and assured Bouquet that the Six Nations were trying to stir up ill will against the English because they felt that the English were not treating them properly. Although the Beaver was certain that the western Indians would not support the Six Nations, and believed that the whole affair would end harmlessly, Bouquet called the Indians around Fort Pitt together and told them that he was ready if any of them wished to make an attack. They disclaimed any knowledge of the plot, however, and promised that they would have nothing to do with it.

As a result of earlier warnings to the Indians to return their English prisoners, they had been making such returns fairly frequently. But the wily sons of the forest were too shrewd to return all their captives. They were well aware of the value of hostages in dealing with a real or a potential enemy, and they could not be stampeded into giving up their advantage completely.

While Trent was in the East, the Pennsylvania provincial agent at Fort Pitt, a Quaker by the name of James Kenny, made some disparaging comments in his journal regarding Trent, his business partners, and their practices. He wrote that the trade at Fort Pitt was in such condition that only those merchants who were willing to grant credit to the Indians could do business with them. The store operated by

Trent and Levy "(Franks being Concerned & its thought Croughan) ventures much on trust, being some of Croughan's Polliticks & he & all his Instruments endeavours to draw all ye Custom to that Store; that is a Point they have ye advantage of the Province Store in." Kenny declared that despite orders to the contrary, Levy, the Jew, had sold two "Ceggs of Rum" to the Beaver's son on July 20. The Quaker had also heard that Levy had sent word to the Indians on the Muskingum River that he would sell them liquor if they wanted it. Kenny charged that Levy was endeavoring "to set ye Indians against me." It is not known to what extent Trent personally approved of these practices of his partner—if, indeed, the charges were true.

In the forenoon of July 23 Croghan returned to Fort Pitt from a trip to Sir William Johnson's. Before another day had passed, he was busy sending out messengers to the Delawares, Shawnee, Twightwees, and other western nations, inviting them to meet him at Sandusky, from which place they would proceed to Detroit to meet Sir William in conference. A Six Nations Indian arrived at the fort on July 25 from the Seneca country. He declared that the Six Nations in general, and the Seneca in particular, thought themselves very poorly used by the English military authorities. At the start of the war they had been neutral, but had nevertheless supplied the English with information; later they had joined the English side, had helped General Abercromby with five hundred men at Ticonderoga, and had afterward assisted Sir William Johnson at Niagara with all their warriors. It was their belief that Fort Niagara could not have been taken without Indian assistance. Subsequently a large force of their warriors had offered their services to General Amherst, but since he had displayed little interest in them, they had returned home. The Seneca Indians charged that in spite of all those services in the hour of need, the English had insulted them as soon as the French had been defeated. They had forbidden them to travel through their own country, refused to allow traders to come among them, denied them powder and lead when they wished to make purchases, and given their land away to be settled, notwithstanding the English King's promise that he would keep their land inviolate. All these things, the messenger said, had made the Seneca believe that the English wanted to wipe them from the face of the earth; hence their attempts to arouse the western Indians against the English.

On the very same day that this warrior made his report, the deputies of the Six Nations who had been sent as messengers to the Indians at Detroit came to Fort Pitt and asked to talk with Colonel Bouquet and Croghan. The requested audience was granted on July 27. When faced with the charge that they had tried to incite the western Indians against the English, the deputies issued a denial. They contended that the only statements made to the western Indians were that the English had not been treating the Iroquois kindly since the conquest of Canada, and that as the Iroquois feared that the English had designs against all Indian nations, they wished to warn those tribes living about Detroit. Naturally, in view of the story he had heard a few days previously, Croghan did not believe the deputies. Therefore, he decided to use his knowledge of Indian psychology to get at the facts, and he invited the messengers to visit him at his house in the evening. When they arrived he gave them some presents and then engaged them in private conversation. Finally, two of them admitted the whole plot. First, they said, it had been planned that the Indians about Detroit were to seize the traders, murder the garrison, and take all the plunder obtainable; second, the Indians settled between the Ohio River and Lake Erie were to attack the posts between Pennsylvania and Fort Pitt (these Indians probably shared the view of some people of that day that Pennsylvania's western boundary was east of Fort Pitt) ; third, all the scattered tribes of the Six Nations settled on the upper Ohio and Allegheny rivers were to attack Presque Isle, Le Boeuf, and Venango; and fourth, a body of Susquehanna and Six Nations Indians was to seize control of the communication lines between Niagara and the German Flats. The Indians believed that once they had cut off all communications, any fort that did not succumb to force could be starved into submission. Thus they hoped to be able to win their country back again. The last point in their strategy involved the sending of one hundred warriors of the Six Nations to encourage the Cherokee in the South to continue their war against the English; and, as a French army was expected to retake Canada, the northern Indians were scheduled to join that army, while the western and southern tribes were to ravish the frontier settlements. (The Wyandots, however, had refused to support this scheme.) This was the Seneca plan of 1761, and with the knowledge of it in his possession, Croghan started for Detroit the next morning—July 28.

As the Indian agent and his party proceeded toward Detroit by way of the mouth of Beaver Creek, the upper Muskingum, and Sandusky Bay, they were joined by various Indian chiefs and warriors who had been invited to the forthcoming conference. The party arrived at its destination on August 16 and was welcomed by the various tribes living around the fort. Croghan announced the expected arrival of Sir William Johnson and sent out messengers to invite some outlying natives to the conference. On the following day a group of Wyandot women made Croghan a present of some roasting ears, thus putting him in the position of being unable to refuse a delegation of principal men of the Wyandot,

Ottawa, Potawatomi, and Chippewa tribes who appeared a few hours later and asked him for a keg of rum.

At a council on August 21 between the Delawares and the other Indian nations, to which Croghan and Campbell were invited, the Delawares informed the western Indians that they were happy concerning the peace that had been established with the English. They promised to do all in their power to keep it and asked their hosts not to believe stories to the contrary that might be circulated. About a week later, the western tribes met the Delawares again and made much the same promise in return. On September 2 Sir William Johnson arrived. By September 18 Croghan's duties at Detroit were completed, and Johnson ordered him to return to Fort Pitt. As he proceeded southward past the Indian villages that he had visited on his way north, he accepted the return of at least two dozen white prisoners.

When Croghan arrived at Fort Pitt on October 3, he learned that dozens of other English captives had been released during his absence. Every few days the various nations returned a few prisoners, but the number was not large at any one time. Seventy Seneca warriors stopped at the fort on October 17 on their way south to make war on the Cherokee. They brought a few presents, expecting war supplies in return; but Colonel Bouquet neglected that opportunity to allay some of the suspicion in which the Seneca held the English, by giving them a paltry fifty pounds of lead, with an equal amount of powder.

During the last week in October, the Beaver, with some Delaware warriors, came to the fort, delivered eight captives, and presented Croghan with a belt of wampum. The wampum was intended to seal the chief's promise that in the spring of 1762 all the English prisoners held by his tribe would be released. Croghan was asked to send the wampum with the Beaver's message to Sir William Johnson. Less than two weeks later a party of Shawnee Indians liberated twelve prisoners, with the guarantee that all English people held by them would be delivered in the summer of 1762. They, too, requested that the news be relayed to Johnson Hall. Their speech differed from that of the Delawares, however, in that they declared that although they had emancipated all their English captives, only five had been willing to return to their relatives. All these Indians were given presents as an incentive to keep their promises. Within the next few days both the Shawnee and the Delawares made the earnest plea that traders be sent among their people. After communicating with Bouquet, who saw no harm in satisfying this demand, Croghan dispatched traders to the Indian towns. Four days later, on November 15, he departed from Fort Pitt for Philadelphia, according to instructions.

CHAPTER VIII

LIFE AROUND FORT PITT, 1762-1763

Friction between Trent and the provincial storekeeper, James Kenny, continued. The trader was accused of having spread the rumor that the goods in the provincial store were to be sold out as quickly as possible, and the store closed. In addition, Trent had made a distasteful comment concerning "Quakerism on this side ye Alegheny Mountain." Kenny gloated over the fact that despite the rumors his store was still very much in evidence.

On April 22, eighty Six Nations Indians, with two Cherokee prisoners and eight scalps, stopped at Fort Pitt on their way home. Several of their number asked for powder, lead, and vermilion. Croghan informed Colonel Bouquet of their request, but, although the colonel had no objection to granting it, he was unable to do so, because General Amherst had issued orders that very few gifts were to be bestowed on the Indians. When this news was conveyed to the warriors, they appeared in a body and declared that it had always been the custom of the French and the English to supply them with the necessary commodities when they were going to or returning from a war. No words were minced by the Iroquois in their statements regarding the change in the attitude of the English toward the Indians since the conquest of Canada. It seemed to them that the English were trying to evade their promises to the red men. They contended that as it would take them twenty days of travel to reach home, and as there were so many of them, some were likely to starve on the road. Bouquet refused to violate his orders, in spite of their earnest plea; but Croghan, unrestrained by military limitations and with one eye to the business of the future, gave them the needed supplies at his own expense. It is easy to surmise that the Indians' opinion of the private traders rose, as the result of such diplomacy, while their opinion of the Crown dropped accordingly.

Several war parties of from twenty to twenty-five warriors stopped at the fort on their way south during the last week in April. That same week Kenny again complained of the unfair competition that the Levy-Trent store furnished him. Some Delaware Indians claimed that Levy gave them better prices on stroud cloth than Kenny, and accused the Quaker of trying to cheat them. Just when the argument was hottest,

Levy happened to walk into Kenny's place of business. When faced with the charge, he denied that his prices were lower than the Quaker's.

On April 30 both the Delaware Indians and the English suffered a serious loss in the death of Delaware George, who had always been a loyal friend of the British cause. All the efforts of the French to win him to their side had failed; nor had they been able to make any headway with the Delawares who had come under his influence. He was given a decent burial near the fort, and after the ceremony his people mourned for three days at his grave before departing for their village.

On May 10 Croghan left the affairs of the Indian department at Fort Pitt in the hands of Edward Ward and set out for Easton. He made this trip primarily to be present at some Indian councils. Trent was in the East on business at this time, too, and on May 31 he took out two warrants for a total of 650 acres of land in Cumberland County. Toward the end of June Croghan attended an Indian conference held by Sir William Johnson and Governor James Hamilton, now in his second term as governor of Pennsylvania, with a number of Delaware Indians led by Tedyuscung. At this Easton treaty making on June 28, 1762, both sides agreed to bury their land disputes over the old "walking purchase" of 1686. (According to an alleged deed granted to William Penn by the Indians in 1686, Penn was to have as large a portion of certain lands along the Delaware River as "A man can go in a day and a half." When Penn's heirs surveyed this land in 1737, they cruelly cheated the Indians by hiring runners instead of casually walking as the Indians had intended them to.)

Trent remained in the East long enough to participate in an important Indian conference at Lancaster, which opened on August 12. Present were Governor Hamilton; several members of the provincial council and of the assembly; a number of Quakers; and over five hundred Indians from the Six Nations, the Ohio Delawares, and the Twightwee, Shawnee, Kickapoo, and lesser tribes. Trent served as the secretary and recorded the minutes.

The Pennsylvania governor had called the Indians together chiefly for the purpose of arranging for the delivery of the English prisoners, a great number of whom were still held by the Indians. At least thirty captives were surrendered at the conference, while the usual promises were made that the rest would soon be freed. With that important business disposed of, Hamilton presented a request that was the special interest of the Philadelphia merchants and traders. These men desired permission of the Six Nations to open a trade route along the west branch of the Susquehanna River toward the lakes, and to build storehouses at the head of that stream to facilitate the Indian trade. It was argued that the Indians would be able to buy their goods more cheaply if they were transported by water, rather than by land over the King's roads. But the Indians interpreted the governor's request in another light. To them it appeared to be an attempt of the English to get control of more land for purposes of settlement, and they flatly denied the merchants the sought-for privileges. A number of Quakers appeared at this treaty making, and they did their best, privately, to stir up new land disputes, but the Indians refused to be influenced. Instead, they ratified the arrangement made earlier in the summer by Tedyuscung, by which all old land disputes were dropped. The lengthy conference finally came to a conclusion on Sunday morning, August 29, after many presents had been distributed among the Indians by Governor Hamilton.

By September 15 Croghan was back at Fort Pitt, ready to resume, for a time, his duties with the Indian department. Two days after his arrival he was visited by a delegation of Kickapoo and other western Indians, who asked for clothing and "colors" (paint) because, they said, they were poor. They also asked that Hugh Crawford, whom they knew, might be sent among them to trade. Colonel Bouquet, voicing his belief that these Indians had always treated the English well, agreed to supply them and to permit Crawford to be sent. On September 21 Croghan renewed the English friendship with them and gave each a suit of clothes and a set of "colors." They immediately displayed disappointment and anger; it had been their expectation that a present large enough for their whole tribe would be given them. In a fit of rage they declared that they could get along without the English and would not take home the speeches that had been made. They said that since the English valued their friendship so lightly, the English traders already in their country could be called home. The next day the tempest had subsided, and the Indians appeared with an apology and asked that all might be forgotten. Before they departed for their villages they told the English that the French people who lived and traded among them were always speaking ill of the English. Such casual reports, seemingly insignificant in themselves, might have served as a barometer for the future, had their warnings been heeded.

Four days after the departure of the Kickapoo deputies, the last of the Indian bands that had attended the Lancaster Conference came straggling past Fort Pitt. The Indians were in a disagreeable humor, because on their way west they had been robbed of almost all their horses and presents. The next day some of the Iroquois dwelling above Pine Creek came to the fort and asked what had transpired at the council. After Croghan had enlightened them they requested powder and lead. Croghan told them that there were no goods in the King's storehouse and suggested that they go hunting and use the skins they collected to pay for what they needed. He then gave the warriors a belt of wampum and informed them that their young men were still stealing horses around Fort Pitt, and that as long as this practice continued, they need not expect any presents.

During the night of September 28 a reputable Indian from the western country near Detroit called at Fort Pitt with the news that a great Indian council had been held at the Ottawa town above Detroit during the past summer. In attendance had been the chiefs and principal warriors of the Ottawa, Wyandot, Chippewa, and Potawatomi tribes, and two Frenchmen in Indian dress. The affairs of the council had supposedly been kept secret from all except the leading men in each tribe. The informant said that after the council had adjourned, messengers had been sent to all the tribes dwelling between the lakes and the Ohio River, with one exception—the messengers had been especially instructed not to communicate with the Six Nations. These actions had led him to conclude that a conspiracy was being hatched against the Six Nations and the English. It was his opinion that the French were trying to stir up a general Indian war. Croghan asked the Indian several questions, but the latter refused to answer.

After considering the report for two days, Croghan told some trustworthy Six Nations warriors about it. They said that they had heard the same intelligence from a Shawnee Indian, who had stated, in addition, that a Frenchman whom he had met along the Ohio had told him that the English were planning to cut off all the western Indians. For proof the Frenchman had pointed to the fact that the English would not give them any powder and lead and only allowed their traders to sell them a little. He had said that the French were always generous because they loved and pitied the Indians, and he had promised them that if they were strong and would join the French in the spring of 1763, when the frogs began to croak, the French would clothe and arm them, and they would then proceed together against the English and drive them out of the country (though probably a fabrication, this tale indicates the fear of the natives). According to the Shawnee, the Frenchman had then given the Indians two English scalps, with the counsel that they should never kill Indians but should always kill the English wherever they saw them. In a few days a report of these threats was sent to Sir William Johnson.

On November 22 a letter arrived from an English trader located at the Lower Shawnee Town, verifying the report of the Indian council meeting north of Detroit. This same trader reported on December 1 that all the western Indians were discontented; that they were growing jealous of the English; and that they publicly charged that the English intended to move against them and for that reason alone had asked for the return of all prisoners. The Indians believed, he said, that English action would start as soon as the last captives had been surrendered, and they had again referred to the fact that the English allowed them only a small amount of powder and lead.

About a week later, additional proof of Indian discontent was presented. A band of forty Six Nations Indians appeared at Fort Pitt and asked for supplies. They reminded the English that when the French had been in the region, and the outcome of the war had been doubtful, the English had given the Indians gifts and had told them that they wanted to build at the forks so that they could supply them in the future. But the English had forgotten their promises since that time. They had helped to scare away the game, thus bringing distress to the red men, and had further contributed to the difficulties of the Indians by not giving them ammunition or allowing the traders to sell it to them. The Indians also referred to their love for rum and wanted to know why it, too, was forbidden them. Croghan presented a reply to the Iroquois complainers in council the next day. He told them that the English were sorry for all the Indians' troubles, and that despite the fact that the King's stores were very low, the English would give them some ammunition, clothing, and blankets. He expressed surprise at their charge of a breach of promise and assured them that the English had kept the promises they had made. The giving of presents had been stopped because the war was over, and the Indians were now expected to hunt and pay for needed supplies with their furs and skins. As for the rum question, when the Indians refrained from behaving as they did when drunk—stealing horses and abusing the white prisoners among them—they might have some liquor. They were reminded, too, of their own unfulfilled promises, such as the guarantee that all English captives would be given over to the white authorities.

That the various threats and signs of dissatisfaction among the natives had their effect on the English officials is proved by the orders issued by Colonel Bouquet near the end of 1762. His proclamation stated that there was to be no hunting or trading west of the mountains without a license from the general or from one of the provincial governors. Settlements in that region were also forbidden. At about this time Bouquet departed from Fort Pitt, leaving Captain Simeon Ecuyer in command.

At the close of the year a party of Six Nations Indians, on their way south for a battle with their old enemies, paid a call at Fort Pitt. Captain Ecuyer consented to their request for powder, lead, knives, and vermilion. On New Year's Day, 1763, another band of warriors stopped at the fort on its way southward and was similarly treated.

Nothing more of interest transpired about the fort until January 22, when a number of Indians of the Delaware and Six Nations tribes came to the forks to trade. Among them was Michel, the trusted son of the late chief, Delaware George. He, too, verified the reports of Indian unrest and stated that a war belt was being carried among the western nations in an effort to arouse them to make war on the English in the spring. Up to the present time, he said, no nation had definitely decided to follow the suggestion, although there was among the tribes a great and growing suspicion of the English, because of their neglect of the wants of the Indians. It was his opinion that that neglect, and the fear engendered by it, were all that kept the tribes from returning their prisoners.

The first entry in Croghan's journal for February must have given Trent and Croghan some secret pleasure. It was noted that several Indians had complained that goods sold to them by Josiah Davenport, the provincial agent who had replaced Kenny, were damaged and not fit to wear. Nevertheless, Davenport had refused to exchange any of the commodities.

On February 6 a message was received from General Amherst ordering the commander to notify the Indians that all hostilities between the French and the English were officially at an end. Croghan proceeded to carry out the instructions by sending messengers to the various tribes. Less than a week later two Shawnee warriors came into camp with the good news that their chiefs, with all their English prisoners, would be at Fort Pitt in the spring. Several days later this report was corroborated by Alexander McKee, Croghan's deputy, who had been stationed for a time at the Lower Shawnee Town.

Perhaps no document better illustrates Trent's interest in the development of the frontier by Pennsylvania than a letter written by him in the winter of 1763. In it he stated that he had often thought how advantageous it would be to establish a town somewhere on the communication lines near the frontier. The fact that the Virginians were planning to settle a town near Fort Cumberland caused him to mention the matter, since he believed that there was still time to get ahead of them. In his judgment, Raystown, where Fort Bedford was situated, was the most suitable location. Several reasons were advanced: the proprietors already possessed an extensive tract of land there; a large branch of the Juniata River passed through the village, "where they are now preparing to build Battoes to carry Merchandise from there to John Harris's Ferry on Susquehannah & back"; part of the work of laying out the land had already been done by the commander in charge of the fort; and the site was only about thirty-five miles from Fort Cumberland, with which it was connected by "a good Waggon Road." The village, he wrote, already possessed at least fifty dwellings, "amongst them some good ones." In addition, he said, the road through Raystown was the one most used by vehicles going to and from Pittsburgh. He believed that if the proprietors would lay out a town around Fort Bedford, it would develop into a place of "considerable" importance, and its establishment would go a long way toward "keeping a great Part of the Trade over the Mountains within this Province." Another advantage, he thought, was the "thick" settlement of "industrious People" in the vicinity who would probably trade in and through such a town.

Baltimore, Trent argued, although a new community, was likely to become an important center, and was so situated that its business would logically go through Raystown. He said that a town at Fort Bedford *"provided our Assembly make no more Trade Laws, to oblidge the Traders to leave the Province & Seek Employment in the other Governments will* effectually secure the greatest Part of the Trade to this Province & keep our Communication open." Another matter that troubled Trent was the unsettled boundary, which made for laxity of law enforcement regarding settlement. With reference to the region around the forks, he declared, "There is scarcely any Doubt of Pittsburg being within this Province"; but a definite line, he thought, would make for more uniform legal restraint.

Between the last week in February and the middle of April, Croghan made few entries in his journal. Those that he did make referred for the most part to visits paid Fort Pitt by warriors of the Six Nations bound to or from battle with their southern enemies, and to the fact that supplies were given to most of them by Captain Ecuyer. There was one exception, however. On April 2 he recorded the arrival of Alexander McKee with a report from the Lower Shawnee Town. As a trader, and as an assistant in helping the Shawnee to collect their English prisoners, McKee had been among the Shawnee people since the last week of January. He reported that on February 20 the Shawnee, in a good humor, had informed him that they would set out for Fort Pitt on March 1 to meet Croghan and deliver their prisoners. On February 26, however,

McKee had received word from Croghan that all hostilities had ceased, and that France had surrendered all the conquered region of North America to the English. When he had relayed the news to the Indians, their temper had immediately changed. They had wished to know how France could give up something that she did not own. Without further ado they had told McKee that they would not be able to free all their prisoners that spring. McKee's efforts to effect a change of mind had been futile. The Indians had said that they would proceed to Fort Pitt at once with the prisoners already collected; but this move had been decided on more because they wanted to learn about the treaty of peace than for any other reason.

After much delay on the way, due to swollen streams, the Shawnee delegation finally arrived at Fort Pitt. There were about 125 in the Indian party, and on April 16, Captain Ecuyer and his officers opened a council with them. After the usual preliminaries, the Indians declared that they had delivered fifty prisoners since they had first been asked to relinquish their captives, and that they had five more with them to be surrendered. Again they assured the English that they intended to give up all the captives they possessed. They had noticed, they said, that bateaux were being built on the river, and they hoped that the English were thinking of nothing but peace! The usual objection was made to the high prices charged by the traders for their supplies.

Two days later, the English replied to the Indians' speeches. The red men were informed that there had been too much delay in the delivery of prisoners, and a final date for completing the job was requested. The officials then relieved the minds of the Indians about the boats. If necessary, they said, the English might have to go down the Ohio on business, but they would be going in peace and would probably notify the Indians before they started. As to the high prices, they were blamed on the war, with the suggestion that since the war was over now, the prices might drop. Finally, Ecuyer promised that as commandant he would do all in his power to promote Indian peace and friendship. The Indians then assured the captain that they would go home and collect all their prisoners; they said that it was impossible to set a date for delivering them but that the delivery would be made sometime in the summer. Thus the conference ended in more or less of a stalemate.

On May 9 Croghan left Fort Pitt for a brief sojourn in Philadelphia, in order to settle his accounts for the past year, and during his absence McKee was placed in charge of Indian affairs. Trent was still carrying on his trading operations at the forks of the Ohio and keeping a close check on Indian activities at the same time. On May 27 two men returned to the fort from the Munsey Indian villages located seven miles up the Allegheny River from the forks. They reported that all the Indians had departed from their towns the night before, had taken all their possessions with them, and had left their cornfield unprotected. Such actions were most unusual, and the people at the fort immediately became suspicious that some trouble was brewing. Their fears were accentuated later in the day when a party of restless Delawares came to the fort to trade a large quantity of skins. Instead of casually engaging in the usual harangues over prices and quality, the warriors appeared to be in a great hurry and did not seem to care whether the bargains they received were good or bad. Their main concern was to get the business done and be gone. The result was that the inhabitants about the fort began arming themselves in expectation of trouble.

The soldiers and settlers at Fort Pitt did not have long to wait. At daybreak on May 29 three men came in from Colonel William Clapham's residence, located about twenty-five miles up the Youghiogheny River at a place called Oswegly Old Town (near West Newton, Pennsylvania), and declared that Clapham, one of his men, two women, and a child had been murdered the previous afternoon by some Delaware Indians. The women had been brutally mutilated. They alleged also that the day before, the same Indians had robbed a Mr. Coleman of more than £50 as he was traveling between Fort Pitt and Fort Ligonier. On the same evening that this distressing news was brought in, two soldiers were killed and scalped at the sawmill, not far from Fort Pitt. The conspiracy of the great Ottawa chief, Pontiac, had definitely moved closer to Fort Pitt.

CHAPTER IX

THE SIEGE OF FORT PITT, 1763

For safety, all the inhabitants of the little town of Pittsburgh moved into Fort Pitt on May 30, 1763. That afternoon an Englishman, Thomas Calhoun, arrived from a Delaware village on the upper Muskingum River, with the story that he and thirteen other traders had been told by the Indians living there that they had better go to Fort Pitt, since an Indian uprising had started. The Indians had sent three of their warriors to accompany the whites to the fort; but Calhoun believed that the Indians had plotted their destruction, for, as they had been crossing Beaver Creek the previous day, a withering fire had struck them from ambush, killing all the white men except Calhoun and three others. The Indian guides had disappeared.

On the receipt of this news, an express was dispatched eastward over the mountains to inform General Amherst of the dangers on the frontier, and other messengers were sent in the direction of Venango. The scouts who were dispatched up the Allegheny got no farther than Shannopin's Town, where they were fired upon, and one man was wounded in the leg. They hastily reported back to Fort Pitt on the morning of June 1. About noon two men from Fort Burd, or Redstone, reported at the forks. That night they were sent back with orders for the sergeant to come to Fort Pitt at once with all the country people living about Redstone, together with eleven hundred pounds of powder and lead stored at that post by a trader. On the same day Captain Ecuyer ordered all the houses outside the fort pulled down and burned, so that they would not furnish cover for the Indians.

Fort Pitt in June, 1763, had about 250 men in its garrison, the regulars and the militia being about equally divided. All were reported to be in high spirits and willing to work or die as necessity demanded. There was little flour available, and the inhabitants were put on half-rations of bread and meat, while the poorer women and children received some Indian corn and meat. The animals of the inhabitants were collected and brought close to the fort. So that the post would be prepared for any eventuality, as much game as possible was secured from the near-by woods, and the livestock was reserved. Each inhabitant was given a tomahawk, and all the beaver traps that the people possessed were collected by the commandant and set along the unfinished rampart.

111

That Captain Trent carried his share of the burden is proved by Ecuyer's statement concerning him: "The merchant Trent is an excellent man, he has been of great help to me. He is always ready to assist me, he has a great deal of intelligence and is very worthy of recommendation."

Ecuyer altered his original order and had most of the lumber carried into the fort from the dismantled houses on the lower side of the town, but the torch was applied to those situated on the hill. All the people were then forced to reside inside the fortification. Ecuyer, ever a diligent and efficient officer, had the fort made ready for a concerted attack. Weak spots were strengthened with barrels of earth; trenches were dug; the ramparts were covered by strong planks; the traders' powder was stored in the King's magazine; two ovens and a forge were built; and, as a safeguard against fire, casks of water were distributed at various places, and the women were assigned the duties of "fire-lassies" in case of a conflagration. Ecuyer wrote to Bouquet, "I have made Trent Major Commandant of the militia, but as that does not agree with my fancy, I have incorporated the militia in our companies." The change of mind was based on the belief that better service would result from mixed companies. Three companies were detailed to each twenty-four-hour period in order to eliminate any possibility of surprise. Ecuyer told Bouquet that he had but ten shillings in his pockets, about which he did not intend to complain; but he wished very much that he did have a little more rum for his faithful men, who, nevertheless, understood the conditions and were patient.

Rumors and reports of all sorts filtered in to the fort and were relayed over the mountains. The Indians were reported to have taken Fort Detroit and the post at Sandusky, and to have captured a great many traders and their goods, including Trent's partner, Levy, and some of Trent's men, so that the merchants east of the mountains, who had a considerable sum invested in the Indian trade, were much concerned. Fort Burd was declared to be in a deserted condition; it was thought that the garrison had fled to Fort Cumberland. (The report concerning the capture of Detroit proved later to be false. That fort was attacked in the general move against the western posts in May, but withstood a siege that lasted several months. No record has been found to confirm the story of Levy's capture, so that was probably a false report also.)

On the morning of June 7 a trader by the name of Wilkins arrived at the forks of the Ohio from Venango with some intelligence that had been brought to Venango from Presque Isle on the day before his departure. According to this information, Lieutenant Cuyler, of the Queen's Rangers, with a force of 100 men, had been escorting 10 bateaux and 139 barrels of provisions to Fort Detroit, when, near midnight of May 28, his force had been attacked at the mouth of the Detroit River. He had lost over half his force and all his supplies, except two bateaux and five barrels of pork. Cuyler had immediately retreated to Fort Sandusky, which he had found destroyed. Not able to find refuge there, he had continued his retreat to Presque Isle. After a rest, all but six of the defeated detachment had moved on to Fort Niagara.

Every precaution was taken at Fort Pitt to guarantee its invulnerability. Regulations, which bring a smile to the reader of today, were far from a laughing matter to those responsible for the safety of the fort and its occupants during the first two weeks of June, 1763. Since the dogs about the fort made a great deal of noise, which it was feared might interfere with the giving of orders in case of attack, Ecuyer ordered a dog-catching squad created for the purpose of killing all canines not tied up by a specified hour. He also ordered the animals of the fort's menagerie, consisting of a bear and a wolf, killed or freed outside the fortifications at once. The cattle had to be watered once every day and fed with spelts (a hard-grained cereal, somewhat similar to wheat) twice a day—at ten o'clock in the morning and four o'clock in the afternoon. In addition to supplying the men on duty with drinking water, the women in the fort were expected to go out to the fields on certain days to cut spelts; any who refused were to be confined to the guardroom. In case of an alarm, certain prearranged assignments were to be carried out, for example, "The Lieutenant-colonels, the reserve, [were to be] under Major Trent's orders." Likewise, no women were to be allowed on the ramparts, or out of their rooms, except those engaged in carrying water to the men. The chimneys were ordered swept on a certain day, but they were not to be cleaned by setting them on fire. Those women with a propensity for keeping their laundry in good order were instructed to do no more washing in the rooms of the barracks or in the governor's house. A concession, however, was made to them: on Sunday, June 12, an order was issued that they might go outside the fort twice a week, on Mondays and Thursdays, to the bateau shed in the lower town, and launder their clothes. They were assigned a corporal and six privates for protection on wash days.

Profiteering, one of the scourges of all wars, was in evidence at Fort Pitt. Those who had Indian corn for sale began charging exorbitant prices for it. The practice was quickly stopped, however, as soon as Ecuyer heard of it, and the profiteers were ordered to return the purchase price over and above six shillings per bushel. Later this price had to be raised somewhat, because the owners of the corn flatly refused to sell at the price fixed by Ecuyer.

Several scattered dwellings located within a few miles of the fort, including George Croghan's, were soon burned by the Indians. It was never safe to go far from the gates of the fort, since enemies were ever lurking near, seeking the opportunity to murder and scalp an Englishman. At times the marauders became quite bold and would fire on the militia or the inhabitants as they were engaged in repairing the fences, or in harvesting grain, less than a mile from the fort. To limit the defensive operations, Ecuyer sent out a party to tear down the chimneys and fences that had been left standing in the upper town. Once in a while some soldier paid for his carelessness, or disobedience, with his life. Such an incident occurred on June 15, when a sergeant and three privates of the militia force, in violation of orders, decided to view the country from Grant's Hill. Just as they gained the summit, the officer was killed by an Indian bullet. In that instance the quick arrival of a rescue party from the fort prevented the Indians from taking the soldier's scalp. Near midnight of the same day an express, who had killed an Indian on the road, arrived from Bedford. As he was challenged by a sentinel from the rampart of the fort, the redskins opened fire, but both men were able to gain safety in the fort.

The middle of June found Captain Ecuyer in good spirits. He felt that his fort was too formidable to be captured by the Indian rabble around it. In addition to the light arms and ammunition, of which there was a sufficient quantity to double-arm each man and equip him with enough powder and lead for five hundred shots, the fort possessed sixteen cannon, all well mounted. Ecuyer had a number of crow's-foot traps built and placed in the moat, with points sharp enough to pierce the moccasins of an attacking savage. To those he added a line of beaver traps, placed outside the palisades. He wrote to Bouquet, "I would be pleased to send you one with the leg of a savage, but they have not given me this satisfaction." Despite the exercise of care, smallpox broke out in the fort, and the commander had to build a hospital in which to house the victims. Writing of co-operation, or the lack of it, he commented, "No one has offered to help me but Mr. Trent, to whom I am much obliged, as well as Mr. Hutchins."

Four Shawnee Indians, accompanied by a Frenchman, appeared on the opposite side of the Allegheny from the fort on June 16 and asked to speak with McKee. To him they admitted the capture of some traders a short while before, but promised to care for them until the war ended. The Delawares, they said, had refused to listen when the Shawnee had requested them not to accept the hatchet for war against the English. Under cover of night, an express was sent east over the mountains with this and other information from the fort. The following day the Shawnee Indians again appeared on the riverbank and called for a chat with McKee. But this time he refused to cross the river. Then they requested him either to return to the settlements at once or to join them for safety, as all the Indian nations had taken up the hatchet against the English. They declared that the Indians intended to attack Fort Pitt in a "great Body" in a few days. The Shawnee warriors announced that Venango and all the other posts on the frontier had already been captured, and that their nation would have to join in the war since practically all the other tribes had become involved. McKee believed them, but Ecuyer scoffed at their tale. Toward midnight, two expresses came through safely from Ligonier with correspondence from General Amherst. After spending about twenty-four hours at the fort, the messengers set out again at one o'clock in the morning with dispatches for Ecuyer's superiors in the East.

During the next few days the Indians increased their activities in the vicinity of the fort. On June 19 a few were routed as they attempted to creep along the bank of the Monongahela. Two days later some others on the opposite side of the Monongahela amused themselves by repeating "All's well" after the sentinels on the ramparts. The next forenoon, smoke was seen beyond Grant's Hill where some Indians had made a fire, and that afternoon, about two o'clock, several Indians appeared in the spelts field and began driving off the horses and cattle. A short time later, James Thompson, who had gone out in search of a horse, was killed and scalped within sight of the fort. This killing was the signal for a great number of Indians to appear on both rivers and on Grant's Hill, where they shot down the cattle and horses grazing in the vicinity, and began firing at the fort. They were dispersed by three well-placed cannon shots. The English had one man killed and one wounded, while the loss among the attackers was undetermined.

The sudden bold appearance of the Indians around Fort Pitt at this time was doubtless a result of their recent success at the English posts between Fort Pitt and the lakes, although news of those events had not yet reached Captain Ecuyer. On June 18, as it was learned later, Ensign George Price, in command at Le Boeuf, was attacked by a band of Six Nations Indians after they had failed to gain entrance to his fortification by a ruse. The Indians took possession of a storehouse near the fort by picking stones out of the foundation, and, with it as a cover, set fire to Price's blockhouse. After extinguishing the flames several times, the officer decided to flee. He was able to make his escape through a window, accompanied by seven men; the other six men of his little garrison, and a woman, were believed lost. Early in the morning of June 20 his party passed Venango. All was quiet there, for the rapacious Indians had already destroyed Lieutenant Gordon and his men at that post and had burned the blockhouse to the ground.

The fate of Presque Isle differed little from that of the posts to the south of it, although the story might possibly have ended less disastrously had an officer of higher rank and greater experience than Ensign John Christie been in command. At daybreak of June 20 the fort was surrounded by over two hundred howling Ottawa, Chippewa, Wyandot, and Senaca warriors, who shortly began shooting at the blockhouse. Soon they resorted to the use of fire arrows in an effort to burn the garrison out. They kept up their attacks all during the day, and after nightfall proceeded to dig holes along the lake edge, from which they were able to shoot without being hit themselves. On the slope above the fort they built a barricade of logs, which served them effectively on that side. The next morning the attack was resumed as vigorously as ever. The blockhouse was set on fire so many times that all the water reserve in the barrels was used. There was a well on the parade ground, but it would have been suicidal to try to reach it. In the meantime the Indians had practically undermined an edge of the blockhouse. The firing continued until midnight, when one of the Indians who spoke French called to the garrison that it would be useless to try to hold out longer. Ensign Christie began a parley. The Indian said that his people only wanted the blockhouse; that if Christie surrendered, he and his garrison might go where they pleased. A reply was promised in the morning if the Indians would cease their attack, which they did. One of the ironies of the situation was that an English schooner was hovering off the peninsula, sounding the bottom, but was unable to come in close to relieve the fort because the water was too shallow. Another was that the storehouse at the wharf was said to have contained eight hundred barrels of provisions, which the schooner intended to carry to Fort Detroit, but which were destroyed by the Indians instead. Ensign Christie capitulated on the morning of June 22. Contrary to their assurances, the Indians immediately made prisoners of the entire garrison. Christie, one soldier, and a woman were eventually delivered to the English at Detroit on July 9. The others of the garrison either were killed or were divided among the various tribes as captives.

The first reports of the destruction of the English frontier posts were brought to Fort Pitt on June 24 by two leading men of the Delaware tribe. McKee went out of the fort to hear what the Indians had to say. They declared that all the western posts, except Ligonier, which had been unsuccessfully attacked, had been destroyed, and that great numbers of Indians were headed for an attack on Fort Pitt. Out of regard for the English, they said, they had succeeded in getting the Six Nations to withhold their attack on Fort Pitt so that the English might have a chance to escape. Therefore, they urged the occupants of the fort to flee over the mountains as quickly as possible. Captain Ecuyer thanked them, but said that the garrison was well able to defend the fort and did not intend to leave. He informed the Delawares that three large armies were marching to punish the Indians for attacking the English, and he told them to go and care for their women and children but not to tell any other Indians what he had said. The spokesmen retired for a few minutes to talk with their people; when they returned, they stated that they had decided to hold fast the chain of friendship with the English. Major Trent wrote, "Out of our regard to them we gave them two Blankets and an Hankerchief out of the SmallPox Hospital. I hope it will have the desired effect." It appears that the dreaded scourge did break out in epidemic proportions among the Indians within the next nine months, but whether or not the disease developed from the contaminated blankets is impossible to say. At any rate, Trent and Levy were able to make a little profit out of selling two blankets and a handkerchief to Captain Ecuyer to replace the ones given to the Indians.

On June 25 a Shawnee Indian crossed the Allegheny River and told McKee that a large band of warriors was marching toward Fort Pitt and that the Delawares who had recently visited the fort intended to join them. Late in the afternoon two soldiers from Le Boeuf arrived and said that Ensign Price would be at the post in the morning. True to the announcement, the ensign, with five men, appeared at six o'clock on the morning of June 26, and told the story of his miraculous escape. He also stated that Fort Detroit had been attacked in May, but that it had withstood the assault. Twelve hours later a soldier who had escaped after the surrender of Fort Presque Isle arrived at Fort Pitt with the first report of the destruction of that post. Captain Ecuyer immediately forwarded the news to Colonel Bouquet by two runners.

The next evening four of the supposedly lost group of six men and one woman of the Le Boeuf garrison came in to Fort Pitt. With them was another soldier who had escaped from Presque Isle, who confirmed the news of the fall of that fort. Indians were seen everywhere around Fort Pitt on June 28, and that night several were discovered in the ditch along the riverbank. As a result, the garrison was ordered to the various alarm posts and remained there until midnight. No more Indians were seen until July 1, when several showed themselves in the garden.

Early the following morning some Indians appeared on Grant's Hill; at noon they moved into the cornfield, and later they proceeded to drive off the cattle and to shoot at some of the animals. That day was a significant one for the female population inside the fort. Since nearly 420 of the 540 occupants were being fed at the expense of the Crown, Ecuyer decided to compel the women, who numbered more than 100 of the total population, to do more to earn their livelihood. Therefore, he issued an order that all women who got provisions from the army must carry water to fill the casks around the ramparts. Any who refused were to be struck from the list of those entitled to food supplies and were to be ejected from the fort as soon as the road over the mountains was clear. Ecuyer hoped that the women would perform their duty without grumbling, since it was for the good of the service. Owners who kept horses and cattle within the fort were ordered to clean the stalls daily as a sanitary precaution.

A party that went into the garden for greens on the morning of July 3 was fired upon by some Indians who had been hidden within sixty yards of the fort. Some soldiers from the fort opened fire on the attackers and killed or seriously wounded one of them, who was then carried away by his comrades. Shortly after noon, four naked, painted Ottawa warriors appeared on the opposite bank of the Allegheny and wanted to speak with McKee. Finally they came across the river and talked to him a short distance from the fort. They declared that peace had been made at Detroit and that they had come to renew the chain of friendship. While the palaver was going on, a number of Indians came running down Grant's Hill. Others appeared along the Allegheny River. The soldiers in the fort fired on those coming from the hill, and the fire was returned. These actions created the greatest alarm. That night the entire garrison was on guard until one o'clock, when all except the regular guard went to bed and slept on their guns. The next forenoon a small band of Ottawa succeeded in enticing two soldiers across the Allegheny, allegedly so that the soldiers might conduct the Indians over to the fort for a parley. When the soldiers landed on the other side, one was severely stabbed, but both succeeded in getting back to the fort under a curtain of fire laid down by the muskets of the garrison and a volley of grapeshot from a cannon on the rampart. Shots were exchanged with various Indians in the afternoon without any casualties on either side.

During the next week only a few Indians were seen, at a distance from the fort. The nights were quiet, and the people began to be careless and to wander about the fields as if they had nothing to fear. Major Trent wrote that he was afraid that they would pay for their carelessness. Official regulations were relaxed enough to permit the commander to order special detachments out to cultivate the garden, collect wood, and perform various other necessary chores. At about this time Trent and other traders who had allowed their bales of deerskins to be piled up as barricades discovered that their pelts were being stolen. Ecuyer issued an order that the stealing was to stop; that all who were found with skins in their possession would be severely punished; and that a reward would be given to any informer who disclosed the identity of the thieves. It is interesting to note that on July 13 Trent considered conditions safe enough for him to remove his clothes when he went to bed—the first time he had done so for over two weeks!

In the meantime Colonel Bouquet, who was at Carlisle .with his little army, was doing his best to persuade Governor Hamilton and the Pennsylvania Assembly to take some steps toward defending the frontiers, but with little result. Help was promised, but showed no signs of appearing. Finally, in the deepest disgust, Bouquet told Hamilton that he would push on toward Fort Bedford with the insufficient force at his command. It was highly necessary, in his opinion, that Forts Pitt, Ligonier, and Bedford be strengthened, and the way opened for the removal of the marooned inhabitants for Fort Pitt. Thus about the middle of July, Bouquet, determined to carry out his purpose or die in the attempt, turned his face and forces resolutely westward.

The lull in Indian activity at Fort Pitt was broken on July 14 with the mortal wounding of a member of the militia while he and some comrades were herding the cattle within two hundred yards of the fort. This incident led Captain Ecuyer to make the request that all inhabitants sell their cattle to the commissary for the benefit of the garrison, as three lives had already been lost in caring for the beasts. That same day Ecuyer took the opportunity to praise the militia highly for the excellent support given him and to assure them that in the future their duties would be as light as possible. A number of Indians were seen in the vicinity of the fort during the next few days. On July 18 Major Trent was given orders to collect a party of thirty militia to cut and tie the corn, and another detachment was assigned the task of cutting the spelts. The workers soon set forth, guarded by ninety regular soldiers equipped with cannon and howitzers. But before the field work was finished, a large band of Indians appeared at the mouth of Sawmill Run (West End, Pittsburgh), and the men were all ordered back to the fort. Soon after their retreat another large band of Indians moved into the upper end of the field, near Grant's Hill, where the harvesting had just been stopped. Three Delawares from the Sawmill Run group and one from the Grant's Hill party came close to the fort and were unmolested because they came in peace. In addition to delivering news about some of the white prisoners among them, they said that they desired peace with the English and were willing to go to war against the Ottawa and the Chippewa. Ecuyer thanked them, but said that he could not hold any council with them at that time.

On July 20 a number of Indians passed by the fort in canoes and on horseback, apparently engaged in the transportation of Indian corn. Trent was of the opinion that they were trying to make the garrison believe that their numbers were greater than they actually were. The reappearance of large groups of Indians about the fort caused Ecuyer to check more carefully the conditions of his defense. His surprise can be imagined when he found his guards asleep at their posts at three o'clock one morning. That discovery led him to issue a caustic command that all guards were to remain alert under arms from two o'clock until daybreak, lest the fort be surprised by the numerous Indians who were skulking about the fields and woods.

The next morning some Shawnee warriors waded part of the way across the Allegheny to a point opposite the fort and asked for provisions for their chiefs. Ecuyer said that he had none, and that he would not speak to the Indians unless their chiefs came. In the afternoon a Shawnee chief appeared and told McKee that his people were holding a council and would come for a parley as soon as it was concluded. He stated that a report had come from Detroit that the commander there had made peace with the Indians. Ecuyer was suspicious, however, and sent a warning to the Indians not to pass back and forth in front of the fort, either on land or on water, carrying arms. Despite the warning, the Indians continued their movements back and forth with canoe- and horse-loads of corn and leather from the deserted plantations and the tan-yard—or, as some thought, with loads of plunder from the frontier settlements. A second warning was soon issued to them to stop these activities under penalty of drawing gunfire from the fort. Only two Indians were seen the next day, although tracks along the riverbank indicated that some of them had paid the fort a visit under cover of darkness. At dusk on July 24, three Indians appeared across the Allegheny and called to the fort that their chief, Custaloga, had arrived. While the conversation was being carried on, three ghastly "death halloos" rang out across the water. When questioned as to the source, the Indians said they did not know who had made the disturbance.

On the following day, four Indians attempted a violation of Ecuyer's order by going up the south side of the Monongahela River in a canoe.

As a result, a six-pounder loaded with grapeshot was fired at them. They all escaped, but their canoe was left afloat. Several of the militia recovered the craft and confiscated its contents. There were four rifles, horns and pouches full of powder and lead, eight pairs of new Indian shoes, eight pairs of leggings, and five blankets. Trent said that such equipment was "a sure sign they were going to War." That night there was additional Indian activity in the vicinity of the fort. Two Indians called and asked why their people had been fired upon, and were told the reason. Then they asked if their chiefs would be heard if they came to the fort. An affirmative answer was given, with the specific condition that the chiefs come alone.

Thus several of the chiefs and principal warriors, including Shingas and Grey Eyes, appeared before the fort on July 26 and made a speech. They asked the English to leave Fort Pitt and charged that their presence there had brought on the war. The English were then warned that they were soon to be attacked by a body of Ottawa and Chippewa, who were approaching for that purpose. The chiefs were promised a reply on the morrow. During a council at the fort on the following morning, another death yell was heard from the direction of the sawmill. Soon fifty-seven warriors, mounted on horses, followed by some on foot, were seen going down the road along the river. Later some of them returned and began cutting grain in one of the fields with knives and scythe. Trent attributed their actions to hunger. Shortly a signal gun was fired at the fort to call the chiefs from across the river to hear the answer to their speech of the previous day.

When the chiefs had assembled, Ecuyer's message was delivered to them. He declared that Fort Pitt had been taken from the French and was now the home of the English. The Indians were assured that the British force intended to defend the fort to the last; further, that the English had ammunition and provisions enough to hold the post for three years against all the Indians in the woods. "I wish we had for three months," was Trent's parenthetical comment on this statement. Ecuyer told the Indians that he did not fear the Ottawa and the Chippewa, since a force was being sent against them in their own country that would keep them busy. The Indians were bitterly denounced for posing as friends at the same time that they were engaged in killing the English traders and settlers and in stealing goods and horses. Ecuyer warned them that if they wished friendship they would have to return to their villages and sit quietly, or send someone to see the general, since he was the only one who could make peace. In reply to this speech, the Indians promised that they would think over what had been said and would return an answer the next day. But before leaving, Yellow Bird, a Shawnee chief, asked for the four rifles confiscated from the canoe. He was informed that they would be returned later, or paid for, when the Indians had demonstrated that they could behave themselves. This rejoinder enraged the redskins, and their countenances underwent a complete transformation. They hurriedly departed, after refusing to shake hands with the English.

Ecuyer's speech had the effect of a stone tossed into a hornet's nest. The next morning, that of July 28, the Indians were seen some distance up the Allegheny, crossing eastward over the river by swimming and on horseback. About the middle of the afternoon they began firing on some people who had strayed out into the garden in spite of Trent's request "not to stray as I was positive they [the Indians] were coming down but they paid no regard to it." One of the group was wounded before shelter was reached. Then the siege began in earnest. Throughout the remainder of the day and all that night, the frenzied denizens of the forest continued their attack. Not only guns were used, but bows and arrows as well; Ecuyer suffered the misfortune of getting an arrow in his leg, and a corporal and two privates received head wounds.

There was no decrease in the ferocity of the attack on July 29. The Indians intrenched themselves under the bank of the Allegheny River and poured a merciless fire into the fort from that side. Several shells were thrown among them, but they had little effect, since the warriors simply shifted their positions. Three English soldiers were wounded on that day; the casualties among the Indians were undoubtedly greater, but there was no way of determining the exact number. Considerable damage was done to the roofs of the barracks and the other houses by well-aimed shots. Time and again the Indians attempted to set the buildings on fire with flaming arrows, but generally the blazing torches fell short of their targets. Trent estimated later that in the two days of fighting, fifteen hundred small arms had been fired from the fort.

On the night of July 29 the Indians gathered under the riverbank, and it was feared that a concerted attack was intended. Although the attack was not made, random firing continued, and during the following twenty-four hours the garrison was kept under arms day and night. Desultory shots were directed at the fort all day on July 31; not all of them were returned by the garrison, since the defenders followed a policy of conserving their ammunition whenever possible. In the evening the Indians called to the garrison that they had letters from Colonel Bouquet and George Croghan and asked that Major Trent be sent out to get them; but Trent knew the wiles of the enemy too well to be caught in that trap. When he failed to appear, the Indians resumed their firing and continued it during the entire night.

At about this time, firewood began to get scarce at the fort, and on August 1, Ecuyer issued an order that the women were to be allowed only enough wood to wash their clothes and were to forego ironing them until further instructions were given. The shooting on that day continued without abatement until afternoon, when the Indians withdrew. Soon they were seen in large numbers crossing back over the Allegheny with their baggage, but without any plunder from Fort Pitt. In that moment the Indian women and children, who had accompanied the warriors to carry home the loot, must have been a bit disappointed in the performance of their fighters. The invested garrison was given a rest from Indian molestation until the following day, when two Indians and a white man called from across the river and stated that they were expresses who had been captured by the Indians as they were carrying letters from Bouquet and Croghan to the fort. One of them said that the Wyandots in a council had declared that they would carry on the war against the English as long as one of them remained alive. The Delawares and the Shawnee had been told that they might do as they pleased.

When the siege of five days and four nights came to an end, Ecuyer sent a report to Bouquet. The attack, he said, had ceased just in time. Although no one had been killed, and only seven men had been wounded, an extended investment might have precipitated a starving condition among the people in the fort. There was no flour in the commissary, and only four legs of beef remained when the Indians raised the siege. The supply of that essential commodity in all military garrisons of that day —rum—was completely exhausted.

But relief was almost at hand. During the last two weeks in July, Bouquet was slowly but surely pushing westward with his force of 560 soldiers, many of them convalescents recently discharged from the hospital. At Fort Bedford he detached thirty men to strengthen that post, and he assigned a like number to Fort Ligonier when he arrived there on August 2. Because of lack of information regarding the enemy, he decided to leave his wagons at the latter fort and to use, instead, four hundred pack horses, on which he loaded flour. On August 4 the little army departed from Ligonier for Fort Pitt. Everything progressed smoothly until the afternoon of the following day, when the force was approaching Bushy Run (Jeannette, Pennsylvania). Then, as if by a hurricane, Bouquet was attacked by over four hundred Indians—the same ones who had failed in their attempt to take Fort Pitt a few days before. It was in that decisive engagement, fought in the most ferocious manner in the open woods, that the leadership of Bouquet and the fighting ability of his brave Scotch Highlanders proved more than a match for the Seneca, Shawnee, Wyandot, and much-vaunted Delaware warriors. The attack continued until nightfall and was resumed again at daybreak. Shortly after the noon hour on August 6, the tide was turned against the Indians when Bouquet out-maneuvered them. After suffering heavy losses, they broke and ran for their lives. The English followed them for two miles, then gave up the chase and sought a cool spring to refresh themselves. After resting awhile, they moved on toward Fort Pitt in a more leisurely fashion. Their losses—fifty men killed and sixty wounded—were heavy, but the fruits of the victory were sweet in view of the fact that of the major forts in the entire Ohio Valley and lakes region only Fort Pitt and Fort Detroit had been able to survive the savage attacks of the Indians.

In the meanwhile, life at Fort Pitt had been comparatively quiet and peaceful after the Indians had left that post to engage Bouquet's approaching troops. Three expresses from Fort Ligonier on August 5 had brought news of shooting, chopping, and bell-ringing near Bushy Run, but the messenger had not realized that a battle had actually been under way. Trouble was suspected, however, and two expresses were immediately sent from Fort Pitt to meet Bouquet's troops. Fear for the safety of his force was felt as four days passed without a word of news. Not until daybreak of August 10 did any intelligence of the Bushy Run battle reach the fort. Then an express arrived and stated that Bouquet was approaching. An honor guard was sent out to escort the victorious colonel and his brave men to the fort, where they arrived in the afternoon.

On the following day Bouquet ordered his thanks to be given to all the officers, soldiers, and inhabitants for the splendid way in which they had defended the fort against the numerous Indian attacks. Regarding Trent, the order said,

> The Colonel takes a particular Pleasure in expressing to Major Trent, how agreeable his Services and those performed by the brave Militia under his Command are to Him; and returns Him his sincere Thanks for the ready assistance He has constantly given to the Commanding Officer; desiring He will inform his Officers & Men of the greatfull Sense the Col: has of their Behaviour.

Bouquet proceeded to divide his little army into two detachments; one was sent down the Ohio to cut off the Shawnee retreat, and the other was sent back to Ligonier to escort the wagons to Fort Pitt. He himself remained at the fort, awaiting a strong reinforcement with which he expected to carry the war to a successful conclusion among the Indians in their own villages.

With the worst of the Indian danger past, the various routine duties about Fort Pitt were attended to as usual. Trent submitted a bill for over £85 to Captain Ecuyer for goods purchased of the Trent and Levy partnership during the siege. Not an Indian was seen for a week after Bouquet's arrival, and the people in the fort made the most of their opportunities. The remainder of the grain was harvested and hauled into the fort; wood was cut and transported inside the walls; a supply of coal and lime was brought from the south side of the Monongahela; and some ground was plowed in preparation for the planting of turnips. Trent was ordered to assist one of the royal officers in taking an inventory of the food supplies available on August 16. Less than a week later Major Donald Campbell arrived with a provision train from Ligonier. On August 25 news was received from Detroit that the French were keeping the Indians stirred up to attack the English there.

For those at the fort, the day of August 27 must have been both happy and sad, depending on individual associations; for it was on that day that Major Campbell and his detachment left Fort Pitt to act as an escort for the women and children, together with the wagons and pack horses, on their journey back east to the settlements. Two days later an express was sent to Presque Isle to ascertain whether the English were rebuilding that post, but he returned in a few days with an adverse report. He said that he had encountered four Wyandot Indians near Venango, who had told him that there were no white men at Presque Isle, but that 150 Ottawa were waiting there to ambush an English detachment expected from Niagara.

On September 5 it was reported by a Shawnee Indian that all the Delawares had left their towns, and that some of them were on the warpath. Additional rumors of Indian opposition about Fort Detroit drifted in by the Indian grapevine. The Indians soon began to appear more frequently about the fort. One night a band of at least thirty encamped on Chartier's Creek not far from the forks. Three days later, on September 15, several of them opened hostilities by firing on the soldiers detailed to herd the bullocks. Although the soldiers returned the fire, no one was hurt on either side. The following morning the sentinels discovered ten more redskins sneaking about the fort, and Bouquet ordered an attack made if they appeared again.

Major Trent was not idle during those weeks and served in various capacities; but the sparseness of his journal entries indicates that private rather than public business occupied a large part of his time. An exception occurred on October 5 when he was detailed to command the company assigned to picket duty. A week later he rendered Bouquet a bill for over £22 for goods that the colonel had purchased of Trent and

Levy since his arrival in August. Trent's last official duty at Fort Pitt of which there is any record was that of commanding sixty men who were sent across the Monongahela on October 17 to guard a party that had been detailed to dig and bring back a supply of coal. Some Indians were seen, but they fled on the approach of the soldiers. The last entry in Trent's interesting journal was made on October 19, when he noted that a Highlander, appointed to sentinel duty with the bullock guard along the Monongahela, had been shot and scalped.

Presumably Trent left the public service at this time and took up the onerous task of trying to straighten out his private affairs as a merchant. The struggle between the Indians and the white men had practically ruined him financially, as it had the other traders engaged in business on the frontier.

CHAPTER X

Trader's Losses and Land Speculation

From the time of the destruction of the trading post at Pickawillanee in 1752 to the end of Pontiac's Conspiracy in 1763, Trent had sustained heavy losses as an Indian trader. Most of his enterprises had been conducted on a partnership basis, so that he had not been the only sufferer, but as he had been one of the largest operators in the field, his penalty had been unusually severe. Washington had contributed to the financial distress of Trent and Croghan when he had impressed their horses in 1754 to carry his cannon and supplies from Gist's plantation to Fort Necessity, for the traders had been unable to recover the horses in time to get their goods away from the frontier before the storm broke. Later attempts to get restitution from Virginia, as well as from General Braddock, for their losses (which amounted to about £370) had been unsuccessful. Even the original statement of their account had been lost in Braddock's cart with his baggage on the occasion of his defeat in July, 1755.

This discouraging treatment had led Trent and a number of other Indian traders in 1756 to draw up affidavits of the losses that they had incurred in 1754, in the hope that the Crown might reimburse them from funds secured from the sale of French prizes that had been seized on the high seas. The sheaf of sworn statements had been signed by Governor Morris of Pennsylvania as a final proof of their validity. In the lists of accounts those of the partnership of Trent and Croghan and of that of Trent, Croghan, Callender and Teaffe were the largest; the combined accounts totaled over £8,700.

Because of the development of French and Indian hostilities into a real war between 1756 and 1763, the promotion of these efforts had been delayed; but the plan had not been forgotten. As a matter of fact, the need for restitution had become greater. As soon as there had been a lull in the Indian attacks, after the fall of Canada, the lure of large profits had led the merchants on the seaboard to grant additional credit to the already burdened Indian traders in the West, and the assumed risk had led to tremendous additional losses on the part of the gambling traders when Pontiac had unleashed his fury on the frontier.

The partial suppression of the Indian menace by Colonel Bouquet in 1763 gave Trent and his fellow-sufferers hope that some constructive measures might be taken to salvage their losses, and they were not long in concocting a scheme to further that end. George Croghan had decided to go to London on business, and the traders felt that here was an opportunity to have their case presented to the King. Their creditors, the eastern merchant groups, agreed to the plan, since they realized that before their own accounts could be collected, the traders would have to receive reimbursement for their losses from some source. Accordingly, in December, 1763, a representative group of traders and merchants, consisting of Trent, Croghan, Robert Callender, Samuel Wharton, David Franks, and several others, met in the Indian Queen Tavern in Philadelphia and laid their plans. It was decided to delegate the task of presenting a memorial to the Crown to George Croghan and Moses Franks, who was a brother of David Franks and a merchant in London. To Trent and Wharton was assigned the job of drawing up the memorial, which they proceeded to do. But the despoiled traders and merchants feared that these tactics might not be sufficient, and they made additional plans to seek the assistance of every influential character whose help could be secured.

Not satisfied to await the outcome of this endeavor, Trent immediately busied himself with his land speculations in Pennsylvania. On December 22 he formed a partnership for speculative purposes with John Baynton and Samuel Wharton, members of the important Quaker merchant firm of Baynton & Wharton in Philadelphia. There were over 1,700 acres of Cumberland County land involved in the proposed transaction, and a written agreement was drawn up assigning to Trent one-fourth of any profits realized. Less than a month later, in January, 1764, Trent was engaged in a much larger real estate venture with Joseph Spear and William Peters, which concerned over 3,800 acres of land in that section of Cumberland County that is now Bedford County. The wily trader was also keeping a business eye open for trade at the frontier store on the forks of the Ohio. Attempting to capitalize on his acquaintanceship with Colonel Bouquet, he asked the latter to buy any supplies needed for his army from the Trent and Levy establishment at Pittsburgh. He pointed out that the stock was large, and that the firm would be glad to make any necessary additions to it that Bouquet might wish.

During the remainder of the year 1764, Trent concerned himself with the task of collecting a list of the names and the losses of the traders operating in 1763. In that effort he was assisted by Callender and Wharton. This tabulation was necessary in order to ensure a proper division of any money secured from the Crown. The year drew toward a close, however, with more than a possibility that the efforts of Croghan and Franks in London would fail. In the meanwhile, Trent's personal responsibilities had increased rather than decreased. A fourth child, Mary, had been born in December, 1762, while Trent was absent on the frontier, and now, on November 29, another daughter, Sarah, was born at Carlisle, where the family was now living.

Croghan's return from England after he had failed to get any restitution for the traders' losses led to the adoption of a new plan of attack. On January 5, 1765, the Trent and Levy Company, joined by Callender, Alexander Lowrey, Thomas Michell, Thomas Smallman and Company, and some other traders, sent a memorial to General Thomas Gage, now commander-in-chief of the British army in America. They asked him to recommend to Sir William Johnson, who was to hold a conference with the Indians in the spring, that the Indians responsible for the depredations against the traders in 1754, and again in 1763, be made to pay reparations. Another memorial was sent to Sir William himself with the same request. Johnson expressed himself in favor of the idea of making the Indians responsible for the trader losses of 1763, but he refused to ask them to pay for the losses suffered in 1754. It was his contention that although Indian responsibility could be claimed for the troubles of 1763, it could not be claimed for those of the earlier period. His opinion had a tendency to split the two groups of traders. Despite the fact that Trent belonged to both groups, he had much more to gain by promoting the cause of the 1763 sufferers, and to that business he devoted more of his time in the future.

While the restitution plan was smoldering, Trent continued his sporadic activities in the field of private land speculation. A venture in which he agreed to participate during March, 1765, illustrates his tendency to be ever on the alert for an opportunity to make some money. At that time he entered into an agreement with two young men, Thomas Ferguson and William George, by which the locations of any lands that they found not surveyed or warranted in Pennsylvania would be turned over to him, and he would have the tracts surveyed, warranted, and sold, if it were within his power to do so. In consideration for his services, he was to receive one-half of the profits from the transactions. But the public land office was closed, and in order to carry out this plan he had to do some conniving with a friendly politician. He wrote to Joseph Shippen, the secretary of the province, and proposed that Shippen obtain an order from the governor for the surveying of the unwarranted lands, or arrange to have them entered in the land office so that warrants might be issued as soon as the office opened. It was

Trent's opinion that about 3,400 acres of good land would be included. The secretary was to advance the money for purchasing the shares of the young men and for paying half of Trent's expenses in getting the land surveyed, although nothing was to be paid until the surveys had actually been made. In return, Trent was to throw his half-interest into the pool, and he and Shippen were to split the profits two ways after the expenses and interest money advanced by Shippen had been deducted. The whole plan was to be kept secret. Trent painted a rosy picture regarding the possible profits and informed Shippen that if he liked this proposal, he had another to make for the next summer whereby they could realize "several Thousand Pounds." Apparently Shippen did not avail himself of the suggestion, but the offer serves to illustrate Trent's frantic attempts to recoup his lost fortune by any sort of shoe-string operation. In a little over a month he was so low financially that he found it necessary to borrow several hundred pounds from Joseph Spear of Carlisle.

Sir William Johnson held the scheduled Indian conference with the Six Nations and the Delawares at Johnson Hall from April 29 to May 22, 1765, to consider a number of matters, including the request of the 1763 traders for a tract of land in payment for the losses that they had suffered at the hands of the Indians. As the result of the fair way in which Sir William presented the matter, the Indians accepted his contention and promised to make restitution to the traders at a future meeting by awarding them a tract of land near Fort Pitt. That promise cleared the air somewhat and gave the traders new hope. Trent, however, seems to have spent several months that summer and fall in various other business dealings before he earnestly began the task of handling the general trader troubles. The store in which he had an interest was evidently still being maintained at Pittsburgh, for a consignment of furs and skins, purchased with his goods, was forwarded to him from the forks of the Ohio in July. His correspondence for the year indicates that his old business partner, David Franks, was included in some of his real estate deals, but his various partnership operations did not prevent him from making entries for hundreds of acres of land in his own name.

By the Christmas season, Trent was ready to begin the business of collecting affidavits of losses sustained by the 1763 traders, as well as the powers of attorney to act for those who submitted their claims. He offered to buy the claims of all traders who would sell them at about one-third to one-half of their face value, although he protected himself by specifying that he would be bound to pay only if a grant of land was actually made by the Indians. Trent was charged at this time with limiting his interest to those who were willing to be fleeced by his scheme, and with refusing to have anything to do with the claims of those who would not deal with him. Despite these accusations, which seem to have contained some truth, the artful trader was able to collect a number of claims and powers of attorney between December, 1765, and August, 1766. Among the accounts collected, his personal account of £4,500 represented one of the larger individual losses, while the losses of the Franks, Trent, Simon and Company partnership, which totaled almost £25,000, were more than three times the total of the next largest account listed. Thus it may be seen that Trent had a very real reason for assuming the leadership in the attempt to secure restitution. The same list also shows that the Quaker firm of Baynton & Wharton had become responsible for the collection of several traders' accounts, which were second in amount only to those of the Jewish firm. This in turn explains the later close relationship that existed between Trent and Samuel Wharton.

The suffering traders were not Trent's only interest, however, during the period from 1765 to the spring of 1768. Numerous sources indicate that he continued his real estate speculation in thousands of acres of land, both as a private operator and in partnership with others. The land concerned was apparently all in what was then Cumberland County, and ranged in location from the valley east of the Allegheny Mountains, in what is now Bedford County, to the town of Carlisle, where Trent invested in some lots. Not every title was sound, and Trent, as well as other operators, encountered quarrels and litigation on occasion. When the trouble involved others, Trent was sometimes called in as appraiser or examiner to help validate the holdings in dispute. Lack of good communication facilities do not seem to have hindered the extensive activities of this ambitious man of business.

Trent's plans of operation as a real estate projector, written in his own hand, exist today and serve as an interesting and valuable illustration of the methods evolved by the frontier realtors of the eighteenth century. For example, at about this time the trader drew up a plan for a land company that was to take over some 15,000 acres of land that he held in Cumberland County. He wrote that the land was all good soil and well watered, and was located for the most part on Middle, Jack's, Wills, and Canoe creeks. He asked £22 for each 100 acres "free of every Expense to the Day of executing the Deeds. The Lands from that Time are subject to the Proprietors Quit Rents." In glowing terms he described the opportunity offered, pointing out that frequent experiment had proved that there was no way whereby an individual at small expense could so easily and so certainly build an estate for posterity as by the purchase of lands in America. He stated that he proposed to form a company with a capitalization of £4,050, divided into 30 shares based upon the £22-per-hundred-acre valuation of his land, plus £750 as additional advancement for improvements. Each share would, therefore, contain 500 acres of land and sell for £135. Any person could hold as many shares as he liked. Trent said that he would be a member of the company and also the manager, if the members so desired, on condition that he be allowed some of the shares; in that event, the company was to advance the money for whatever shares they allowed him (the money to be repaid without interest at the time the partnership was dissolved), and his expenses were to be paid by the company when he was engaged on company business. His plan even included detailed suggestions as to the best methods of new land development. It was proper, he said, to build a small log house, clear and fence a field of ten or twelve acres, and then lease the tract for a number of years to a farmer, who would not only give the owner a share of what he raised, but would also clear a number of additional acres during each year of his tenancy. Trent pointed out that by these means it would be possible to create a good improved plantation with land worth three or four times what had originally been paid for it. No record has been found to indicate that any such land company was ever formed. Presumably it was not, since more important affairs were urgently demanding Trent's attention.

In the summer of 1768, Trent learned that Sir William Johnson had received instructions to settle the boundary question with the Indians, and he therefore started for Albany, in company with Samuel Wharton. Upon their arrival in the Mohawk country, the men learned that Sir William had gone to the seashore at New London, Connecticut. Not to be turned away from their purpose, they, too, started for the seashore, but not for their health! The hospitality of the popular Sir William was proverbial, and the two friends of the baronet spent several weeks at New London as his guests, promoting the interests of the 1763 traders' claim all the while. On September 1 they set out with Sir William for Fort Stanwix (Rome, New York), where an Indian conference was to be held on September 20. Although Trent and Wharton presented their claims and powers of attorney on September 21, the Indians were slow in gathering, and almost two full months elapsed before the Indian deputies were ready to do business. Johnson had taken great care to send invitations to all the Indians concerned, including some Canadian tribes, as well as the tribes dwelling hundreds of miles down the Ohio. The long interval consumed in convening gave Trent and his friend an excellent opportunity to do some missionary work for the traders among the Six Nations. Trent's long absence from Philadelphia, however, tended to cause some of his creditors to become skeptical, and he was forced to do a bit of corresponding to allay their suspicions.

Finally, on Monday, October 24, the famous Fort Stanwix treaty making started. Johnson took great care to explain the English claims to the assembled red men, and then left them to hold their council in private. But the Indians needed advice on numerous points, and during the nine days of conferring they frequently found it necessary to call in Sir William and George Croghan to clarify or advise on some doubtful matter. While the Indians were thus engaged, Trent; Governor William Franklin of New Jersey (son of Benjamin Franklin); Joseph Galloway, an attorney of Philadelphia; and Amos Ogden of Hunterdon County, New Jersey, availed themselves of the opportunity to enter into a partnership to develop three separate tracts of land along the Susquehanna River, on which they believed there were deposits of silver ore. Apparently this was another of Trent's fancy schemes that never materialized. Thereafter the Englishmen had but a few days to wait before the Indians announced on November 1 that they were ready to assemble in a general meeting to give their reply to Sir William's requests.

It has been said that the Fort Stanwix Indian Conference was the largest ever held in North America. In addition to some thirty-four hundred Indians, there were in attendance at one time or another during the negotiations, commissioners from Pennsylvania, New York, New Jersey, Virginia, and Connecticut. The most important political characters present, aside from those connected directly with Indian affairs, were Governor John Penn of Pennsylvania and Governor William Franklin of New Jersey. The former had come to help arrange for the purchase of a tract of land from the Indians, and the latter, because he had developed a lively interest in New York lands, as well as in the affairs of Trent and the other 1763 traders.

Partially surrounded by twenty boatloads of presents and thousands of dollars piled on a table on the parade ground of the fort, the participants in the great Indian conference met together during the first week of November, 1768. Although the major business of the council was the settling of a permanent boundary line between the Indians and the English colonies, the Six Nations decided to deal first with the matter of the land grant to the traders. Accordingly, on November 3 there was awarded "To and for the Only use Benefit and Behoof of the Said William Trent in his Own Right and as Attorney" for the traders of 1763, a tract of land that included much of the area of

present-day West Virginia, as restitution for the losses of £85,916
10*s*. 8*d*. worth of goods and property destroyed by Indians tributary to
the Six Nations. The boundaries of the immense grant were as follows:
starting at the south side of the Little Kanawha River where it empties
into the Ohio, the line ran southeast to the Laurel Hill, then along that
mountain until it struck the Monongahela River, and from there down
the Monongahela and the several branches thereof to the southern boundary of Pennsylvania. There it turned west and followed that boundary as far as it extended, then continued west by the same course to
the Ohio River and followed down that stream to the place of beginning.
The twenty-two traders and merchants for whom Trent acted as attorney at Fort Stanwix, in addition to himself, were: Robert Callender,
David Franks, Joseph Simon, Levy Andrew Levy, Philip Boyle, John
Baynton, Samuel Wharton (both in his own right and as administrator
for John Welch, deceased), George Morgan, Joseph Spear, Thomas
Smallman, Edmund Moran, Evan Shelby, Samuel Postlethwait, John
Gibson, Richard Winston, Dennis Crohon, William Thompson, Abra-
ham Mitchell, James Dundas, Thomas Dundas, and John Ormsby.

The troubles of the 1763 sufferers did not end, however, with the
successful negotiating of the land grant at Fort Stanwix. In fact their
greatest difficulties were still ahead. The ink on the 1768 deed had
scarcely dried when the 1754 group of traders and merchants began
efforts to block the confirmation of the grant, or, failing that, to secure
a part of the tract of land for themselves. Trent declared that the 1768
tract was very valuable, and that as early as December 1, he and his
partners had received applications from "several Thousand People in
New England to Settle, at prices which will certainly make us all happy
and forever independent." The risk of losing what already seemed to
be within grasp led him and his business associates to take drastic
steps. Trent wrote to a friend: "Mr. Wharton and Myself at the earnest
Desire of all our Friends have Determined to Embark for London with
all possible Dispatch in order to have the final Stroke given to the
Grant." He hoped thus to remove the threat of trouble, and he stated
that he and Wharton expected to carry recommendations to London
that would be as good as any their opponents might have, although the
chief reliance for winning a confirmation by the Crown would be placed
"on the Justice and Reasonableness of our Cause."

Not all the 1754 traders had lost faith in Trent, and at least one
allowed him to retain his power of attorney in preference to giving the
same authority to creditors who wished to drive an even harder bargain
than Trent. But some of the merchant creditors of Trent and Croghan,
especially David Franks and Jeremiah Warder, whose accounts also

dated back to 1754, were not so trusting, and they issued some statements designed to impugn the motives of Trent and Croghan in regard to the payment of their old debts. In a pointed letter, penned apparently by Trent, Croghan reminded Franks and Warder that under the law, not a penny was owed to them, because of an artfully worded release that the creditors had signed for the traders following a partial payment of the Trent-Croghan account; he added, however, that he and Trent, if they received any compensation for their losses, would gladly pay the portion of their obligations that remained unpaid. Another difficulty of a similar nature immediately presented itself. Either by intent or by accident, the name of Alexander Lowrey, one of the 1763 traders who had lost heavily at the hands of the Indians, had been left out of the 1768 grant. Lowrey demanded that he be included, and to silence him, Trent, Croghan, and Wharton drew up an agreement promising to pay him over £4,000 within four years after the ratification or confirmation by the Crown of any land grant to the three signatories of the bond. Trent was obliged to deal with some other, but less formidable, creditors, before he could begin the task of preparing for the proposed ocean voyage to England.

By the end of December, 1768, the various obstacles had been so far removed as to enable Trent and Wharton to meet with their financial backers for the London expedition. Articles of agreement were drawn up whereby William Franklin, George Croghan, John Baynton, George Morgan, and Robert Callender pledged themselves to provide the two men with expense money for the trip to Great Britain. In return for this promise, Trent and Wharton agreed to give the five financial backers a share in the 1768 land grant when its title had been cleared. According to the arrangement, £500 in notes or specie were to be paid to Trent and Wharton in addition to a letter of credit for a similar amount on some responsible house in London. All passage charges from Philadelphia to New York and London, as well as for the return trip, for Trent, Wharton, and their servant were likewise to be paid by the backers, as were all fees charged for securing the confirmation of the land title and for clerical hire. It was stipulated that the £1,000 advanced was to cover the expenses of the two men and their servant for one year in England. In the event that the work could not be completed in a year, the financial support was to be continued at the rate of £83 for every additional month. Little did those optimistic underwriters realize what a large assignment they were giving themselves! The financial responsibility was to be divided: Croghan agreed to supply three-tenths of the funds, and Robert Callender, one-tenth; the other six-tenths were to be evenly divided among the other three gentlemen. On their part,

Trent and Wharton promised to make all haste possible to get the grant confirmed at the earliest moment. They further agreed to refund £500 to their sponsors if the job was completed within six months; otherwise there would be no refund. They also consented to assume two-tenths of the expense of the confirmation fees, and, finally, they engaged to repay any part of the £1,000 not used for living expenses.

The promise of Trent and Wharton to do something for the 1754 group of traders, as well as for the 1763 group, led to a change in the attitude of the agitators against them. In January, 1769, several individuals who had previously been most ardent in petitioning the Crown for a separate grant and had subsequently tried to block the moves of the 1763 traders, reversed their positions and stated that they felt "satisfyed there has been no unfairness in the proceedings of the sufferers of 1763 and that therefore, it would be more proper and Just to make an application to the Crown for a Tract of Land distinct from theirs, than to attempt to interfere with their Grant." In order to win this concession, Trent, who was still the legal attorney for the 1754 group, had found it necessary to deed a part of the proceeds from the sale of any lands that might be granted to the 1754 traders, to their merchant creditors. It was a shrewd move on Trent's part to arrest for a time at least the pressure on his nerves of continuous badgering by the creditors. As a result of the foregoing arrangement, Moses Franks, in London, was empowered to act as *"Sole Agent"* for the 1754 traders in presenting an application to the Crown for a separate grant of land. Franks was instructed to consult with, and seek advice from, Trent and Wharton when they arrived in London.

After his stroke of diplomacy had been consummated, Trent set about the task of renewing and adding to his powers of attorney from the 1754 traders. This was a difficult job in those days of poor communication, and he had the additional problem of securing trustworthy messengers to assist him. But the doughty trader and politician was not to be stopped, and he ended by securing no less than twenty powers of attorney from the despoiled traders of 1754 alone.

Other problems now presented themselves. The prospective voyager had to make arrangements for his family, which had been increased, in November, 1768, by the birth of a sixth and last child, John. In addition, he was compelled to raise money to appease certain troublesome creditors whose judgments could not be sidestepped before his departure.

Various methods were used to raise the necessary funds. First of all, Trent appealed to his old friend and partner, George Croghan, who did not fail him in the hour of need. Croghan agreed to lend him £1,000, for which Trent and his wife gave Croghan a mortgage on a town lot in Carlisle (on which was a stone house, a log stable, and another building), on an improved plantation of 244 acres not far from the town, and on over 9,000 acres of unimproved lands scattered over Cumberland County. To free himself from the toils of his debt of over £4,000 to his partners in the firm of William Trent, David Franks, Levy Andrew Levy, and Joseph Simon, Trent assigned to Franks and Simon, as security for the debt, his share in the 1768 grant to the 1763 traders, or whatever part of his share might be needed to pay off the obligation to his partners. The debt was made payable in one year. In addition, he gave Franks and Simon a mortgage on the same lot in Carlisle on which Croghan held a mortgage, as well as on 7,500 acres of Cumberland County land.

From Joseph Morris, Trent arranged a loan, secured by over 2,200 acres of Cumberland County real estate, of over £200, £150 of which were to be paid to his wife, Sarah, in monthly instalments of £10 each, and the remainder of which was to be paid to Trent. Another loan of £400 was made by Morris to Trent in the spring of 1769; this was secured by a mortgage on a tract of 10,000 acres of land in Albany County, New York. The land was part of a 30,000 acre tract granted to Croghan by the Indians at Fort Stanwix in 1768, which had been transferred by Croghan to Samuel Wharton, who in turn had deeded it to Trent.

Toward the end of March, 1769, Trent was still trying to clear up his financial difficulties, and Croghan was doing what he could to help him raise enough money to take care of a judgment for £400 levied against him. Regardless of the trouble Trent was having in arranging his affairs, and his misgivings about making a journey that would necessitate leaving his property and business, and moving his wife and family to Trenton, Croghan still thought it "absolutely Nesesary to Inshure Success" for Trent to go to London.

Further to fortify his finances and provide for the future, Trent, along with Charles Reade, Thomas Wharton, Sr., and some others, petitioned the authorities in New York for a large tract of land, later known as the Otsego Patent, along Adigo Creek, a tributary of the Susquehanna River. The patent to these lands was not granted for almost a year after the application was presented, but before Trent left America he had the property mortgaged to still other creditors located in Burlington, New Jersey, and in Philadelphia, who had formed, with Trent, a land speculating organization known as the Burlington Company.

Sometime in April, 1769, Trent finally got his affairs temporarily in order, his family moved to Trenton, and his journey to London started. Samuel Wharton had apparently sailed earlier. Both men left the shores of America with high hopes of success for a reasonably early confirmation of the title of the 1768 Indian grant. Little did either one realize how long it would be before he would again be permitted to look upon his beloved homeland.

CHAPTER XI

LAND COMPANY PROMOTION IN LONDON

Since Moses Franks had been designated as the individual responsible for promoting the cause of the 1754 traders in London, and since Samuel Wharton had been the first to make the voyage to England, Trent had transferred all the powers of attorney that he had collected from the 1754 traders, along with his own, to Wharton. In this way it was hoped that the interests of the 1754 group might be taken care of promptly. Information had already been received in America that the King had approved all the various transactions at the Fort Stanwix Conference, and it was therefore believed that Trent would encounter little difficulty in getting a confirmation of the title to the 1768 grant. As for Wharton, his financial affairs before his departure from America had apparently been in almost as precarious a condition as Trent's, for he had not been in Europe six months before his creditors started agitation for payment of his debts.

When Trent and Wharton joined forces in London, the outlook did not appear bright. Trent, after conversing with Benjamin Franklin, Moses Frank, and Henry Dagge, who had been hired as the solicitor of the traders, was aware of unexpected opposition and was very downcast. He wrote to Croghan that he was "thoroughly convinced" that all the time, labor, and money spent on the land project was "wholy lost," and that he and Wharton would be plunged into "inevitable Ruin." What was even worse, in his opinion, was the fact that he and the other promoters of the land-grant idea had involved their wives, children, and friends and reduced all to penury and want. In his distress he appealed to Croghan to exert his influence to the utmost in an effort to get the land title perfected. To spur on the jovial Irishman, he reminded him that his (Croghan's) private grant—made at the Fort Stanwix Treaty also—was on the same footing as the traders' grant. If one was not confirmed, the other would not be upheld either. Then, almost in a hysterical vein, he pleaded, "I beseech you by all the Ties of Friendship, Our Wives & our Children have all their Eyes fixed on you Our and their future happyness depending entirely Upon your bringing this affair to a happy Conclusion." Trent thought that he would be "forever a Beggar" if Croghan and Sir William Johnson did not help him and Wharton to cope with the opposition, which Trent was sure was coming only from Lord Hillsborough, president of the Board of Trade. Up to this time, Croghan, believing that Trent and Wharton formed such a congenial team that everything would move along smoothly under their guidance, had been complacent, but the arrival of his old partner's letter caused him to lose his calm assurance that all was well across the ocean.

The optimistic opinions of Dr. Franklin, Lord Camden, and other dignitaries of the law in England, that a royal confirmation of the 1768 grant was unnecessary, together with the almost certain opposition of Lord Hillsborough, led Trent and Wharton to defer the pressing of their case. Moreover, Hillsborough's opposition was not the only factor that threatened the interests of the traders' group of 1763, which was now officially designated as the Indiana Company. Other land companies, such as the Ohio Company and the Mississippi Company, composed for the most part of Englishmen and of prominent Virginians —among them the Lees and the Washingtons—tried either to block the efforts of the Indiana Company or to secure grants for themselves. Faced with possible failure, Trent and Wharton sought a new approach to their problem.

It was believed by Benjamin Franklin, as well as by several prominent Englishmen, that the purpose of the Indiana Company could be achieved by other than direct means, and Trent and Wharton were easily converted to this point of view. It was suggested that a new company be formed, and that the Crown be petitioned to allow the purchase of about 2,500,000 acres of land in America. The land in question was to include most of the area purchased by the Crown from the Six Nations Indians at the Treaty of Fort Stanwix in 1768, as well as the region granted by the Indians at the same time to the traders of 1763. This plan was finally adopted. The company that was formed was sometimes known as the Walpole Company, because of the leadership of Thomas Walpole, but usually carried the more dignified title of the Grand Ohio Company. On July 24, 1769, Walpole, Franklin, and several others of the new group petitioned the King to grant them 2,400,000 acres of land lying back of the colony of Virginia.

The summer and autumn passed before the usual difficulties incident to the handling of such petitions were partially removed. During that time Trent's friends in America were doing what they could to ease his financial burdens and were keeping him informed regarding the condition of his immediate family. Croghan's communications were anything but encouraging. He said that in order to raise funds to cover Trent's and Wharton's expenses in London and to save his own estate in America, as well as Trent's, which was mortgaged in large part to the Burlington Company, it would be necessary for Trent and Wharton to try to sell a portion of Croghan's property to someone in England, or at least to mortgage it. As an inducement to a prospective buyer, he suggested that he would be willing to take payment half in goods and half in cash. Trent was told that if something of the sort could not be arranged by him in London, both he and Croghan faced ruin.

At a meeting of the Grand Ohio Company held on December 27, 1769, in the Crown and Anchor Tavern in London, the assembled members were told that some changes in the purchase plan had been "thought of by Mr. Wharton" as the result of a hint dropped by Lord Hillsborough to the company committee when the committee had appeared before the Board of Trade on December 19. Wharton briefly explained the idea to the assemblage and intimated that it might be to their advantage to enlarge the company petition to include a tract of land extensive enough to be created into a new colony. An incentive to the adoption of this procedure was the fact that the hint had originally come from one of the chief sources of opposition. Accordingly, it was decided that the company be reorganized along these lines.

The affairs of the Indiana Company had by January, 1770, taken such a turn that one of the original underwriters of the London scheme became worried. And good reason he had for being troubled, too, although he was not to learn the worst for some time. John Baynton, of the Quaker mercantile establishment in Philadelphia, and his son-in-law, George Morgan, had apparently fallen behind in their payments on the expense account of Trent and Wharton. Wharton had sent Baynton a request for funds, but the old gentleman had replied that he was facing bankruptcy himself and could not contribute his share. His failure to meet Wharton's demands was to prove unfortunate for him. Trent and Wharton, who were by this time playing fast and loose with their powers of attorney, used the inability to pay, on the part of their financial backers, as an excuse for practically deserting their cause. Among the names of those Americans who were included in the reorganized Grand Ohio Company, or Vandalia Company, as it came to be known, those of John Baynton and George Morgan were conspicuous by their absence. The American group was represented by Willaim Trent, five members of the Wharton family (including Samuel), the two Franklins (Benjamin and his son, William), Sir William Johnson, George Croghan, and Joseph Galloway. The roster of Englishmen in this organization of more than fifty-odd partners, included such outstanding characters as Lord Hertford, Lord Camden, Richard Walpole, Robert Walpole, John Robinson, Moses Franks, Thomas Pownall, and Lord Gower. Baynton, although he felt that some things were transpiring about which he was in the dark, was unaware of his position. Robert Callender learned a little later that he, too, had been hoodwinked.

Shortly after his arrival in London, Trent,had practically dropped out of the picture as a dominant personage and had assumed, more or less, the role of secretary and adviser to the more polished Wharton. His reasons for doing so are not known, but a plausible explanation can be formulated. Trent was a provincial in the broader sense of the word. He understood both the colonial society of the seaboard and the coarser, cruder civilization of the frontier, but the final machinations of British politics and society must have been outside his accustomed sphere. On the other hand, Samuel Wharton seems to have been of the smooth, suave type of colonial merchant, and his many business transactions gave him contacts with influential London merchants, who were willing to participate in any venture that might mean added profits to them in the future. Whatever the real reasons for Trent's eclipse, the fact remains that Wharton, with Trent in the background and Benjamin Franklin in the foreground, proceeded to work with the leading English politicians to carry out the Vandalia project.

On January 4, 1770, a committee of the Vandalia Company delivered a proposal to the Lords of the Treasury for the purchase of a tract of land lying, roughly, between the crest of the Appalachian Mountains and the Ohio River, south of Pennsylvania's southern border and north of the Kentucky River and North Carolina. Details regarding the proposed bounds and the quit rents to be paid were presented. The Lords reserved their approval of the proposed grant until they could make various investigations. On April 7, however, they approved both the price offered and the schedule of quit rents submitted. That was as far as their jurisdiction extended, and they passed the proposal on to the other departments of the government whose business it was to determine questions of policy.

The Vandalia operations had been under way several weeks before the colonial agent of Virginia, stationed in London, became aware of them. As soon as he learned what was happening, he did what he could to block the grant, as did also Colonel George Mercer, the agent of the Ohio Company in England. George Washington and other members of the latter company saw their opportunities for profitable land speculation on the frontier melting into thin air, and they became bitterly opposed to Vandalia. But Colonel Mercer, evidently without instructions from America, finally agreed to the absorption of the Ohio Company interests into those of the Vandalia Company, in return for two of the seventy-two shares into which Vandalia was divided. This merger brought about the withdrawal of the Ohio Company petition for a separate grant within the proposed bounds of Vandalia. Mercer's decision to consolidate the claims of the two companies may have been facilitated by the judicious dropping of a hint that he might receive the nomination for governor of the new colony. It was not possible, however, to turn aside the opposition of Virginia so easily. A running fight between the Old Dominion and the promoters of Vandalia was carried on for almost a year, and a temporary truce was not arrived at until the latter group agreed to recognize the rights of Virginia, and of her soldiers of the French and Indian War period, to a portion of the Vandalia tract.

While Trent and Wharton were assiduously playing politics with British politicians and statesmen in London, in an effort to bring the affairs of Vandalia to a successful conclusion, their friends in America were expressing varied feelings regarding their methods. John Baynton was still complaining about the lack of information concerning the land transactions in England, and he accused Trent and Wharton of treachery toward himself and George Morgan. Since he had heard rumors that the grant was practically confirmed, his anger was the greater. Croghan, too, found occasion to complain about the difficulties that Trent and Wharton had left him in, so far as their financial affairs were concerned; but his expressions were couched in kindlier language, and he voiced his belief that the two men were putting forth their best efforts in London.

Croghan had found it necessary to transfer Trent's mortgage to the Burlington Company in order to save himself, and this step caused Trent considerable worry, for he had submitted as security his valuable lands in Cumberland County and was apprehensive lest the mortgage be foreclosed during his absence, with a heavy loss to himself. He therefore wrote to Thomas Wharton, Philadelphia merchant and brother of Samuel, and asked him, on behalf of his brother and on Trent's own behalf, to do everything possible to delay the threatened sheriff's sale until Trent returned from London. He indulged in glowing promises to pay off the mortgage to the Burlington group, as well as to pay what he owed Thomas Wharton. He promised to send a consignment of goods to Wharton large enough to cover his obligations to him and still allow a commission for his kindness. He then asked another favor: Wharton was to have a deed drawn from himself to Trent and sent to London to care for the transfer of the title to Trent's New York lands, which the trader had been unable to have patented before he left America. For this assistance Trent promised, upon his return home, to give his friend a good tract of land in Cumberland County. To spur the Quaker to action in the land transaction, Trent informed him that he intended to pay for Wharton's proposed consignment of goods by selling some of his New York lands! Two weeks later he again wrote to the Philadelphia merchant and assured him that the contract for the goods had been made.

The new year brought a little relief to Trent from some of his financial worries in America. Governor William Franklin of New Jersey notified him from Burlington that he had talked with one of his creditors and had explained that it would be unfair to sell the trader's lands during his absence. Franklin said that his plea had elicited the statement that although some members of the Burlington Company would like to have their money, the company had never intended to dispose of Trent's property without giving him sufficient notice and would not proceed against him within the period of grace that he had requested. Franklin complained that he had lived to regret his trip to Fort Stanwix, which had involved him in the land speculation deals.

Some months later, when the fortunes of Vandalia seemed to be rising, Franklin might have had occasion to feel better about the prospects of profit from that venture, had not his informant been tactless in the conveyance of the news. William Strahan, a partner in Vandalia, and the source of the optimistic report, was profuse in his praise of Samuel Wharton's great accomplishments in London. He said that Wharton, through his energy and personality, had succeeded in interesting a number of the greatest men in England in the land-promotion business; "without the *least Assistance,* that I know of, from *any other Quarter,*" he wrote, "he [has] found means to connect himself with many of the great names in this Country." That Wharton possessed ability and a winning personality there is little doubt; but there is cause for skepticism regarding Strahan's statement about his lack of assistance. Concerning the Quaker merchant and politician, Strahan wrote further: "His own and Major Trent's great Knowledge of the Subjects in Question . . . not only completely removed such Objections as hath been thrown out . . . but every obstruction to the Policy of such a grant that could weigh with Government." Then, with something akin to rudeness, he continued, "In truth, he [*Wharton*] hath acquired better *Connections* here, than *any other American* . . . ever did. Your Father [*Benjamin Franklin*] could not stir in Ohio Business as he is not only on bad terms with Lord Hillsborough, but with the *Ministry in general.*" Strahan charged that the elder Franklin was getting too old and inactive and had once even suggested, while visiting Strahan, that Wharton's name ought to be struck from the Vandalia Company list, "as it might be of prejudice to the Undertaking." Strahan's epistle concluded with a warning to Franklin to be circumspect about what he said and did, since in England there was a feeling in some quarters that the governor and his father held "the same political Opinions" and the same ideas concerning Anglo-American relations. Governor Franklin prepared a reply to Strahan's reflections on his father, but on second thought did not send it. Instead, he merely told Strahan that he still doubted whether the Vandalia venture would be "eventually advantageous" to him. In writing to Thomas Wharton about a year later, however, he was less reticent.

By the first week in June, 1771, certain false rumors had reached America that the charter for the new colony had been granted and that Samuel Wharton was to be the governor. When Croghan heard this news he made the comment that he hoped that the report was true, but that he had heard nothing from his friends in England for about six months. Trent and Wharton were not similarly negligent in their correspondence when they needed funds, as William Franklin could well testify. He had failed to pay his fifth of their expenses, and in July they sent him an urgent request to make good his promise. Not waiting for a reply, they made a draft for £200 on Wharton's brother in Philadelphia. This action was unauthorized by Franklin, and apparently he felt justified in ignoring Thomas Wharton's requests for repayment.

So far as Trent was concerned, the money shortage must have been exceedingly acute during this period. It is almost inconceivable that a man of Trent's breeding could have been as neglectful of his family as he was during a part of the time he was in London. Yet the cold facts remain. Thomas Wharton came to the rescue near the end of the summer of 1771, when the family was facing dire circumstances in Trenton. Mrs. Trent, in her letter of thanks to Wharton, wrote, "I have Received no money these fourteen Months but what you Sent me." In a postscript she wanted to know "where Mr. Trent Lodgeth that I may know where to direct my Letters."

Those most interested in the land grant on both sides of the Atlantic did what they could to help the cause along. Others, like William Franklin, who had lost his interest, or like Lord Hillsborough, who was bitterly opposed to the idea almost from the beginning, tended to block the progress of the promoters. Croghan and Thomas Cresap exerted all the pressure they could against Hillsborough's stand on the land question and toward the end of the year were somewhat optimistic concerning the outcome of their efforts. Regarding the rumored threat that the Penns would oppose the granting of the title on the grounds that it might infringe on their province, Croghan wrote to Thomas Wharton that the latter could "farther be ashurd" that the western boundary of

Pennsylvania would fall far short of Fort Pitt. Cresap took an even more conservative view regarding the Quaker proprietors' claims. To him it seemed "Monstruous" of the Penns to claim any lands west of the Laurel Hill, and he was certain that their western boundary would never reach the "big Meadows." After conversing with a great many of the settlers living west of the mountains, he was sure that they thought they were within the bounds of the new colony, and was convinced that they were satisfied.

But the petty efforts of a few provincials, sincere though they were, had practically no effect on the land situation, and by the winter and early spring of 1772, the political maneuvering of Trent and Wharton had failed completely. Something drastic had to be done. Lord Hillsborough had effectively blocked the path of progress of the Vandalia Company's petition. In so doing, he was not merely checkmating a few American colonials, but was flying directly in the face of powerful British politicians and statesmen who were members of the Vandalia organization and who hoped for its success. As early as February, 1771, Benjamin Franklin had indicated his personal dislike for the haughty lord and had commented that Hillsborough's colleagues did not like him any better than he did. It was Franklin's opinion at that time that Hillsborough would not be able to continue "much longer" as head of the Board of Trade.

No opportunities were missed by Franklin and the other friends of Vandalia to undermine Hillsborough's position and force him to release the report on the Vandalia petition, which he had been withholding. Finally, in April, 1772, the pressure became so great that the Board of Trade report was delivered to the Privy Council. The report, however, so distorted the real facts in the case that the promoters of Vandalia sought and secured the privilege of defending their cause and refuting the arguments of the Board of Trade before a committee of the Privy Council. Wharton, doubtless assisted by Trent, probably prepared the Vandalia defense. On June 5 the principals were ready, and the committee convened to hear what they had to say. Present were Trent, Wharton, Thomas Walpole, Benjamin Franklin, and Colonel Mercer. Walpole opened the discussion, but apparently the burden of the argument was brilliantly presented by Wharton, who, in the opinion of one observer, was the hero of the occasion. At any rate, the committee was favorably impressed, and the Privy Council issued instructions for the Board of Trade to pave the way for the granting of the petition with the proper reservations and guarantees.

This turn of events made Lord Hillsborough's position untenable, and he decided to resign rather than accept the rebuff. His move was not forced, however, until a successor had been chosen to take his place. When Benjamin Franklin was asked by a high English politician if he could name someone to succeed Hillsborough, he immediately suggested Lord Dartmouth, who had occupied the position satisfactorily some years before. As it turned out, Dartmouth did get the appointment in August. Franklin, although inclined to gloat over Hillsborough's downfall, was fearful that something might yet happen to check the completion of the Vandalia business. He cautioned his son in America to be careful of his words, lest he and his father look "ridiculous" if the whole venture should fail. The accuracy of his intuition, however, was not to become apparent for some years.

At this point it is of interest to note the attitude of General Thomas Gage toward the proposed idea of the new colony in America. As commander of the King's military forces on the North American continent for a number of years, he was in a position to pass judgment, although by 1772 the trend of events in New England may have colored his thinking. Be that as it may, he expressed a bitter opposition to the plan for the colony in the West. In the first place he doubted if silk, rice, indigo, cotton, and wine could be produced there; and even if they could, what, he asked, would the people do for a market? He expressed his belief that it was to the English interest to keep the American settlers near the seacoast as long as possible and "cramp their Trade as far as it can be done prudentially." The growth of American trade and the development of manufacturing in the colonial cities were additional sources of worry to him.

But the land speculators were a hardy set, and, encouraged by the direction of events in London in the summer of 1772, they even went so far as to make plans for a new Indian land purchase north of the Ohio River. Trent and Samuel Wharton were both concerned in the new plans, as were a number of Englishmen, and George Croghan's opinion was sought regarding the handling of the scheme. The Irish trader had never ceased his land-speculation activity, and he was continually attempting to ascertain by survey the location of Pennsylvania's western boundary. The end of the year 1772 found him still of the opinion "that Fort Pitt Lays about twenty Miles to the Westward of ye Western bounds of pensylvania." This conclusion, had it been correct, would have proved of great advantage to the land speculators and traders, as it would have lessened the possibility of undesirable interference by eastern interests.

That there was to be further delay in the completion of the Vandalia project quickly became evident. Soon after Lord Hillsborough had resigned, and the affirming order regarding the land grant had been given, a great many of the most influential British officials left London for their country seats. For months thereafter, no constructive action was taken. But on January 21, 1773, Trent wrote a hurried letter to Moses Franks, who was away from London at that time, telling him that Lord Dartmouth finally "is come to Town, and is doing American Business." Trent wanted to see Franks before the Board of Trade assembled, to "consult on the properest Method" to pursue in appealing to the Crown for restitution for the losses suffered by the American traders in 1754. Apparently Franks had not enjoyed much success in fulfilling his assignment as representative of the 1754 group. Despite Trent's own seeming indifference at times, his correspondence indicates that he still had the interests of that group in mind, although he was never able to be of much service to its cause. Meanwhile, as his London sojourn lengthened from months into years, the problem of meeting his living expenses became increasingly serious, and he was forced to call on his good friend, Croghan, as well as on others, to arrange additional loans in America. Nevertheless, he was still able to retain much of his land, though it was heavily mortgaged.

During the winter and spring of 1773 the skeins of governmental red tape involving the Vandalia project unwound slowly in London. In America, where there was less formidable opposition, the same inertia did not prevail. Instructions issued earlier to the superintendent of Indian affairs to inform the Indians of the proposed establishment of a new colony west of the mountains were carried out to the letter. During the first week of April, Alexander McKee held an important conference with the chiefs of the various western Indian nations on the plains of the Scioto River. There he told the natives that the British King proposed to permit the formation of a new colony on the land purchased by the Crown from the Indians in 1768. The chiefs declared themselves pleased with the proposal. It was their belief that the creation of a new colonial government west of the mountains would tend to control the influx of settlers into the western country, a migration that was already, they declared, causing alarm among the Indians and threatening to break the chain of friendship with the colonies of Pennsylvania, Maryland, and Virginia.

Another month elapsed, however, before any signs of energy in regard to the new colony were displayed by the British officials. Finally, on May 6, the Lords of Trade submitted to the King their report on the proposed land grant. The report opened with the admission that the land in question was "at present a Part of the Colony of Virginia," but proposed that since it was in no position to enjoy the privileges of that colony's constitution, it "be separated from the Colony of Virginia and erected by Letters Patent into a distinct Colony under the Name of Vandalia." The government to be established was to exercise jurisdiction over an area greater than that of Vandalia alone. Its power was to extend over all the lands inhabited, or to be inhabited, by British subjects in the trans-Appalachian region.

Executive authority in Vandalia was to be vested in a governor possessed of all the powers enjoyed by the governors of the other English colonies. He was to be assisted by a council of twelve, which was to be appointed by the Crown and was to have the same powers as similar councils in other colonies. Below that body there was to be a representative assembly consisting of two deputies, elected by the majority of freeholders, from each of the counties into which Vandalia might be divided. Until such division should bring about the creation of twelve counties, the assembly was to be limited to twenty-four members, elected by the freeholders of the province at large, considered as one county. Every person possessed in his own right, or that of his wife, of one thousand acres of land in fee simple, if he were a Protestant and over twenty-one years of age, was eligible for election to the assembly. Meetings of the assembly were to be called and dissolved by the governor, and the period of time between meetings was not to exceed twelve months. The clerk of the representative body was to be appointed by the King (presumably in order to guarantee an accurate record of the transactions of that popular group). Power of veto was vested in the governor as well as in the Crown; all laws passed by the assembly were to go into effect at once unless vetoed. As to religion, it was decreed that the Church of England should be the legal church, although all Protestant dissenters were to be tolerated. (Failure to mention toleration for Catholics would seem to imply that they were not to be welcomed.) Civil and criminal justice was to be dispensed in a superior court, presided over by a chief justice and two associates, all appointed by the King. Local justice was to be cared for by justices of the peace in each created county. Each year the superior-court judges were to submit to the governor a panel of three names of freeholders from each county, from which county sheriffs were to be chosen. These officers were to possess powers similar to those of English sheriffs. Money due the Crown was to be collected by a receiver-general appointed by the King.

It was stipulated that on the day of the completion of the grant, the Vandalia associates were to pay to the Crown the sum of £10,000 7 *s.* 3*d.*, which was the exact amount that had been paid to the Indians by the English in 1768 for the Ohio River tract of land. Two shillings quit rent were to be paid for every one hundred acres of land settled, the payments to start twenty years after the granting of the title. All land claims, legal or otherwise, that had been secured before January 4, 1770, were to be reserved to the occupants. In addition, two hundred thousand acres were to be set aside for the officers of the Virginia regiment of 1754. Mineral rights were reserved by the Crown, as was the right to build fortifications wherever they might be deemed necessary.

In America there was both sorrow and joy over the fact that the land title was so close to confirmation. George Morgan was still seeking information; in a letter to Samuel Wharton he stated that John Baynton was at the point of death, and that Baynton attributed his illness to Wharton's poor treatment of him. George Croghan, of course, was among those who welcomed the tidings concerning the land grant. It was reported in Pittsburgh about the middle of May that the "New Colony Was fixed, Trent immediately expected and the Governor to be over in June." Another rumor had spread about the town that Croghan was to be empowered by the proprietors of Vandalia to grant lands and build houses around Pittsburgh, "which . . . Will be 12¾ Miles out of Pennsylvania." Before the end of the first week in June, Baynton had died as a result of his double burden of worry and illness, and had left behind him twelve children as well as much financial trouble, which his son-in-law, Morgan, felt in duty bound to share. In order to help clarify the situation, Morgan sought Benjamin Franklin's assistance in London. Through Franklin's influence he hoped to get a statement from Wharton as to Baynton's share in Vandalia. He complained that he had written at least eight letters to Wharton between 1769 and 1773 and had never received a single reply.

By July 16 the attorney-general and the solicitor-general of Great Britain had prepared and laid before the Privy Council committee entrusted with the consideration of the American land-grant business, a proper legal document covering Vandalia and its proposed government. At last it seemed that the land-promotion scheme was to be a success. In August, Trent, who had expected to start for home in the spring found himself still in England. Well might his ears have burned about that time had he known what George Morgan was writing about him. It seems that Trent had made a disparaging statement to Croghan about Baynton and Morgan and had advised Croghan to be guided by Samuel Wharton's advice, as it would be much more valuable than that of the other two men. When Morgan heard of this, he penned a letter to Croghan in which he said, "Don't you think that I have sufficient Spirit to wring Capt. Trent's Nose for writing this & such like to you. I shall Serve the Rascal as he deserves . . . I most ardently long for the Opportunity." But the chance that Morgan sought was to be denied him for many months to come, since Trent found it necessary to continue his stay in London.

Nothing of significance concerning the land grant seems to have transpired for some weeks after the legal document had been drawn up, but on October 28 the Lords Commissioners of the Council for Plantation Affairs issued an order for the attorney-general and the solicitor-general to prepare the final legal forms for the transaction. The affixing of the legal seal of Great Britain was then all that was necessary to complete the business.

Trent evidently spent most of the year 1773 rather well behind the scenes. Doubtless he was continually making plans for his return voyage to America, but the usual delays in governmental procedure prohibited their fulfillment. As he bided his time in England, his erstwhile friend, Morgan, became more and more angry at his silence regarding the statement to Croghan. At last the hot-headed Morgan wrote a curt letter to Trent in which he threatened to take appropriate action for the redress of his grievance, unless Trent availed himself of the opportunity to "Appologize." To encourage him to act on his own initiative, Morgan made the suggestion that

as you have often freely communicated your private Sentiments of Mr. Wharton, I hope you will not suffer his Influence over you now, (which is well known,) to govern you in this Matter-Take the Advice of some Men of *Princeple* & *Honour*—And let me beg as speedy an Answer as convenient.

Regardless of the threat, there is no evidence that Trent paid any attention to Morgan's demands.

Other people in America connected with the land-speculation scheme were having their troubles too. Croghan, who was a sort of Jack-of-all-trades for the speculators, found himself in a dilemma in the fall of 1773. Because of the rumor, spread in the spring, that Vandalia was to be established and the governor to arrive shortly, the Indians began to drift toward Pittsburgh for an expected conference. No one seemed interested in doing anything about feeding and caring for them, with the result that the burden fell on Croghan. Since his reputation among the Indians was at stake, he fed them as best he could, using up the winter supplies that he had collected for his own household. At length the numbers became so large, and the demands for food so great, that in order to meet the situation he was forced to pawn his plate and other valuables and to use his credit with the local merchants. He finally convinced the chiefs that the governor was not coming that autumn, and succeeded in starting them for home with the tentative promise that the

Vandalia executive would be in Pittsburgh in the spring with a "handsome present." When it became apparent that this promise could not be kept, Croghan blamed the affair on his American and English speculator friends in England, who had told him that the grant had been made and the Indian presents packed; he was justly angry and declared that the statement about the goods must have been false. It was his opinion that at least sixty thousand people were settled on the Vandalia tract already. That condition, added to the state of affairs in the American colonies at the time, made him apprehensive regarding the ultimate success of the new colony.

In England the early months of 1774 were fraught with exasperating delays that blocked the last step necessary to the confirmation of the Vandalia title. Finally, in August, Thomas Walpole and his associates sent a memorial to the Crown asking that the granting of the title be not longer put off. In closing, they referred to the great inconvenience suffered by two of the outstanding memorialists—Trent and Wharton —who had been kept away from their families for years, patiently waiting for the government to complete their business. An even more urgent plea was sent to the Board of Trade by Croghan. He pointed out that the year before, Sir William Johnson had been ordered by the Crown to inform the western Indians that a new colony was to be established, and declared that unless some relief presently arrived on behalf of the new province, he would be forced to leave the forks of the Ohio because of the trouble and expense involved in placating the Indians. In that event, he said, hundreds of innocent English families would undoubtedly be slain, because there would be no one in whom the Indians had confidence to restrain them.

George Morgan, driven almost frantic by the continued silence of Trent and Wharton, bitterly criticized the land speculators for not following his advice. He contended that the Fort Stanwix trader grant should have been occupied immediately after it had been made in 1768, and that sales should have been made on it at a nominal figure of about £5 for each one hundred acres. In a letter to Wharton he accused the latter of wishing to "strike some great Stroke in England to make a grand Fortune," and added, "With regard to *that contemptible Wretch Trent,* my treatment of him will depend on your Conduct; for of himself he is not worth giving a Kick in the Breech to, or a Pull by the Nose."

Not all the British officials remained quiet throughout this trying period. News had reached the ears of the president of the Board of Trade of the illegal land grants being made in the Ohio Valley by Lord Dunmore, governor of Virginia, and of the resultant Indian hostilities in that region. It was these hostilities that precipitated the struggle between Virginia and the Shawnee Indians known as Dunmore's War. Dunmore's lame reply to the charge made against him angered Dartmouth. In no uncertain terms he flayed Dunmore for pretending ignorance of the prior claims of the Vandalia Company to that region and of Lord Hillsborough's order that no settlements were to be made west of the 1763 boundary line. But fate was to play into the hands of the Virginia group ere long, and in the meanwhile Lord Dunmore did much as he pleased.

The winter of 1775 passed without any positive action being taken by the British officials toward completing the Vandalia Company grant. In February of that year it was reported to the London agents of the company that an impostor by the name of Lewis was traveling about through the proposed Vandalia region, selling locations to the ignorant people and representing himself as having authority to do so. It was feared that such practices might seriously injure the cause of the Vandalia promoters.

By the spring of the year the outlook for success in the land-company venture looked so hopeless that Trent resolved to return to America. Accordingly, he and Wharton attempted to collect written statements from high legal authorities in England to prove that titles to land grants made by the Indians were valid. They succeeded in getting signed statements from Henry Dagge and John Glynn, two of the ablest legal minds in England at that time. Another step in the preparation for the voyage was to call a meeting of the executive committee of the Vandalia Company, a group consisting of Thomas Walpole, Samuel Wharton, Benjamin Franklin, and John Sargent. Acting on behalf of themselves and their associates, these men constituted Trent their lawful attorney to manage and superintend all their interests in the lands supposedly to be included in the proposed grant. Trent was empowered to lease or sell the lands, or make any other deal that seemed advisable in regard to them, and he was instructed to try to make the best possible bargains in rents or sales.

Before Trent left London his old friend, Colonel George Mercer, borrowed several hundred pounds from him, giving him two notes, which apparently were never repaid. On the same day that the loans were arranged, Trent drew up his "last will and testament." Ocean voyages were rather precarious in those days, especially in the spring of the year when there was danger of icebergs and storms. Although this will was not to be Trent's last, it is of interest in that it gives some hints regarding his attitude toward his family and toward life in general. First, he ordered the payment of all his just debts and funeral expenses. After the cost of these obligations had been deducted, the remainder of his estate was to be divided into six parts, of which his wife, Sarah, was to receive one-sixth; his son, John, two-sixths; and his daughters, Ann, Mary, and Sarah, one-sixth each. (Evidently the other son, William, Jr., and one daughter, Martha, had died during Trent's absence.) His wife was appointed executrix. Trent stipulated that from each child's share enough money was to be taken each year—not in excess of £50 for the girls or £100 for John—to provide food, clothing, shelter, and education for that child. After John had reached the age of fifteen years, his yearly allowance was to be increased to £150. No division of the estate was to take place until the eldest daughter had arrived at the age of twenty-five years. All of Trent's lands in Pennsylvania and New York were to be sold, if necessary, to carry out the foregoing plan. Should the lands not provide sufficient funds, the deficiency was to be made up by the sale of whatever other parts of his estate the executrix desired to sell. If his wife should remarry, she must apply to a county court to appoint two men to assist her in executing the will; all three were to keep accounts relating to the transactions. If she remained single, no accounts were to be required.

On April 21, 1775, several weeks after Benjamin Franklin's departure for America, Trent boarded a packet for home. In his effects he carried a letter from Samuel Wharton to Franklin. In the missive Wharton asked Franklin to assist Trent in securing from such men as Galloway and John Dickinson, and from the leading Virginia lawyers, legal opinions that would concur with those already secured from Dagge and Glynn. On his journey to America, Trent carried all sorts of documents, but not the precious one confirming the title to Vandalia, which he had spent so many long years in trying to obtain.

Benjamin Franklin had departed from England with a heavy heart. To the very last he had hoped that the friends of America would be able to overthrow the ministry of Lord North and restore amicable relations with the thirteen American colonies. But the English liberals, led by such able men as Edmund Burke, had failed in their attempts to get the British government to heed the threat of a civil war as set forth in the acts of the first Continental Congress.

CHAPTER XII

FINALE AND FAILURE

Major Trent's arrival in Philadelphia was the signal for George Morgan to resume his efforts to secure an apology from him. Since Trent continued to ignore him, Morgan finally called Trent a liar and accused him of being a scoundrel. The old trader remained unperturbed for some time, but his anger was aroused when in one of Morgan's letters, he read a veiled challenge to a duel. That was too much; he said that if a duel was what Morgan desired, he was ready, and that Morgan should name the time and the place. Morgan replied that he had not meant what Trent had inferred, but had merely suggested that they meet Robert Morris and John Cadwallader and let them arbitrate the dispute. Nevertheless, he was willing to settle the quarrel on the field of honor, and he named a time to meet Trent at Cadwallader's. The mutual friends of the two men evidently succeeded in bringing about a peaceful settlement, for the quarrel was finally dropped, and friendly relations were again established.

With the Morgan feud out of the way, Trent proceeded to the more important business of promoting the land company. Benjamin Franklin gladly wrote his opinion in support of the validity of Indian grants: "Having long since carefully studied these Points, I concur fully with Counsellor Dagge & Serjeant Glynn, in their Opinions as above delivered." Some weeks later Trent was able to add the opinion of Patrick Henry to his bag of legal trophies: "From principles which appear to me very clear, I concur in the above opinions." But the securing of legal co-operation was just one of many angles in the land-speculation game.

George Croghan, whose advice had been sought some years before regarding the possibilities of a new Indian land purchase north of the Ohio, was again approached on the subject in July, 1775. He told Trent that he thought the whole idea had been dropped, because of the trouble between the colonies and England. He admitted, however, that he had talked with a number of Indian chiefs about purchasing a tract of land for himself and Trent's group, and that as a result the Indians had agreed to sell him one and one-half million acres for six thousand "Dollars." He had raised the purchase money with "the greatest Difciulty [sic]" and had secured a title to the land, containing the clause that the tract was not to be settled for fifteen years, unless the Indians

155

decided to move down the Ohio to better hunting grounds. He only wanted one-third of the tract for himself, he declared, and would gladly sell the other two-thirds to Trent and his partners. It was the opinion of the Irish trader that a larger purchase might be made later from the Indians, but that the promotion of such an enterprise would take time. In the meantime he offered to sell to Trent and his friends one million acres of his purchase for the sum of four thousand dollars. Trent was invited to collect the money and proceed to Warm Springs, Virginia, where Croghan had scheduled a conference with some Southerners who had asked him to buy some land for them. Croghan said that if Trent could not raise the necessary funds, he would have to transfer a part of the land to the Virginians. But Trent was no longer in touch with the Englishmen who were interested in a new land tract. Sir William Johnson was dead, and Samuel Wharton was still in England. As for himself, he had too many creditors who wanted money that he did not have. Furthermore, Croghan's statement that "the Indians will take Nothing butt Mony Now a Days for land" destroyed the hopes of Trent and his partners that they might be able to use a consignment of goods from London in making the proposed purchase. Thus the affair apparently ended in a stalemate.

For the next few weeks Trent was engaged in attending to various business affairs in the East, but on August 1 he set out for the trans-Appalachian country to view the Vandalia region. A few hours before he started on his journey, he wrote a letter to his friend, Anthony Todd, of London, describing the state of affairs in the colonies. He informed Todd that the colonies had an army, some fighting vessels, a government organized, and foreign assistance offered in the event of separation from the mother country. His feelings on the subject of independence may be gathered from his statement: "I hope to God! that the King may attend to the last Petition sent Home, to prevent the Ruin of the English nation.—A Reconciliation is wished for by every good Man on this Side of the Water." Trent told Todd that he planned to talk with Croghan at Warm Springs and from there proceed to the Ohio region, where in September the Indians and the Virginians expected to settle their disputes.

While Trent was on the frontier, George Washington, to whom the trader had applied for information regarding the possibilities of collecting his debt from Colonel George Mercer's estate, wrote to Trent from Cambridge telling him that the estate had been sold, but that because of the heavy mortgages against it and the unsettled condition of the country, he doubted whether Trent would be able to realize anything from the sale. During the same week Samuel Wharton wrote from London to his brother, Thomas, beseeching him and Major Trent to appeal to Dr. Franklin and "other members of the Congress" to have the legislative body enact a resolve or declaration, at the earliest moment, indicating the validity of titles to land obtained from the Indians. Wharton explained that he would be willing to enlarge the number of shares in the Vandalia Company by four more, if the giving of a half-share to eight members of Congress would facilitate the business at hand! In connection with this proposal he stated specifically that Patrick Henry was not to be one of the eight considered eligible for a bribe. He asked his brother to work with Trent in carrying out the task of winning the congressmen over to the idea. Wharton feared that Franklin, in spite of his great interest, was too old to be of real service; and for that reason he warned Thomas that it "will be necessary for you & Major Trent, with his [*Franklin's*] concurrence, to take an active part with the other members of the Congress."

As the relations between the colonies and England had almost reached the breaking point, the possibility that a title to Vandalia would ever be granted became more and more remote. This situation led Trent and Robert Callender to suggest the possibility of reviving the old Indiana Company in the hope that a purely American title might be secured for it if a successful break for independence were made. George Morgan was assigned the task of making contacts with some of the other influential members of that company in order to secure their opinions. Through Morgan, Benjamin Franklin asked his son, William, to express his judgment concerning the idea of opening the Indiana lands under the government of Virginia. In his letter to William, Morgan proceeded to outline a plan whereby a central land office would be created with a board of trustees to receive money and pay annual dividends. The position of land agent for the Indiana Company was sought by Morgan, and he asked the younger Franklin's assistance in securing the appointment. Franklin was informed that the Whartons were doubtful of his right to a portion of the land grant, since he had not paid his share of Trent's and Wharton's expenses in London, but was assured that Morgan understood the arrangement to have been that Franklin was to give only his influence and not his money. Morgan said that the Whartons thought £20 for each one hundred acres a fair price to ask for the land, but that he believed £15 to be a fairer figure. Mention was also made of the desire of a number of the Indiana partners to call a meeting in the near future at Pittsburgh.

William Franklin replied with a word of caution to his father. He declared that after reading the letters of Thomas Walpole and John

Sargent from London, he felt certain that his father and Trent should move slowly in attempting to put into effect the plan described by Morgan. He said that the Vandalia partners had received every assurance that a title would be granted to the Walpole group, just as soon as the colonial disturbance ended. Therefore, if the whole subject should be opened at once to public view, by starting a land sale, serious prejudice against the granting of a title might develop in England. He then changed the subject of his letter and voiced his disapproval of Trent, accusing him of trying to avoid payment of the debt he owed to his financial backers in New Jersey.

After meditating for a few weeks upon the affairs of the Indiana Company, Trent decided to visit Pittsburgh and study the situation at first hand. Arriving there on September 13, he met and talked with the commissioners of the Continental Congress who had been sent to treat with the Indians in behalf of the United Colonies. Discussions were also held with the delegates from Virginia who had been sent to make peace between the Shawnee Indians and the Old Dominion. Trent reported to a friend in England that there were undoubted proofs that the Indians were being encouraged by the British officers in Canada, and at Detroit, to attack the inhabitants settled on the frontier. The officials had also told the red men that the colonies were sending an army against them, but the Indians refused to believe that tale. During Lord Dunmore's War, Trent said, upwards of one hundred palisaded forts had been built west of the mountains; on his way to Pittsburgh he had "lodged in one of them, that had Barracks sufficient for a compleat Regiment." According to Trent, disputes between the Pennsylvania and Virginia elements were rife around Pittsburgh in the autumn of 1775, and he added:

> In short Unanimity prevails only, in opposing the present despotick Ministerial Measures. Implicit Obedience is paid to the Orders of the Congress; and when the Inhabitants meet to consult on Measures for the publick Good, private Animosities subside, and no Passion seems to animate their Breasts, but that of serving their Country.

Regardless of William Franklin's advice and of the general confusion that prevailed, Trent proceeded to call a meeting of the members of the Indiana Company at Pittsburgh on September 21. Present at the meeting were Trent, Robert Callender, John Ormsby, Thomas Smallman, Joseph Spear, and George Morgan. Trent made the announcement that upon his arrival in England he had been told by eminent legal authority that the King's confirmation to the 1768 grant was unnecessary. All that was required, in the opinion of the lawyers consulted, was for him to return to America and take possession of the grant, since he was the legal attorney for the traders. Then the old trader briefly recited the story of Hillsborough's opposition and of the evolution of the Vandalia Company to circumvent the president of the Board of Trade and secure a land title.

After listening to Trent's speech, the group entered into a lively discussion of plans, which finally ended in the adoption of a series of resolutions. Trent, John Gibson, Smallman, and Morgan were empowered to act as commissioners to determine, with the aid of the Indians, where the eastern boundary of the Indiana grant was located. They, or any two of them, were to assume the responsibility for having the tract surveyed. A general land office was to be opened at once and to remain open until January 1, 1777, at some convenient place on the tract, with an administrative land agent in charge to care for the surveys and sales. Fifty dollars for each one hundred acres was to be the price, with some additional fees for warrants and surveys. Squatters who complied with the land-office regulations were to be permitted to remain in possession of their lands so long as the tracts did not exceed four hundred acres. The above commissioners were to supervise all activities of the land office. George Morgan was chosen as the agent and entrusted with the task of devising an official seal for the Indiana Company. It was also agreed that the grantees should write a joint letter to Samuel Wharton in London with the request that he immediately send over the copy of the "Original Grant," which Trent had left with him, so that it might be recorded in Williamsburg, Virginia, at once. Callender and Morgan were instructed to call a general meeting of the Indiana partners at Carlisle in January, 1776; but that date was later changed to the second Monday in November, 1775.

In the opinion of the Whartons, the Pittsburgh meeting was a mistake. As soon as Thomas Wharton heard of it he wrote Trent a letter in which he roundly scolded him and the others present at the meeting, for acting on the land-company affairs without consulting all the grantees. He declared that so far as he and Samuel were concerned, the resolutions enacted at Pittsburgh would not be binding. But Trent at the moment was deeply agitated by a personal matter that allowed no room for the consideration of Wharton's feelings. On September 28 a newspaper article had appeared in the *Maryland Gazette* that was very damaging to Trent's character. The item, which had originated in Williamsburg, stated that "Captain Trent, a native of Pennsylvania, left London about the beginning of May being intrusted by Lord North, with the . . . sum of 40,000 l. to see the Indians to cut our throats."

This false report startled and worried Trent, for he feared that in his travels about the country he might be murdered by someone ignorant of his true interests. In a letter to a friend he stated that he had no fear of those who knew him well, since they were aware "that I am as strongly attached to the Interest of my Country as any Man in it." Nevertheless, as he had reason to believe that many people were not cognizant of his motives, he decided, despite a painful injury suffered when his horse fell and rolled over on him, to start for Philadelphia as soon as possible to appear before the Continental Congress, so that the delegates from all the colonies might receive a clear impression of his political opinions.

Before making arrangements to depart from Pittsburgh, Trent asked for and received a statement from Lewis Morris, James Wilson, and Thomas Walker, commissioners from the Continental Congress for Indian affairs, to the effect that he was a patriot and not a loyalist. The statement indicated that Major Trent, since his arrival in America, had disposed of part of the Indian goods that he held in trust for the Vandalia Company (at Georgetown), and had offered to sell more. This fact the commissioners felt was good proof that he had no funds or commission from Lord North, because if he had, he would have been buying and not selling goods. A much stronger credential in support of Trent's patriotism to the colonies was given him at the same time in the form of several resolutions passed by the committee of correspondence of the County of West Augusta, Virginia, of which George Croghan was chairman. The report and resolutions praised Trent for exerting his influence on the side of the colonies at the recent council with the Indians, and recorded the fact that he was well known to all citizens west of the mountains as a friend of his country. Unanimously, the committee resolved that the Maryland news item was false and scandalous; that the injury done to Trent was apt to cause considerable mischief both among his white friends and among the Indians; that printers should be more careful in what they published; that as Major Trent had ordered the author of the article to be sued, all Trent's friends should help in trying to apprehend the culprit; and finally, that the committee's resolves be published in the Philadelphia papers and be copied by all other papers on the continent. Thus armed, Trent was ready to start for the East to defend his character; but for some reason he delayed his departure from the frontier indefinitely, in spite of the fact that he had originally been most anxious to leave.

At last the time arrived for the proposed Indiana Company meeting at Carlisle. The group assembled on the day appointed, but was forced to adjourn to meet in Lancaster in December, because Trent failed to appear. The trader gave no reason for his absence, and some of his old friends and partners were mistrustful of his actions. Levy Andrew Levy wrote to him that his unexplained absence "leaves room for a good deale of Suspicion," and reminded him that he had "ever Maintained the Character of an honest Gentlemn [*sic*] and I hope you will Still Maintain the Same." Then Levy expressed the hope that Trent would be present at Lancaster and give a full explanation to the sufferers of 1763 "of what you have done." Thomas Wharton, in writing to his brother, Samuel, was not so lenient in his opinion of the "One Ey'd Major," as he was wont to call Trent, who, in some unknown manner, had lost the sight of one eye. Wharton stated that a number of the Indiana grantees thought that Trent had misused their powers of attorney and that they should be taken from him. He mentioned Trent's absence from the Carlisle meeting and said that an express had been sent after him to tell him to be sure to appear at Lancaster in December; despite that precaution, he declared, he had learned that Trent would not be in Lancaster. After complaining bitterly about all the trouble the land business had brought him, Wharton told his brother, "I most Cordially wish that Person [*Trent*] had remained in England till you could have [come] together, He is not equal to the Task & I am therefore persuaded He will do much more Harm than Good." According to Wharton, many of the grantees wanted to know what the "Major's Designs" were, since "many Things are in the Dark."

In the meantime Trent was still tarrying at the forks of the Ohio, where on the last day of November he purchased several hundred acres of land on the Allegheny River, near Pittsburgh, from Thomas Smallman. If Thomas Wharton's extensive correspondence is to be relied on, Trent was also engaging in certain forms of intrigue with regard to the Indiana Company. Wharton believed that Trent was violating his promise not to pursue the Indiana affair until he returned to Philadelphia. He further accused him of damaging the rights of many grantees by injudiciously raising the land question before the proper papers had been prepared. The traders, he said, wanted fifty shares in the company, instead of the thirty reserved for them. He wrote Trent that as a result of an examination of the powers of attorney granted to the latter, he and Morgan were of the opinion that Trent had violated his authority by the measures he had adopted at Fort Pitt. In concluding, he warned Trent to be "circumspect" and to meet him in Philadelphia as soon as possible.

No business was transacted at Lancaster on December 11, and the conference was adjourned to meet at Philadelphia on December 15. The session held on that date was the first of a number of meetings and discussions, which, by January 1, 1776, ended in the evolution of what seemed like a good working policy. Trent, Thomas Wharton, and Morgan were chosen to present a summary of the latest plan to the company members on January 19. Under the new arrangement a deed was drawn up by which the proprietors of Indiana transferred all their rights to a board of three trustees—Richard Bache, son-in-law of Benjamin Franklin; Owen Jones, Jr.; and Isaac Wharton—who were to administer the company affairs for the best interests of all. In that manner personal business failures and unforeseen accidents would have the least effect on the whole organization. An additional agreement was drawn up "to guard against all frauds and Clandestine Combinations, and other Mischiefs and accidents whatsoever which may tend to obstruct or Frustrate the present Designs of the said Proprietors," and the grantees obligated themselves "to be just true & faithful to one another in all things relating to . . . their common Interest." For every three hundred shares held, a partner was entitled to one vote, although the maximum number of votes allowed any one person was limited to ten. On the official schedule Trent was listed as holding 7,147 shares in his own right, and as a partner in another account, he was entitled to a portion of 784 additional shares. After a fundamental policy had been formulated, the meeting was adjourned until March.

Trent proceeded to keep himself posted regarding the various land transactions of Croghan and others of his friends, and to engage in some minor trading in Philadelphia. He was also concerned about the disposal of the Vandalia goods still stored at Georgetown, and planned a trip to that port. But the business that caused him the most anxiety was the suit that Alexander Lowrey brought against Samuel Wharton, Croghan, and himself in February, for payment of their debt of over £4,000 contracted in 1768. Trent was saved from jail by the unwilling intervention of Thomas Wharton. Since Samuel was still in London, his brother was obliged to look after his affairs in America, although Trent's residence in Trenton made close co-operation between the trader and Wharton somewhat difficult. Nevertheless, when the Lowrey case was tried in March, the defendants were able to establish the fact that payment of the bond in question had been contingent upon confirmation of the 1768 land grant by the Crown, and since that confirmation had never been made, the debt was not due. Thus Lowrey lost his suit because of the shrewd wording of the bond.

At the meeting of the proprietors of the Indiana Company in Philadelphia on March 20, 1776, Joseph Galloway was elected president, and Thomas Wharton, vice-president. George Morgan was appointed secretary of the land office and receiver-general of funds, while Robert

Hooper was made surveyor-general. It was decided to open a land office, and the surveyor-general was instructed to have all unsettled land in the grant surveyed in four-hundred-acre lots. By the middle of April, Morgan had published an announcement of the forthcoming opening of the Indiana Company land office and had called upon all "squatters" to secure clear titles. The announcement brought almost instant action from Virginia. The Virginia delegates to the Continental Congress in Philadelphia immediately communicated with Morgan and Thomas Wharton. They demanded an explanation of the advertisement and declared that the land offered for sale was a part of Virginia's property ceded to her by the Indian treaty of 1744. The Virginia delegates then asked that nothing more be done about the land sale until they could take the matter up with the Virginia Constitutional Convention, which was in session at that time. Its resolutions, passed a few weeks later, tended to block the western land companies for the time being.

In April, Trent laid plans to take a pack-horse train of Vandalia goods from Georgetown to the frontier. It is not clear what his purpose was, but by the end of the month he was at Pittsburgh, from where he and Croghan supposedly made a journey down the Ohio River to trade with the Indians and make some observations of the surrounding land. Trent reported that the English had called the western Indians to a conference at Niagara, and he imagined that as soon as the council was over, the Indians would begin murdering the inhabitants, in the back country. In May, Morgan was also at Fort Pitt, on Congressional business, and he wrote from there that he had been tendered applications for land purchases in Indiana to the amount of twenty thousand acres, all of which he had refused to accept. Trent, he said, was at the moment opposed to the idea of applying to the Virginia convention for permission to develop Indiana; in Morgan's opinion, the trader was not likely to visit Philadelphia in the near future.

In keeping with Morgan's prediction, Trent remained in the vicinity of Pittsburgh for some time. On July 6 he was present at an Indian conference held at Fort Pitt after the return of the Indians from their meeting with the British at Niagara. The Indian leaders informed the American officials that the Six Nations had determined on a neutral position in the war between England and her colonies and had called upon their western tributaries to do the same. Accordingly, the western Indians would not permit any American army to cross their territory to attack the English. The Americans replied that they would respect the Indian territory so long as no British army moved across it to attack them. The Indians then asked that the Americans refrain from getting angry if any depredations were committed by their younger warriors, who had been ordered to stay neutral or proceed to Canada to do their fighting.

During the last week in July, Virginia appointed four commissioners —John Harvie, Charles Simms, James Wood, and Abraham Hite—to gather evidence regarding the claims of the Indiana proprietors. Morgan was notified to appear for the company, but refused, saying that he had no authority to do so. He did agree, however, to place a copy of the 1768 deed in the hands of the Virginians. Presumably Trent was not in Pittsburgh at the time the investigation started, for he was not asked to appear. Within the course of a month he was back at his home in the East, volunteering helpful information to the secretary of the committee of public safety in Philadelphia concerning the location of supplies of sulphur and flints. Thomas Wharton heard rumors of certain land transactions made by Trent while the latter was on the frontier, and he confided the belief to his brother, Samuel, in code, that the money that the old trader was using had certainly come from the sale of a part of the Vandalia goods at Georgetown. But in September the dissension among the Indiana Company proprietors was buried long enough to permit them to meet together and draw up a memorial to Virginia on behalf of the 1768 land grant. The petition was sent to the Virginia Assembly on October 1. Whatever may have been the true nature of Trent's activities throughout this period, it is certain that he continued to be alert in the field of business, for he succeeded in retaining some of the lands that he had acquired many years before, and at the same time was ever on the lookout for new bargains.

The war complicated the affairs of the Indiana Company considerably and at times brought about a complete cessation of its activities. Trent found his residence in Trenton so disadvantageous to him in the winter of 1777 that he sought and secured from General Howe a certificate of protection. He declared that this procedure was necessary in order to protect himself and his property, since his enemies, some of whom had joined the British, had labeled him a dangerous person because of certain patriotic actions committed in the interests of the United Colonies. Thus it was imperative that he submit his credentials to General Caesar Rodney when the latter appeared as the commander in Trent's home county in February, 1777.

Because of his advancing years and his many financial troubles, Trent began, in the spring of that year, to reorganize his estate, selling land in one place in order either to buy something more attractive elsewhere, or to secure funds to pay off a pressing obligation that could no longer be delayed. In order to carry out one of his schemes, he had a survey made of over six hundred acres of land on the Jersey side of the Delaware River. After the completion of that transaction, he made arrangements to visit Cumberland County, where he sold one of his tracts of land in June, and engaged in some business conferences with his merchant friends before returning to Trenton. British troop movements in the fall caused him considerable worry, as he feared that his private papers, many of which were scattered about in the possession of his friends, might fall into the hands of the English. He said, "I would not for any Concideration that they should have got my Papers"; for some of the things that he had written about the British, including General Howe, might have made his position difficult had they been known. In November he planned a journey to Georgetown to examine the goods in stock there, and made arrangements for some trading operations with Barnard Gratz. He could not go to Philadelphia to conduct business, he said, since the British had the city. In fact, he does not seem to have been involved in any significant affairs until the late spring of 1778.

With the departure of the British from the area in and around Philadelphia, the clouds of Loyalist suspicion rested so heavily on a number of leading citizens that they found it necessary to take an official oath of allegiance to the United States in order to clear themselves. Trent was in that group, and on May 29, 1778, he took the oath of allegiance at Burlington, New Jersey. During the remainder of the spring and summer, he seems to have divided his time between his plantation near Trenton and his business interests in Philadelphia. About the middle of September, despite a glowing description of his property, he was unsuccessful in an attempt to sell his large estate along the Delaware. The Indiana Company associates wanted him to go to Virginia later in the same month, but he said that it was impossible for him to do so at that time, because two members of his family were seriously ill. He suggested the hiring of a lawyer to apply for an order of survey from the Virginia authorities. Morgan shared Trent's opinion about the employment of counsel, but he felt that it would still be necessary for Trent to go to Williamsburg, either that autumn or the following spring. He declared that his attempt to call a regular meeting of the Indiana Company had failed, because the notice of the meeting had not been properly announced. Trent was asked to sign and return an application for a new meeting, as there was pressing business to be considered by the partners. As the year 1778 drew to a close, Morgan informed Trent that Indiana shares were being sought after, and that he had been instructed to offer Trent £5,000 for his equity in Indiana. He also told Trent of the action of Virginia in declaring void all land purchases from the Indians. The news found the old trader in low spirits. Several members of his family were still suffering from illness, and he told

Barnard Gratz, in a letter, that he himself was just recovering from a serious illness that had almost ended in his "paying a visit to the other Country."

The first day of the new year, 1779, Trent celebrated by purchasing three tracts of land, containing over seven hundred acres, in Northumberland County, Pennsylvania. Later he found himself in the unusual role of creditor, trying to collect his debts from a debtor who was almost as good at alibi-making as Trent himself. But before the month of January ended, he was engaged in matters of much greater import. The Virginia legislature had decided to give the representatives of the land companies a chance to be heard on the third Monday in May, and Trent was asked to present the case of the Indiana Company at Williamsburg. Thus during the intervening months he was largely concerned in collecting and consolidating all the evidence possible to support the company's claims. Whenever possible, however, he engaged in private business transactions, especially those involving land speculation. Between February 1 and May 1, his real estate operations involved some ten tracts of land located, for the most part, in Cumberland County or in the new counties created from it. From one group of speculators he held a mortgage for £6,000, which again placed him in the position of a creditor. He also dealt in the shares of the Indiana Company. From John Ormsby of Pittsburgh he purchased 280 shares, and on May 1 he sold 900 shares to William Grayson of Virginia for £1,200. The last deal was probably a shrewd one, in that it aligned an influential Virginian on the side of the Indiana Company interests just prior to Trent's presentation of the company's cause before the Virginia legislature.

Trent appeared before the Virginia Assembly on the day appointed and presented the case for the Indiana Company; but his efforts were of little avail. Within a few weeks the legislative body passed a series of resolutions outlawing the claims of the Indiana Company, as well as those of all other companies, to lands within the charter claims of Virginia. The Commonwealth reserved the exclusive pre-emption rights to all Indian lands within her borders as set forth by the Constitution of 1776. And lest, perchance, there might be some doubt as to their meaning, the delegates, in the last resolution, specifically voided the 1768 grant and named Trent as the attorney who had received it. Colonel George Mason stepped into the picture at that time as the defender of Virginia against the machinations of the land companies, and their ultimate defeat was doubtless due in large measure to his masterful efforts. Nevertheless, Trent, as he fenced with Mason, was not greatly impressed with the latter's arguments against the Indiana Company claims.

The notes that Trent took on these arguments indicate that in the last analysis the Virginia lawyer's opposition rested on the rather flimsy legal grounds of *salus populi* and political expediency. Whether legally sound or not, however, the arguments were sufficiently effective to convince the already prejudiced authorities of Virginia. Trent and his fellow partners in Indiana read the handwriting on the wall and retired to try a different tack.

Finally, after due consideration, the land speculators hit upon the idea of petitioning the Congress of the United States for redress of their grievances. Two memorials were presented—one on behalf of Vandalia; the other in the interests of Indiana. Trent submitted the petition asking that a title be granted to Vandalia, while George Morgan handled the Indiana memorial. Trent's document reviewed the story of Vandalia from November, 1768, when the British government had purchased a tract of land from the Indians, down to September 11, 1779, the date that appeared on the memorial. In addition, Trent told Congress that the prosecution of the Vandalia business had cost the proprietors about £20,000, and that confirmation of the title by the Crown had been momentarily expected when the Declaration of Independence had been signed. It was his understanding, he said, that since independence had been declared, all rights to the sale of lands were to be transferred from the British Crown to the United States in Congress assembled. Further to influence his hearers, he reminded them that many of the individuals for whom he spoke as attorney had distinguished themselves in the American cause on both sides of the Atlantic. His group, he asserted, was willing to pay the Congress of the United States the same sum that it had offered to pay the Crown of Great Britain. In closing, he urged Congress to act quickly and, if possible, to allow him or his counsel to be heard before a committee, since Virginia had ordered that a sale of the lands under dispute be started in October. Morgan followed much the same line of reasoning, although he naturally based his arguments on the Fort Stanwix Indian grant to the traders. He also contended that when the King in council had included Indiana within Vandalia, any claims that Virginia had ever possessed to the region had been canceled. Then he, too, pleaded for a speedy hearing as a check to Virginia's proposed land sale. Both memorials were read to Congress on September 14, and were then assigned to a committee for consideration.

As soon as the Virginia delegates sent word to Williamsburg that memorials were being read in Congress from the land companies, Mason and his assistants girded themselves for a contest. The General Assembly was convened in October and enacted a sizzling remonstrance to the United States Congress, which, however, was not delivered to Congress until March 20, 1780. In this document Virginia opposed the idea of Congress accepting such petitions. She further declared that the national body had no jurisdiction in these matters, and that if such powers were assumed, the sovereignty of the states might be threatened at any time in the future. Attempts to make inroads on her domain were being made by other companies than Vandalia and Indiana, she argued. Congress was warned that the contention that a common national fund might be created if Congress took over the western lands and sold them, was only a trick, since Congress did not have any such lands, possessed no power under the Articles of Confederation of acquiring any, and could not do so without the risk of bloodshed.

Toward the end of October the Congressional committee reported on the land companies' petitions. After a heated debate, a motion to recommit the report was lost. Shortly thereafter, Congress adjourned, but not before the committee members had offered the resolution that Virginia and all other states in a similar situation desist from "the sale, grant or settlement of any land unappropriated at the time of the declaration of independence, until the conclusion of the War." The Virginia delegation, through James Mercer, offered bitter opposition to the Vandalia and Indiana petitions, but this resistance was met by strong arguments from the other side of the question, collected from judicial as well as other sources.

The next move on the part of the Indiana Company was the appointment of Morgan as its agent to go to Williamsburg to seek the repeal of the legislation that had been designed to thwart its purposes. Trent wrote Morgan a letter of introduction to Edmund Randolph, which Morgan was to present to the lawyer upon his arrival in Virginia. In it Trent expressed the hope that Indiana might have another opportunity to be represented before the Virginia Assembly. Should that chance occur, he hoped that Randolph would consent to serve as Indiana's advocate. But the ambition to secure another hearing was never realized. Although Morgan continued his activities on behalf of the company, Trent took no active part in its affairs during the remainder of the year. Minor matters engaged his attention, such as the theft of a horse from his stable, for which he offered a one-hundred-dollar reward if recovered.

With the advent of the year 1780, the Indiana proprietors began marshaling all the strength they could from any and all quarters. Samuel Wharton joined with Benjamin Franklin in preparing a long and detailed memorial to the Congress of the United States. The memorial was prepared in Passy, France, in February, 1780, from which place it was sent to America. (Wharton had been forced to flee for safety from England to France because of his revolutionary activities. He returned to America before the end of the year 1780. Franklin had been sent to France on a secret mission, with Arthur Lee, in the autumn of 1776. Together with Silas Deane, who was already in France, they were to direct their efforts to winning the French to the revolutionary cause in America.) Even the trenchant pen of Thomas Paine was enlisted in the cause of the land companies. His thesis began with the same error that had been made by Drake—that of assuming that the Pacific was only a short distance from the Atlantic, a belief upon which Virginia's sea-to-sea charter was based. He argued strongly for the idea of making the unoccupied western lands into a public domain, from the sale of which an income might be derived to defray the nation's debts. It was his opinion that a new state should be laid out over the general Vandalia lines, with land offices in America and Europe. Instead of being a detriment to Virginia, he contended, such a state would be an advantage for two reasons: the new state would serve as a buffer between Virginia and the Indian dangers on the frontier; and Virginia's position to the east of the frontier state would be a boon to her trade, since practically all imports would have to come in by the Chesapeake Bay. With the sending of this memorial the activities of the Indiana Company came to a halt for several months, during which the principals in the affair hoped that Virginia would alter her plans.

When not engaged in public of semipublic business, Trent concerned himself with the management of his plantation near Trenton. As it was located on the edge of the Delaware River, he was frequently troubled with floodwaters and tides that caused the creeks to overflow his meadows. In the summer of 1780 he and some of his neighbors petitioned the New Jersey governor and the assembly to enact a law permitting the construction of some necessary flood walls and dams and requiring each landowner to contribute to their support and upkeep; but the request was apparently not granted. Before the summer ended, Trent again became ill, but recovered sufficiently to participate in the shaping of the regular business of the Indiana Company.

On September 12, Morgan sent Trent some important information that he had just received from the frontier which he believed would help the cause of the Indiana Company and Vandalia if it were secretly given to certain members of Congress. The report stated that there was considerable unrest in Kentucky because of the fact that a number of "nabobs" from Virginia had taken most of the good lands there by office warrants and pre-emption rights. The informer, who, according to Morgan, was a reliable person, had said that hundreds of families were being ruined by the tactics of the Virginians, and that he feared that the region would be lost if the English appeared and offered the settlers protection. Morgan thought it strange that Congress remained passive under these conditions. He said that on the pretext of defending the frontiers, all the states were helping to pay for an army to make possible Virginia's absorption of the back country.

Near the end of September, Trent presented another memorial to Congress on behalf of the Vandalia and Indiana Companies. He reminded Congress of his earlier memorial and charged that although Virginia had been asked to stop her sale of western lands, she had not done so. Then he stated that he and the other memorialists had seen a copy of a motion from the committee appointed to consider the cession of Virginia, North Carolina, and Georgia lands to the United States, recommending that all purchases or deeds from the Indians within the ceded lands be declared void. He made an earnest plea that the motion be acted on promptly, and that Congress give the land speculators a hearing as soon as possible. Every document that could possibly help the land companies was eagerly sought, and in October, Trent was hurriedly summoned to Philadelphia to try to secure some valuable papers from one of the Franks brothers, who had been jailed as a Tory and was about to be taken to New York.

At about the same time, Trent and his associates learned of a petition that Virginia had sent to Congress again protesting that Congress had no jurisdiction in the case of the land companies versus Virginia. Whereupon Trent submitted another memorial in behalf of the Vandalia and Indiana companies, in which he argued that Congress did have the right to adjudicate the land question, that right being the "very Essence of their [*the companies'*] claims." He stated also that the land problem "is of infinite Consequence to the American Union as well as to your Memorialists; and that it ought to receive a speedy and solemn Decission." In concluding, he again sought an opportunity for a hearing.

Despite Trent's age and failing health during these years, he took on added duties as a servant of the public. His name appears as a representative in the General Assembly of New Jersey for the year 1780. Whether he sought that office in order to strengthen his position in furthering his land ventures cannot be determined, but it does seem unusual that at his age he should have desired the office for the sake of either prestige or money. Regardless of the nature of his efforts, the year 1780 proved no more profitable to him than those immediately preceding. Congress took no action in regard to his memorials or to those of Morgan, and the new year offered little more than a dim hope of better results in the future.

After waiting for Congressional action throughout the winter and part of the spring of 1781, which seemed a reasonable time, Trent, assisted by Samuel Wharton and Barnard Gratz, as attorneys for George Croghan, drew up still another memorial to Congress. This one differed somewhat from the others in that it mentioned a specific instance—the case of Charles Simms—in which Virginia, despite all her opposition to the recognition of purchases on the frontier, had supported a purchaser of western lands. Citing that action as a precedent, the memorialists asked for the privilege of locating three of Croghan's tracts within the region granted to the Crown at the Fort Stanwix Treaty of 1768, if the boundary line between Pennsylvania and Virginia should be confirmed. This petition, along with others from the Illinois and Wabash land companies, was shunted off to a committee, where it remained for over a month.

In the meantime Trent again became delinquent in the payment of his financial obligations, and his creditors threatened to use legal means to collect their accounts. Although Trent always seemed to be short of cash, he was actually far from being broken financially. Perhaps he might have been termed "land poor"; because, in addition to his large estate in New Jersey, he owned upwards of three thousand acres in Northumberland County, Pennsylvania, and various tracts elsewhere. But, business gambler that he was, he always looked about for an opportunity to invest any funds that fell into his possession.

Finally, on June 27, the committee report on Trent's latest memorial was presented to Congress. The committee recommended that none of the land cessions of the states be accepted as they stood. Further, it was suggested that Congress establish western limits for the various states and ascertain how much vacant land belonged to the United States and could therefore be used for the common benefit. Saturday, June 30, was set as the day to consider the report, but nothing was done in regard to the matter for over three weeks. Such dillydallying was almost more than human nature could stand, and the result was that Trent drafted and presented yet another memorial to Congress, which was quite bitter in tone. The language used in castigating Congress for the repeated delays and the denial of justice prompted a request from a Congressional committee that the document be returned to Trent for rewriting. Trent agreed, too, when his anger had passed, that some of his expressions should be expunged before the memorial was read. Pointed arguments in favor of the Indiana Company also appeared in the pamphlet, *Plain Facts,* at about this time. Soon the subject of the last two memorials, as well as the question of the land cessions of the various states, was referred to the committee on the cessions of western lands.

Between the time when his last petition was presented to Congress and the time in October when the land-company affair again came up for consideration, Trent engaged in some small-scale land speculation near his home. He purchased the interest of James Hays in two tracts, totaling nine hundred acres, of backwoods New Jersey land that had not yet been surveyed. The arrangement was a typical, shrewd, Trent agreement. Trent was to make an effort to have the lands surveyed as soon as the New Jersey office opened the back country for sale. One month after the deeds had been delivered, he was to pay for the land. Hays, on his part, guaranteed that the tracts would be well timbered and readily accessible to the Delaware River. The old trader was also able at this time to collect some funds on a mortgage that he held against three men who had purchased a rather large amount of Pennsylvania acreage from him over two years before. But in a short while he was back in the midst of the Vandalia-Indiana Company business again.

It seems that Trent spent most of his time during that fall and winter in Philadelphia, in an attempt to bring about a successful solution to the land problem. To judge by succeeding events, his efforts were fairly successful. Shortly after his departure from home, the Virginia delegates in Congress announced that they had refused to attend hearings scheduled by the Congressional committee that was considering the memorials of the various land companies, on the ground that such questions were not within the jurisdiction of Congress. There were some evidences of friction over the stand taken by the delegates, but Congress adjourned for the day without taking any action. On October 28 a document, prepared by Trent and Samuel Wharton and signed by both, entitled, "A few Hints respectfully submitted to the Honorable Committee of Congress upon the Subject of *Vandalia,*" was presented to Congress. In it the promoters reviewed the story of their expense and sacrifice on behalf of the grant and asked that those partners in Vandalia who were "good Citizens of these States, and especially Mr. Trent and Mr. Wharton . . . will be considered, as most justly and equitably entitled to their respective Shares of the Lands contracted for," even if Congress should decide that the British partners were outside the pale of their consideration. Later in their discourse, however, the authors returned to the subject of the English members of Vandalia and made a special plea that their interests also be recognized. In closing, they once more offered Congress the same price for the land that the English Crown had agreed to accept.

Evidently a rumor escaped from Congress at this time to the effect that the land-memorial committee was looking favorably on the petitions, and Trent's spirits rose somewhat. As the tables seemed to be turning for the better, his agile mind concocted a new business scheme. He proposed to sell a voter's share in Indiana for £375, and he wanted the same buyer to purchase a mortgage that he held, for £300. He said that he would be satisfied with £150 in cash on the transaction, and that the remainder could be paid in such commodities as rum, tea, coffee, wine, and sugar. His reason for offering to accept goods in part payment was based upon his tentative plan to start a store at his ferry on the Delaware, near Trenton. There is no evidence, however, that any of his 1781 plans got beyond the imaginative stage. In January, 1782, he asked Barnard Gratz to try to sell one of his Indiana Company shares in Maryland. Trent still held a good deal of land in Pennsylvania, but he apparently made no particular effort to part with it during this period.

By January the Old Dominion delegation had apparently also received an inkling that certain committee members of Congress were smiling on the land speculators, and as anything favorable to the land companies was an anathema to Virginia, her delegates were worried. Patiently they waited for the assigned committee to make its report on the land-company memorials. Weeks dragged by without any report being presented; finally, on May 1, the Virginians demanded that the report be read. The request was complied with, but the results disappointed those who forced the committee to release its findings. The committee asked Virginia to reconsider her act of cession and to give up all claims to the western lands beyond a "reasonable" western boundary. After rebuking Virginia's delegation for not attending the hearings when the land companies had presented their cases, the report went on to state that the purchases of Croghan and the Indiana Company were considered valid. Then the recommendation was made that when the lands were finally ceded to the United States, the purchasers who were citizens of the United States should have conferred upon them their respective shares in the said lands, after a reasonable deduction for quit rents had been made. This report may properly be said to have been the highest achievement of the land companies in their struggle for recognition of their claims. From that point onward, retrogression replaced progression.

What influences Trent was subjected to in the two weeks immediately following the submission of the foregoing report can only be surmised. Possibly he visited his lifetime friend, George Croghan, of near-by

Passyunk, who was in such poor health that he died before the summer was over; or perhaps his own weakened condition, due to advanced age and overwork, greatly discouraged him. At any rate he wrote a new will before leaving Philadelphia for Trenton and home. In it he divided his estate into five parts, giving two-fifths to his son, John, and the other three-fifths to his wife, Sarah, and to his two living daughters, Ann and Mary. His daughters and Tench Coxe, his "Relation," of Philadelphia, were appointed executors. He stipulated that his estate was not to be divided until John reached the age of twenty-one years. "I particularly recommend," he wrote, "the giving to my Son the best Education this Country affords." With that task completed, he retired to Trenton to remain in relative seclusion until late in the year.

About the middle of November, 1782, a rumor was forwarded to Trent that the inhabitants west of the mountains had declared themselves an independent state with the name of "Transylvania." They were supposed to have five thousand good marksmen ready to support their stand; and it was surmised that the situation would bring western affairs to a climax in Congress. Trent was asked to pass the news along to Morgan, and to decide with him whether or not Indiana should take any action. Nothing came of the report, however, and Trent did not deem it necessary to proceed to Philadelphia on Indiana Company business before the Christmas holiday.

Since no constructive action had been taken by Congress in the interests of Vandalia or Indiana for almost a year, the proprietors of the Indiana Company called a meeting for May 1, 1783, to map plans for the future. Between the time when the call for the meeting was issued and the time of its convening, Trent drew up and submitted to Congress still another memorial in support of Indiana. He pointed to the sufferings entailed by those who had been waiting so long because of the indecision of Congress. He said that the war was no longer an excuse for delay and asked that a final decision be handed down quickly. Less than two weeks later he presented another and final petition in the interests of Vandalia, using much the same argument in his quest for speedy justice. But no justice, speedy or otherwise, was rendered by Congress. Thus when the proprietors of the Indiana Company met for their business session in May, no progress could be reported, although Trent, personally, was able to get his organization expense account of several hundred pounds honored.

Even in his old age, Trent never seemed to be able to keep more than one step ahead of his creditors. In the summer of 1783 he and Samuel Wharton found some of their old bonds and mortgages coming due. For a time, however, the holder was diverted from his purpose because, although Trent still owned thousands of acres of land, it was not deemed a good time to foreclose the mortgages against him. Thus he was spared a little longer. The year 1784 found him fairly active both as a creditor trying to collect his own debts, and as a debtor trying to avoid payment of his obligations as long as possible. In both roles he had some measure of success. A reduction in the number of his land-holdings would seem to indicate that he sold some of his real estate, although no deeds have been found to prove the fact.

Early in the year the sages of the Indiana Company met together and evolved a scheme whereby the State of New Jersey would assume the position of plaintiff against Virginia in the Indiana affair. Accordingly, in March, George Morgan, as agent of New Jersey, presented a petition to Congress in behalf of the Indiana Company. But as Congress under the Articles of Confederation was unable to muster a quorum of the states—even to care for affairs of much greater significance than those of the land companies—there is little wonder that the cause of the petitioners was neglected.

Trent in the meantime had removed his family from Trenton to Phila-delphia. There, unfortunately, his creditors could reach him the more easily, and they proceeded to do so, regardless of his failing health. On July 6, 1784, he made what proved to be his final will and testament. In this document he left to Richard Wharton; John Todd, Jr., his "Kinsman"; and James Todd, together, one share of his Indiana hold-ings. To Israel Morris, his "Kinsman," he left one half-share in Indiana in trust for Morris' four children. After providing for another small bequest of £10, apparently to a colored servant, he asked that the re-mainder of his estate be divided equally among his wife and his three children, Ann, Mary, and John. As executors he appointed Samuel Wharton, Israel Morris, John Todd, Jr., and his daughter, Mary. But the end was not yet for the old Indian trader and land speculator. Practically no records exist from which to chronicle the story of the last three years of his life, but he survived to the spring of 1787, when he passed quietly away. Thus a colorful career came to a close.

After Trent's death his heirs and the other proprietors of the Indiana Company continued the fight for recognition under the new Constitu-tion, but with little success. In 1792 their case was taken to the Supreme Court of the United States under the title of "William Grayson & others *vs*. The Commonwealth of Virginia," where it was lost. Possibly the disputes between Virginia and the proprietors of Indiana were more responsible than any other one thing for the addition of the eleventh amendment to the Constitution of the United States.

To estimate fairly the place of William Trent in history is exceedingly difficult. As he was born in a home of good breeding and moderate wealth, one might suppose that a professional career would have attracted him. There are plausible reasons, however, why such a choice was not made. In the first place, his father died when William was a child, and the financial support, as well as the parental pressure, necessary to complete his training for a profession was thus reduced. To that circumstance may be added the fact that his father was primarily a merchant, and the son could easily and logically have developed a desire to emulate his father. Whatever the reason for his choice, he adopted the allied fields of Indian trade and frontier land speculation as a career. He also displayed a willingness to dabble in public service, both in a civil and in a military role, when occasion demanded, or when it seemed most judicious for his own interests to do so.

Evidently Trent felt that there was more money to be made on the frontier than in the more settled seaboard area. That the physical, as well as the financial, risks were greater he undoubtedly knew from the beginning. His entry into the Indian trade about the middle of the eighteenth century, following his first military venture, was made under conditions that would lead one to believe that he possessed little capital. The prospects of success were bright, but the vicissitudes of the period were too great to be overcome by him and his contemporaries, despite their skill and daring.

As a military man, Trent was slightly above the average in ability. In King George's War he performed no outstanding act, possibly because there were few opportunities. But in the French and Indian War, and during Pontiac's uprising subsequent to it, his services were of a higher order and drew the unstinted praise of his superiors. It is only fair to point out, however, that he does not seem to have entered the service by choice at all, but participated in military activities only when necessity dictated.

Trent's record in the Indian trade was a good one. He enjoyed such respect among the highest authorities of both the white and the red men that he was chosen on many occasions to handle the most delicate and important negotiations between them. Had he lived in a different period he doubtless would have amassed a fortune from his merchandising ventures. Even as matters stood, he was shrewd enough to have helped in the evolution of a plan that would have made him and his partners wealthy, had not the Revolution intervened. But for the hard blow that fate dealt his interests, he might have died one of the honored founders of the first state to be carved from the raw frontier.

BIBLIOGRAPHICAL NOTE

MANUSCRIPTS

A. Official

Since William Trent had a long and interesting career and since his life touched the lives of many important people, it is not surprising that pertinent material regarding him is found in a great many different manuscript collections.

The Bouquet Papers, in the Additional Manuscripts Division of the British Museum in London, England, proved valuable, especially for the French and Indian War period and for Trent's connection with that conflict. The Library of Congress in Washington has copies of most of these papers. Photostatic copies of material that bear especially on the history of western Pennsylvania are to be found in the Historical Society of Western Pennsylvania in Pittsburgh. Useful for the same general period, and to some extent for later years, were the Colonial Office Papers in the Public Record Office in London. The Library of Congress possesses transcripts of many of these documents. Included among them are valuable letters and a Trent diary (1753). In the Library of Congress were found photostatic copies of some interesting materials on Trent from two other foreign sources: The House of Lords Library in London, and the Privy Council in London.

By far the most voluminous and generally valuable material on Trent was found in American depositories. The three most significant collections of an official and semiofficial nature containing letters, accounts, and deeds are the Ohio Company Manuscripts in the Historical Society of Pennsylvania in Philadelphia, the Ohio Company manuscripts in the possession of the University of Pittsburgh, and the McAllister Papers in the Manuscript Collection of the Ridgway Branch of the Library Company of Philadelphia. Of distinct value, too, for letters and official materials are the Provincial Papers and the Revolutionary Papers, two large collections in the possession of the Archives Division of the Pennsylvania Historical and Museum Commission in Harrisburg. The Papers of the Continental Congress, in the Library of Congress, proved helpful in following Trent's frantic efforts to salvage something tangible from his grandiose land speculation. The author was particularly pleased that he was able to locate an original Fort Stanwix deed in the National Museum in Philadelphia. The deed was granted to Trent on November

177

3, 1768, and included most of the territory in present-day West Virginia. Some usable letters or items of information were also found among the following collections: the Irvine Papers in the Historical Society of Pennsylvania; the official correspondence and miscellaneous letters of the Penn Manuscripts, and a bundle of unbound deeds, also in the Historical Society of Pennsylvania; the New York Provincial Council Minutes, in the New York State Library in Albany; George Croghan's will and Trent's will, in the City Hall, Philadelphia. Trent's last will and testament, though interesting, did not prove as helpful as had been expected.

B. *Unofficial*

Fortunately, Trent kept a diary on a number of occasions. The author found the original copies or transcripts of two of these. A third exists in print, but the original was not located. Trent's journal for May 14 to October 19, 1763, is especially interesting and valuable. This is the best account in existence of life in and around Fort Pitt during the dark days of Pontiac's Conspiracy. It is thrilling and dramatic in a number of instances.

An extensive journal used for its valuable background material on the frontier, during the period that Trent was in the neighborhood of the forks of the Ohio, was the Croghan diary for the years April 3, 1759, to May 9, 1763. (Most of this journal is in Trent's handwriting. For many years it was believed to be Trent's journal, and it was so catalogued by the Library of the Historical Society of Pennsylvania. Only recently —since this book was set in type—was the author informed that sufficient evidence has been found to establish the document as Croghan's journal. Apparently Trent was responsible for the transcription only, although it must be remembered that he was with Croghan much of the time as an official assistant, fellow trader and intimate friend.) The document is now being prepared for publication by the Historical Society of Pennsylvania.

For more than half of Trent's adult life he was engaged in trying to get restitution for the losses which he and his partners and their friends suffered at the hands of the Indians. Restitution was to take the form of land grants in most cases. On this subject and the problems arising from it a great mass of manuscript material exists. Documents useful in depicting background, Trent letters, letters in which Trent was prominently mentioned, land-promotion business, opinions relating to the validity of land grants by the Indians, deeds, mortgages, wills, an oath of allegiance, and the like were found and utilized in these collections. They include the following: John Baynton Private Letter Book; Baynton, Wharton and Morgan Letter Book; Baynton, Wharton and Morgan Letter Book "A"; Manuscript Letter Book; and the George Morgan Letter Book, all in the Pennsylvania State Archives. In the Manuscript Collection of the Carnegie Library in Pittsburgh are the Trent-Croghan Letters. By far the largest number of useful documents, not yet mentioned, is to be found in that great depository of Colonial Americana, the Historical Society of Pennsylvania. These include: The William Trent, Sr., Ledger, 1703-1708; the Wharton Manuscripts, in which is the Indiana Company Deed Book; the Thomas Wharton Letter Book; a View of the Title to Indiana; Opinions Regarding the Grant to Wm. Trent, 1775, in which appear the legal opinions of leading English and American Lawyers supporting the validity of Trent's title; the Shippen Papers; the Simon Gratz Collection, which contains, among other materials, an early Trent will and his oath of allegiance to the United States; the Gratz-Croghan Papers; the Dreer Collection; and the Etting Collection.

All the following collections yielded some items of value for this study, although they did not prove as profitable as the sources listed above: the Ashmead Papers; the Autograph Collection; the Balch Papers; the Horsfield Papers; the Lamberton Scotch-Irish Manuscripts; the Lancaster County Miscellaneous Papers; the Logan Papers; and the Taylor Papers, all on deposit in the Historical Society of Pennsylvania. The monumental collection of Franklin Manuscripts, owned and preserved by the American Philosophical Society in Philadelphia, proved helpful in throwing light on Trent's land-speculation problems. Of less value were the George Washington Papers in the Library of Congress. At least one or more letters bearing directly on Trent and his business were located in the following: the Draper Manuscripts, in the State Historical Society of Wisconsin, in Madison; the Emmet Collection in the New York Public Library, in New York City; the Gratz Papers, in the Missouri Historical Society, in St. Louis; the Manuscript Collection in the Henry E. Huntington Library and Art Gallery, in San Marino, California; the Manuscript Collection in the New York State Library, in Albany; the Miscellaneous Manuscripts in the Library of Congress; and the Morgan Papers in the Illinois Historical Survey, in Urbana.

PRINTED SOURCES

A. *Official Documents*

For the study of Trent's long, versatile life, the state archival sources proved particularly valuable. Of the nine published series of the *Penn-*

sylvania Archives, the following six yielded materials of value in the form of letters, reports, minutes, and official decisions: First Series (twelve volumes, Philadelphia, 1852-1856); Second Series (twenty volumes, Harrisburg, 1879-1893); Third Series (thirty-one volumes, Harrisburg, 1894-1899); Fourth Series (twelve volumes, Harrisburg, 1900-1902); Fifth Series (eight volumes, Harrisburg, 1906); Eighth Series (eight volumes, Harrisburg, 1931-1935). Indispensable also, because of their wealth of official documents and letters, were the *Pennsylvania Colonial Records* (seventeen volumes, Philadelphia, 1851-1860). For information on Trent's father, and his own land-company promotion schemes, the *Archives of New Jersey,* First Series (thirty-four volumes, Newark, 1880-1931) and Second Series (five volumes, Trenton, 1901-1917), as well as the New Jersey Historical Society *Collections* (nine volumes, Newark, 1847-1916) and the New Jersey Historical Society *Proceedings,* New Series (Newark, 1916-date) proved useful. The *Archives of Maryland* (fifty-two volumes, Baltimore, 1883-1935) were chiefly valuable for the period of difficulty with the French. Letters and papers relating to Trent's experiences in New York during King George's War and to his real estate operations there at a later date appear in the New York Historical Society *Collections,* Publication Fund Series (fifty-six volumes, New York, 1868-1923); the *Documentary History of the State of New York,* E. B. O'Callaghan, editor (four volumes, Albany, 1849-1851); and *Documents Relative to the Colonial History of the State of New York,* E. B. O'Callaghan, editor (fifteen volumes, Albany, 1853-1887). The Dinwiddie Papers, in Volumes III and IV of the Virginia Historical Society *Collections* (eleven volumes, Richmond, 1882-1892), proved particularly valuable for Trent letters, orders from Governor Dinwiddie, and Trent's commission as captain of the forces entrusted with the building of a fort at the forks of the Ohio. Less valuable, but still important, was the *Calendar of the Virginia State Papers,* edited by W. P. Palmer *et al.* (eleven volumes, Richmond, 1875-1893). For scattered Bouquet and Trent letters and Contrecoeur's 1754 summons to Trent's men to surrender, the Massachusetts Historical Society *Collections,* First Series (nine volumes, Boston, 1792-1804); Fourth Series (ten volumes, Boston, 1852-1871) and the Michigan Pioneer and Historical Society *Collections* (forty volumes, Lansing, 1877-1929) were helpful. For background materials and interpretations dealing with the Old Northwest, the Wisconsin Historical Society *Collections* (Madison, 1854-date); and the Illinois Historical *Collections* (twenty-seven volumes, Springfield, 1903-1936), were indispensable. The (British) Historical Manuscripts Commission *Reports* (London, 1874-date) provided a number of useful letters on the land-company question. The *American Archives,* Fourth Series (six volumes, Washington, 1837) and Fifth Series (three volumes, Washington, 1853) contain valuable letters and credentials concerning Trent's status during the Revolution and concerning Indian conference minutes. In the Lancaster County Historical Society *Papers* (Lancaster, 1896-date) was found some interesting material and a sketch of Trent. Not all the data on Trent found therein, however, are reliable. Materials necessary in following the course of Trent and his associates through bankruptcy and the long years of legislative and legal bickering over their land-company schemes are the following: *The Statutes at Large of Pennsylvania, 1682-1809,* compiled by J. T. Mitchel *et al.* (eighteen volumes, Philadelphia, 1896-1915); the *Statutes at Large of Virginia, 1619-1792,* compiled by W. W. Hening (thirteen volumes, Philadelphia, 1823); the *Journals of the House of Burgesses of Virginia, 1619-1776* (thirteen volumes, Richmond, 1905-1915); the *Acts of the Privy Council of England,* Colonial Series (six volumes, London, 1908-1912); the *Journals of the Continental Congress, 1774-1789,* edited by Gaillard Hunt, *et al.* (thirty-three volumes, Washington, 1904-1936); and the *United States Reports,* compiled by A. J. Dallas, second edition (four volumes, New York, 1905-1907).

B. *Writings*

The Writings of George Washington, edited by J. C. Fitzpatrick (eighteen volumes, Washington, 1931) is by far the best work in this field. Because of the letters that have a bearing on western Pennsylvania history about the middle of the eighteenth century, this source was found helpful. Although an earlier work, *The Writings of George Washington,* edited by Jared Sparks (twelve volumes, Boston, 1834) was consulted, it was utilized very little. Useful in following the land-company developments were *The Writings of Benjamin Franklin,* edited by A. H. Smyth (ten volumes, New York, 1905-1907), since they contain some pertinent letters and the full Report of the Board of Trade (Volume V) opposing the petition of the Vandalia Company.

C. *Diaries and Journals*

Among the publications under this heading the most useful was *The Journal of Captain William Trent, 1752,* edited by A. T. Goodman (Cincinnati, 1871). This journal covers Trent's first major assignment for the colony of Virginia and presents a picture of the Indian unrest on the frontier at the time. With the journal, Goodman has included a number of other interesting documentary papers. Perhaps second in importance are *Christopher Gist's Journals,* edited by W. M. Darlington (Pittsburgh, 1893), in which light is thrown on trans-Appalachian conditions. Of most merit for this study was the deposition (1754) of Edward Ward explaining the conditions under which he surrendered the embryo fort at the forks of the Ohio. The diary of George Washington covering his journey into northwestern Pennsylvania for Governor Dinwiddie in 1753-1754 was the most valuable item in *The Diaries of George Washington,* edited by J. C. Fitzpatrick (four volumes, New York, 1925). Beneficial in supplying background and as a verification check on other sources were: *The Journal of Jeffrey Amherst,* edited by J. C. Webster (Toronto, 1931); *Early Western Travels,* edited by R. G. Thwaites (thirty-three volumes, Cleveland, 1904-1907); and *Voyage au Canada dans le nord de L' Amerique Septentrionale fait depuis l'an 1751 a 1761 par J. C. B.* (identity of "J. C. B." is still in doubt), edited by H. R. Casgrain (Quebec, 1887).

D. *Contemporary Accounts*

No careful student can have any real grasp of Indian affairs in North America between 1750 and the Revolution without having consulted *The Papers of Sir William Johnson,* edited by James Sullivan and A. C. Flick (eight volumes, Albany, 1921-1933). *The History of Colonel Henry Bouquet,* edited by Mary C. Darlington (Pittsburgh, 1920), proved useful. Mary C. Darlington's *Fort Pitt and Letters from the Frontier* (Pittsburgh, 1892) were even more valuable because in addition to contemporary letters, the author included a Trent diary for the summer of 1763. It is to be noted, however, that she erroneously ascribed the authorship of that journal to Captain Ecuyer, the commandant at Fort Pitt. No one who has seen the original and possesses any familiarity with the Indian trader's chirography, could doubt Trent's authorship. In *The Olden Time,* edited by Neville B. Craig (two volumes, Pittsburgh, 1846-1848), is to be found, among other items of interest, a copy of Captain Contrecoeur's summons to Trent's ensign, Edward Ward, to surrender the stockade at the forks of the Ohio in April, 1754. Useful, also, in presenting the point of view of the royal officials on pertinent problems of the day is *The Correspondence of General Thomas Gage,* edited by Clarence E. Carter (two volumes, New Haven, 1931). Two other accounts should be mentioned here, chiefly because of their espousal of the land-company cause: Samuel Wharton's *Facts and Observations* (London, 1775); and *Plain Facts* (Philadelphia, 1781), anonymously written, though perhaps—from its nature —the work of Samuel Wharton and Trent.

E. *Newspapers*

Because of the great abundance of original source materials of various types, newspapers were utilized but little in this study. The only one directly used in the preparation of this monograph was the *Maryland Gazette,* for 1775.

SECONDARY SOURCES

A. *Monographs and Special Accounts*

By far the most useful publication in this list was Albert T. Volwiler's *George Croghan and the Westward Movement,* 1741-1782 (Cleveland, 1926), Professor Volwiler has attained a high level of scholarship and skill in this valuable contribution to the history of western expansion. Its special interest for this study arises from the fact of the lifelong friendship that existed between Croghan and Trent. Max Savelle in his *George Morgan, Colony Builder* (New York, 1932), likewise helped to make clear the picture of Trent's character, because of the many friendly, as well as unfriendly, relationships that flourished from time to time between Trent and Morgan. The most recent and probably the best biography of Franklin is, Carl Van Doren's *Benjamin Franklin* (New York, 1938). In a somewhat less significant, but similar, role is *Barnard and Michael Gratz,* edited by W. V. Byars (Jefferson City, 1916). Although his work no longer enjoys the prestige it once did, any study closely connected with the French and Indian War period is not complete without an examination of Francis Parkman's *The Conspiracy of Pontiac* (Champlain edition, three volumes, Boston, 1898).

Other works whose titles generally indicate their usefulness include the following: Neville B. Craig, *The History of Pittsburgh* (Pittsburgh, 1851); Charles W. Dahlinger, *The Marquis Duquesne* (Pittsburgh, 1932—a reprint from Volume XV of the *Western Pennsylvania Historical Magazine*); John Marshall, *The Life of George Washington* (five volumes, Philadelphia, 1836); Kate M. Rowland, *The Life of George Mason* (two volumes, New York, 1892); J. R. Watson, *Annals of Philadelphia* (three volumes, Philadelphia, 1905); H. L. Cooley, *Genealogy of Early Settlers in Trenton and Ewing* (Trenton, 1883); and the Trenton Historical Society, *A History of Trenton, 1679-1929* (Princeton, 1929). Last, but not least, some of the most helpful guides were: *Calendar of the Sir William Johnson Manuscripts,* compiled by R. E. Day (Albany, 1909); *Calendar of the Council Minutes of New York,* compiled by Berthold Fernow (Albany, 1902); *Calendar of the Papers of Benjamin Franklin in the . . . American Philosophical So-*

ciety, compiled by I. M. Hays (Philadelphia, 1907) ; and *The Virginia Historical Index,* compiled by E. G. Swem (two volumes, Roanoke, 1934).

B. *Articles and Essays in Publications of Learned Societies*

Space does not permit the listing of the titles of all the articles used, but materials from the following magazines were of value: *Mississippi Valley Historical Review* (Cedar Rapids, 1914-date) ; *Pennsylvania Magazine of History and Biography* (Philadelphia, 1877-date) ; and *Virginia Magazine of History and Biography* (Richmond, 1893-date).

C. *General Accounts*

Indispensable to any study having to do with the Old Northwest is the exceptionally well-written work of Clarence W. Alvord, *The Mississippi Valley in British Politics* (two volumes, Cleveland, 1917). Of considerable value for general background was Charles A. Hanna, *The Wilderness Trail* (two volumes, New York, 1911). Thomas P. Abernethy's *Western Lands and the American Revolution* (New York, 1937), although somewhat disconnected, is a creditable contribution in its field. For the part played by French Canada, William Kingsford's *History of Canada, 1608-1841* (ten volumes, Toronto, 1887-1898) served the general purpose adequately. The story of New France's highest colonial officers is to be found in L. J. Lemieux, *The Governors-General of Canada* (London, n.d.). The general attention given the unsettled lands west of the mountains in the latter half of the eighteenth century is further attested by the contribution from the pen of the trenchant pamphleteer, Thomas Paine, in his *Public Good* (Albany, 1780), in which he espoused the cause of those who favored the establishment of a national public domain west of the mountains.

INDEX

Amherst, General, 99, 102, 107, 111, 115
Annapolis, 61
Articles of Confederation, 168, 175
Assapausa, 22, 24, 37
Assunpink Creek, 2
Aughwick (Shirleysburg, Pennsylvania), 62

Bache, Richard, 162
Baynton, John, 128, 135, 141, 143, 150
Baynton and Wharton, merchants, 128, 131
Beaver, Delaware chief, 37, 42, 74, 87, 98, 101
Beaver Creek, 35, 36
Bloomsbury Court, 2
Blue Shadow, Cherokee chief, 22
Board of Trade, 25, 26, 140, 141, 146, 148, 152, 159
Bouquet, Colonel Henry, 68, 69, 71, 81, 89; commander at Fort Pitt, 95, 97-99, 102, 104, 106; in the East, 112, 114, 117, 119; at Bushy Run, 123, 124; business around Fort Pitt, 125, 127, 128
Braddock, General, 61, 127
Burd, Colonel, 61
Burge, Mary, 3
Burlington Company, 137, 141, 143, 144
Burnet, Governor William, 2
Burney, Thomas, 19, 20, 25-27, 30
Bushy Run (Jeannette, Pennsylvania), Battle of, 123

Cadwallader, John, 155
Callender, Robert, 10, 26, 44, 135, 141, 157-159
Camden, Lord, 140, 141
Campbell, Major Donald, 92-94, 101, 125
Canasatego, Onondaga chief, 9
Carlisle, 26, 42, 43, 46, 48, 137; threatened by Indians, 64
Carlisle, Major John, 51, 53, 59
Catawba Indians, 38, 56; in English service, 69
Céleron (de Bienville), 11, 12, 15, 16
Chartier's Creek (McKees Rocks, Pennsylvania), 46
Chatacouit (Portland, New York), 29
Cheningue, 26. See also Logstown
Cherokee Indians, 22, 23, 30, 38, 56, 100; in English service, 68, 69
Clapham, Colonel William, 110

Clinton, Governor George, 4, 15, 32
Coddington, Mary, 3
Coddington, Governor William, 3
Congress of the United States, 167, 168, 171-175
Connewango Indians, 30, 36
Conococheague Creek, 60
Conspiracy of Nicholas, 12
Continental Congress, 158, 160, 163
Contrecoeur, Captain Claude Pierre de, 54-56
Cresap, Thomas, 29, 30, 56, 145, 146
Croghan, George, 10, 11, 14, 15, 30-32, 42-44, 47-49, 52, 59-62, 65, 68, 72-75, 80-97, 99-109, 114, 127-129, 133, 135-137, 139-141, 143, 145, 147, 148, 150-152, 155, 156, 160, 162, 163, 171, 173

Dagge, Henry, 139, 153-155
Dartmouth, Lord, 147, 148
Davenport, Josiah, 107
Davison, John, 46
Delaware George, Indian chief, 73, 77; dies, 103
Delaware Indians, 11, 13, 22-24, 29, 31-33, 35, 37-39, 101, 114; pro-French, 53
Denny, Governor William, 65, 67
Dickinson, John, 154
Dinwiddie, Governor Robert, 13, 24-26, 30-33, 37-40, 42, 45-47, 52; commissions Trent, 50, 51; Trent wins lawsuit against, 93
Duquesne, Marquis, 17, 18, 20, 28, 29
Dunmore, Lord, 152, 153
Dunmore's War, 153, 158

Easton conferences, 67, 103
Ecuyer, Captain Simeon, 106, 107, 109, 111-115, 117-123, 125

Fairfax, Colonel William, 42
Finley, John, 30, 31
Forbes, General John, 69; takes Fort Duquesne, 71, 72
Forks of the Ohio, 33, 35-37, 40, 44, 45, 50, 52, 56, 58, 109. See also Fort Pitt
Fort Bedford, 72, 107, 108, 119, 123. See also Raystown
Fort Burd, 111, 112. See also Redstone
Fort Cumberland, 60, 61, 107, 108, 112. See also Wills Creek

185

Fort Detroit, 16, 17, 19, 82, 83, 85, 87, 89, 92, 100, 105, 112, 113, 116, 120, 124, 125
Fort Duquesne, taken by English, 71
Fort Le Boeuf (Waterford, Pennsylvania), 29, 36, 37, 39, 48, 49, 54, 74, 115
Fort Ligonier, 72, 73, 110, 115, 117, 123. *See also* Loyal Hannon
Fort Machault (Franklin, Pennsylvania), 29, 54, 90
Fort Miami (Fort Wayne, Indiana), 12, 16, 94
Fort Necessity, 127
Fort Niagara, 39, 54, 74, 78, 79; taken by English, 81
Fort Pitt, 146, 147, 163; building started, 82, 98, 101, 108-110; condition of in the year 1763, 111-113, 117, 119, 121; ferocious attack on, 122-124
Fort Pitt conferences, 73, 80, 91
Fort Presque Isle (Erie, Pennsylvania), 35, 37, 39, 54, 74, 116, 125
Fort Prince George, 52 and footnote
Fort Sandusky, 113
Fort Stanwix (Rome, New York), conference at, 132-134, 137, 139; treaty of 1768, 140, 171
Fox Indians, rebellion of, 8
Franklin, Benjamin, 43, 133; interested in land companies, 139-142, 144, 146, 147, 150, 153-155, 157, 162, 168, 169
Franklin, Governor William, 133, 135, 141, 144, 145, 157, 158
Franks, David, 128, 134
Franks, Moses, 128, 136, 139, 148
Fraser, John, 32, 33, 36, 39, 45, 47, 50, 51, 53-55, 58
French Creek (Riviere au Boeuf), 29, 36
Fry, Colonel Joshua, 13, 56, 58

Gage, General Thomas, 129, 147
Galloway, Joseph, 141, 154, 162
Gist, Christopher, 14, 42, 45, 47, 49, 50, 53, 54
Gist's New Settlement (Mount Braddock, Pennsylvania), 50
Glen, Governor, 57
Glynn, John, 153-155
Grand Ohio Company, 140, 141. *See also* Vandalia Company
Grant's Hill, 118-120
Gratz, Barnard, 165, 166, 171, 173
Grayson, William, 166
Grayson, William, & others vs. The Commonwealth of Virginia, 175
Great Crossing of the Youghiogheny, 59
Great Miami River (Rock River), 7

Half King, Iroquois chief, 11, 13, 14, 23, 33-35, 37-40, 42, 44, 46-49, 52-56, 58. *See also* Tanacharison
Hamilton, Governor James, 10, 11, 15, 26, 30, 31, 42, 43, 46, 48, 49, 57, 61, 63, 119; at Easton conference, 103; at Lancaster conference, 104, 119
Henry, Patrick, 155, 157
Hillsborough, Lord, 140, 141, 144-147, 153, 159
Hockley, Richard, 60, 62, 64
Holdernesse, Earl of, 40, 45
Hopewell (New Jersey), 3
Howe, General, 164, 165

Illinois Indians, 17
Indiana Company, 140, 141, 157-170, 172-175
Iroquois Indians, 7, 28, 30, 100, 102. *See also* Six Nations

Johnson Hall conference, 130
Johnson, Sir William, 32, 63, 75, 99-101, 105, 129, 130, 132, 133, 139, 141, 152, 156; to attack Fort Niagara, 78
Joncaire, Captain Chabert de, 48, 54

Kanawha River, 43
Kenny, James, 98, 99, 102, 103, 107
Kickapoo Indians, 104
King George's War, 7, 8
Kuskuski (New Castle, Pennsylvania), 47

La Demoiselle, 10, 13, 16, 17, 20. *See also* Piankashaw King
La Jonquière, Governor, 16-18
Lancaster Indian conferences, 8, 9, 12-14, 42, 44, 65, 66, 103
Langlade, Charles de, 19-21
La Salle, 7, 18
Le Mercier, 29, 55
Levy and Company, 62
Levy, Levy Andrew, 161
Little Meadows, 58
Logan, James, 1
Logan, William, 31, 32
Logstown (Ambridge, Pennsylvania), 11, 13-16, 18, 22, 24, 26, 30, 34-36, 39, 43, 46, 47. *See also* Cheningue
Logstown conference, 15
Logstown treaty, 14
Longueuil, Baron de, 17, 18
Lords of the Treasury, 142
Louisiana, 7, 9, 18, 28
Lower Shawnee Town, 19, 21, 30, 31, 107, 108
Lowrey, Alexander, 95, 135, 162
Lowrey, Lazarus, 30
Loyal Hannon (Ligonier, Pennsylvania), 70

McBryer, Andrew, 19, 20
McKee, Alexander, 107-109, 114, 115, 117, 118, 120, 148
McKee, Thomas, 14, 80
Marin, Chevalier de, 28, 29, 47
Maryland Assembly, 57
Maryland Gazette, 159
Mason, George, 67, 166, 167
Maumee River, 8, 12
Meguck, 19
Mercer, Colonel George, 142, 146, 153, 156
Mercer, Colonel Hugh, 71, 73, 75, 80, 90
Mercer, James, 168
Miami Confederacy, 12, 13, 15, 17, 18, 20, 22, 25. *See also* Twightwees
Mississippi Company, 140
Mississippi River, 8, 26, 35
Monckton, General Robert, 89, 91, 98
Monongahela River, 12, 32, 40, 43, 45, 46, 51-53, 56, 61
Montour, Andrew, 10, 14, 15, 18, 19, 21, 22, 24, 36, 40-43, 47, 49, 73, 77, 82, 94
Montour, Lewis, 36, 46, 49
Montreal, 28, 54; taken by English, 92
Morgan, George, 135, 141, 143, 150-152, 155, 157-159, 161-165, 167-171, 174, 175
Morris, Governor Robert Hunter, 61-63, 127
Muskingum, village of, 19

New France, 8, 17, 54
New Jersey Assembly, 2
New River, 7
Norris, Isaac, 43
North, Lord, 154, 160
Nuchecomer, Shawnee chief, 37

Ohio Company, 9, 12, 13, 24-26, 29, 31, 46, 49, 50, 52, 57, 140, 142
Ohio River, 7, 15, 24, 26, 28, 30, 36, 40, 42, 45, 46, 48, 51, 54, 56
Onas, Brother, 26
Onondaga Council, 13, 16, 24
Onondaga Indians, 9
Osage Indians, 10, 17
Obsorne, Governor, 44
Oswegley Old Town (West Newton, Pennsylvania), 110
Otsego Patent, 137
Ottawa Indians, 11, 20, 30, 31
Ouabache (Wabash River), 16, 22

Paine, Thomas, 169
Palmer, Anthony, 9
Patten, James, 13
Patten, John, 48, 49
Pease, Professor Theodore C., 7

Penn, Governor John, 133
Penn, Thomas, 60
Penn, William, 1, 103
Pennsylvania Assembly, 57, 119; passes special bankruptcy law, 62
Pennsylvania Executive Council, 9, 46
Peters, Richard, 11, 43, 63
Pianguisha King (Piankashaw), 15, 26. *See also* La Demoiselle
Piankashaw Indians, 17, 22. *See also* Twightwees and Miami Confederacy
Pickawillanee (Piqua, Ohio), 12, 13, 16, 18, 19, 21, 25
Pine Creek (Etna, Pennsylvania), 31, 32
Pitt, William, post at forks of the Ohio named for him, 71
Plain Facts, 172
Point, The, 40, 45
Pontiac, Ottawa chief, 110, 127
Potomac River, 8, 26, 34, 41
Presque Isle (Erie, Pennsylvania), 29, 36. *See also* Fort Presque Isle
Privy Council, 57, 62, 146, 150
Proctor, Lieutenant, 5

Quakers, 104; lose control in Pennsylvania, 64, 65
Quebec, 17, 18, 54; taken by English, 84
Queen Anne's War, 7

Randolph, Edmund, 168
Raystown (Bedford, Pennsylvania), 70, 107, 108. *See also* Fort Bedford
Redstone, 111. *See also* Fort Burd
Redstone Creek, 50, 52, 54, 58
Reymond, Captain Charles de, 16

St. Pierre, Legardeur de, 49, 50, 54
Sargent, John, 153, 158
Sawmill Run (West End, Pittsburgh, Pennsylvania), 119, 120
Scarouady (Monacatootha), Oneida chief, 32, 34, 36, 37, 39, 42, 46, 52
Scioto River, 19, 23, 35
Seneca Indians, 29. *See also* Six Nations and Iroquois Indians
Seneca Plan of 1761, 100
Shannopin's Town, 13, 35, 48, 55
Sharpe, Governor, 57
Shawnee Cabins (Schellsburg, Pennsylvania), 44
Shawnee Indians, 11, 13, 21-24, 29, 32, 33, 36, 39, 48, 49, 101, 153, 158
Shingas, Delaware chief, 37, 46, 74, 121
Shippen, Edward, 60, 63
Shippen, Joseph, 129, 130
Simon, Franks, Levy and Trent, merchants, 88, 98, 99, 102, 103, 112, 117, 125, 126, 128, 129, 131, 137

Six Nations Indians, 9, 13-15, 21-25, 30, 32, 33, 36-40, 44, 46-49, 57, 82, 98-101, 105-107, 115, 117, 134, 163
Stanwix, General John, 66, 72, 84, 87
Strahan, William, 144

Tanacharison, Iroquois chief, 13. *See also* Half King
Teaffe, Michael, 10, 14, 31, 44
Tedyuskung, Delaware chief, 65, 67, 103
Thomas, Governor George, 3
Treaty of Utecht, 7, 18
Trent and Croghan, merchants, 10, 127
Trent, Croghan, Callender and Teaffe, merchants, 10, 127
Trent, William, Senior, 1-3
Trenton, 2, 137, 138, 173-175
Trent's Town, 2
Turtle Creek (North Braddock, Pennsylvania), 33, 45, 50, 53-55
Tuscarawas River, 19
Twightwee Indians, 9, 11, 12, 15, 18-26, 30, 33, 36, 38, 63, 91. *See also* Miami Confederacy

Van Braam, Jacob, 45
Vandalia Company, 141-148, 151-154, 156-160, 162-164, 167-170, 172, 174; description of, 149-150
Venango (Franklin, Pennsylvania), 29, 32, 33, 36, 39, 47-50, 54, 74, 115, 116

Villiers, Coulon de, 16
Virginia, 8, 9, 12-15, 22, 24, 25, 30-32, 39-41, 45-48, 51, 52, 60; opposes land companies, 143

Walking purchase, 103
Walpole Company, 140
Walpole, Thomas, 140, 146, 152, 153, 157
Ward, Ensign, 54, 56, 58, 103; surrenders to French, 55
Washington, George, 19, 45-47, 49-51, 53, 56, 57, 67, 142, 156; quarrels with Trent, 58, 59; opposes opening of Forbes Road, 71
Weiser, Conrad, 9, 12, 65
Wharton, Isaac, 162
Wharton, Samuel, 128, 131, 132, 134-147, 150, 152-154, 156, 157, 159, 161, 162, 164, 168, 169, 171, 172, 174
Wharton, Thomas, Senior, 137, 143-145, 157, 159, 161-164
Williamsburg (Virginia), 24, 25, 49
Wills Creek (Cumberland, Maryland), 41, 45, 57, 61. *See also* Fort Cumberland
Wilkins, Sarah, marries Trent, 41
Winchester conferences, 38-42, 66
Wisconsin Indians, 19
Wyandot Indians, 22, 31, 38, 100

Young King, Shawnee chief, 37